D0040115

Reading
and
Responding
to
Literature

READING

AND

RESPONDING

TO

LITERATURE

SuzAnne Cole
Jeff Lindemann

Houston Community College

Harcourt Brace Jovanovich, Publishers

San Diego   New York   Chicago   Austin   Washington, D.C.
London   Sydney   Tokyo   Toronto

Copyright © 1990 by Harcourt Brace Jovanovich, Inc.

All rights reserved. No part of this publication may be reproduced or transmitted in any form or by any means, electronic or mechanical, including photocopy, recording, or any information storage and retrieval system, without permission in writing from the publisher.

Requests for permission to make copies of any part of the work should be mailed to: Copyrights and Permissions Department, Harcourt Brace Jovanovich, Publishers, Orlando, Florida 32887.

ISBN: 0-15-575501-3

Library of Congress Catalog Card Number: 89-84145

Printed in the United States of America

Preface

Reading and Responding to Literature will show you that there is pleasure in reading a poem, play, or prose work, and how to freely react to literature — to form opinions, express feelings, and relate the art to your own life.

We believe that there is a deep satisfaction to understanding literature through the study of genres, the elements of literature, and various critical approaches to literature, and through discovering a writer's purpose and craft. There is also the excitement of the class itself — discussions and lectures that stimulate; perhaps seeing a film, a reading, or a production. And there is a personal fulfillment in writing an expressive essay about literature — sharing your message with an audience that cares and seeks enlightenment.

HOW TO USE THIS BOOK

The book is divided into five parts, each giving specific advice on how to read and respond to literature. Numerous student samples provide useful models for writing about literature. Although the parts may be read in any order, depending on the demands of your particular course, you will probably find it helpful to read Parts I and II first.

Part I, "Reading Literature and Making Initial Responses," offers a reading model built on an interactive process between the reader and the literary text. Chapter 1 discusses how to become involved with the text both before and during the reading and gives suggestions on how to engage the imagination, mark the text, and develop an understanding of the text. Chapters 2 and 3 discuss initial responses to literature, including how to keep a response journal and suggestions for activities designed to generate ideas on literary topics.

Part II, "Additional Responses to Literature," builds on initial responses as it offers further ways of responding. Chapter 4 explains how to analyze the parts of a literary work, make close readings, and interpret meaning. Chapter 5 introduces a variety of ways to substantiate your interpretation of what you read, in class discussions and in essays.

Part III, "Discovering and Responding to Elements of Literature," Chapters 6–11, offers advice on such matters as structure, language, theme, character, setting, symbol, point of view, and tone. Each chapter contains student essays to illustrate the role of initial responses in the development of essays. These chapters may be read in succession or independently as the need arises. These chapters also introduce you to specialized approaches to literature that depend on knowledge gained through the study of other fields, such as psychology and history. You may want to use this part of the text to help you select an approach for research or other assignments.

Part IV, "Writing Papers from Sources," has two chapters which follow a student writing her research paper from the first assignment to the final draft and which are illustrated with examples of the work in progress. Chapter 12 explains how to choose and define a topic, reread primary sources, use library resources, compile an initial resource bibliography, write an outline, evaluate secondary sources, and take notes. This chapter provides useful information to prepare informal and formal research projects. Chapter 13 covers organizing, drafting, revising, and preparing the final draft of your paper, as well as putting together a final bibliography. It contains the student's rough draft with the instructor's suggestions for revision, and the final draft. You can follow the student model to write a formal research paper.

Part V, "Final Considerations," offers a helpful review of such matters as study skills, examinations, and manuscript mechanics. The text concludes with a comprehensive glossary and an index.

ACKNOWLEDGMENTS

Because any textbook represents the combined efforts of editors, publisher, colleagues, friends, family, and students, we would like to acknowledge, with gratitude, the following:

Our editors and production staff at Harcourt Brace Jovanovich for their faith in our proposal, and their continued enthusiasm, support, and assistance during the writing process: Marlane Agriesti Miriello, Sandra Carey, Eleanor Garner, David Watt, Christopher Nelson, Cathy Reynolds, Stacy Simpson, and Mandy Van Dusen.

Our reviewers, who read the manuscript in process, preventing any egregious errors and contributing sage advice: Tom Derrick, Indiana State University; Thomas Erskine, Salisbury State University; Peter Gillett, University of Wisconsin; Donald Gray, Indiana University; John McInerney, University of Scranton; Robert Peterson, Middle Tennessee State University; and Barbara Wilson, Frostburg State University.

Our colleagues at Houston Community College for encouraging and supporting us, reading our drafts, and sharing student responses and essays, especially J. Frank Thornton, David Gersh, Rhada Mohini, Cheryl Peters, Martha Weathers, Roger Wood, and Robert Terhune.

Our former professors for their inspiring examples of scholarship and humanity: Frances Harris, Neal Houston, Kirby Duncan, E. Paul Alworth, John Dodds, J. Frank Eikenberry, Donald Hayden, and Gary Tate.

Our students who have read, listened, discussed, responded, written, and rewritten. Because many of our student samples represent compilations, it is impossible to thank all of our students individually; however, we would like to note especially the efforts of Blanca Silva, Donna Montgomery, Katherine Karr, Betty Ellsworth, and Linda Slover.

And finally, our families, to whom we dedicate this book. SuzAnne would like to thank her parents, June and Myrl Chapman, for understanding and support in her early years, and her husband, Doy, and sons, Brad, Wes, and Mike for their love and for allowing her time and space to write. Jeff would like to thank his parents, Ellen and Walter Lindemann, and his brother Cliff, for their enthusiastic support and continuing patience.

SuzAnne Cole and Jeff Lindemann

Contents

READING

AND

RESPONDING

TO

LITERATURE

PART I

READING LITERATURE AND MAKING INITIAL RESPONSES

CHAPTER 1

Reading Literature

WHAT IS LITERATURE?

*I*n the broadest definition, the word "literature" refers to any body of written material, in the sense that one reads "the literature of mathematics" or "in the literature of sociology." However, in this book we restrict the term "literature" to refer to that written work which has a lasting appeal and which is highly regarded and widely accepted by its readers. Usually this acceptance and regard are based on the expression of a universal emotion or idea in an attractive and appealing form. Agreement on what constitutes literature is both cultural and historical; what one people or one century regards as literature may not be so regarded by another. Another way of saying this is that readers, by their regard or disregard, "create" the literature of their times.

How then is literature written? A writer may deliberately attempt to write literature by imaginatively creating an experience or an event and then communicating it through language in one of the recognized forms of poetry, prose, or drama. Or a writer may produce a speech or a history or even a personal letter reflecting cultural values and identity so aesthetically and to such an extent that it also becomes a work of literature. Thus, few would deny that Martin Luther King's "Letter from Birmingham Jail — April 16, 1963" is as genuine a work of literature as Richard Wright's novel *Black Boy*. So the categories (or *genres*) of literature considered in this book include nonfiction prose such as essays, journals, letters, historical documents, and sacred material, as well as poetry, fiction, and drama.

As you read the descriptions of the basic genres of literature below, keep in mind that although each genre has its own methods of recreating experience, these methods do overlap. Thus, plot is characteristic of fiction, drama, and even narrative poetry, while symbols may be found in all genres of literature. Also, note that this chapter is just an introduction, and that the terms mentioned here are discussed more fully in later chapters (see the index). Definitions will also be found in the "Glossary of Literary Terms" at the back of the book.

What is poetry?   Once you've observed that poetry doesn't look like prose because of the way it is arranged on a page, what else can you say? Even poets are not very specific:

> Poetry is the kind of thing poets write.
>
> > Robert Frost

> . . . not an assertion that something is true, but the making of that truth more fully real to us.
>
> > T. S. Eliot

> Thoughts that breathe, and words that burn.
>
> > Thomas Gray

> Imaginary gardens with real toads in them.
>
> > Marianne Moore

> If I feel physically as if the top of my head were taken off — I know that is poetry. Are there any other ways?
>
> > Emily Dickinson

One definition that might be satisfactory is that poetry is literature which recreates experience or creates an illusion of reality by exploiting all the resources of words — their rhythms, meanings, associations, and appearance on the page — more fully than any other genre. Because poetry is compressed, to read a poem and fully experience it is to read for a total impression of its elements.

One way to comprehend this definition of poetry is to contrast a poem, Percy Bysshe Shelley's "Ozymandias," with a prose version:

Ozymandias

I met a traveller from an antique land
Who said: Two vast and trunkless legs of stone
Stand in the desert . . . Near them, on the sand,
Half sunk, a shattered visage lies, whose frown,
And wrinkled lip, and sneer of cold command,
Tell that its sculptor well those passions read
Which yet survive, stamped on those lifeless things,
The hand that mocked them, and the heart that fed:
And on the pedestal these words appear:
"My name is Ozymandias, king of kings:
Look on my works, ye mighty, and despair!"
Nothing beside remains. Round the decay
Of that colossal wreck, boundless and bare
The lone and level sands stretch far away.

Now examine a prose version:

Ozymandias

I met a traveller from an old country who told me that he had seen a statue in the desert. Two large legs of stone rose up out of the sand. And near them, half covered with sand, the rest of the broken statue appeared. Because of the statue's facial features, especially the frown, the traveller surmised the sculptor knew Ozymandias well. The pedestal read, "My name is Ozymandias, king of kings: Look on my works, ye Mighty, and despair!" Nothing else now stands near the statue. All you can see is the flat and lonely desert.

There is a marked contrast between these versions of the same experience that obviously changes your experience as reader. Although both accounts depict the speaker's encounter with a traveller who has seen the statue of the ambitious Ozymandias, Shelley's poem exploits the power of diction, imagery, line, and form. The poetic version communicates to us in a way the prose version cannot.

What is fiction?   Fiction, including the short story, the novella, and the novel, is an invented narration or story whose purpose, according to the Roman poet and satirist Horace, is to inform or to delight or both. The fiction writer creates an imaginary world whose characters are involved in conflict. The important ingredients in fiction are *plot* (the arrangement of the action), *character, setting, tone* (the author's attitude towards his creation and his imagined audience), *theme* (the underlying messages) and *point of view* (who tells the story).

Although imaginary, fiction presents a world which could be, events which may have occurred, and characters one may have met or perhaps will meet in a lifetime. Thus, readers of fiction customarily accept the reality of fictional worlds.

For example, Theodore Dreiser, in his novel *Sister Carrie*, creates the fictional world of Carrie, an ambitious "little soldier of fortune," who rises from a factory worker to a chorus girl and eventually becomes a famous actress. At the end of the novel, all the ambition that has brought Carrie success has really led her nowhere — her life is empty and meaningless. In the last chapter, she sits alone, bored, in her New York apartment at the Waldorf Hotel. Dreiser's novel concludes:

> Oh, Carrie, Carrie! Oh, blind strivings of the human heart! Onward, onward, it saith, and where beauty leads, there it follows. Whether it be the tinkle of a lone sheep bell o'er some quiet landscape, or the glimmer of beauty in sylvan places, or the show of a soul in some passing eye, the heart knows and makes answer, following. It is when the feet weary and hope seems vain that the heartaches and the longings arise. Know, then, that for you is neither surfeit nor content. In your rocking chair, by your window dreaming, shall you long, alone. In your rocking chair, by your window, shall you dream such happiness as you may never feel.

Although Carrie exists only within her fictional world, by the end of the novel that world has become real to the reader. As we experience her ambitious rise, she lives.

What is drama?   A drama (or play) is a story intended to be acted on the stage, a story developed by *dialogue, action, conflict, character, setting,* and *staging.* Since a drama seldom has a narrator to reveal exposition, background, and character details, the characters' speech and actions must reveal the experience (the plot and story). Costumes and music, sound effects, lighting, props, and the audience are all part of the theatrical experience.

Even though a play is meant to be seen rather than read, reading drama can certainly be a rewarding experience; the reader can reread while the spectator can hear the lines of a given performance only once. Perhaps the most satisfying experience of drama is to read and study a play and then see a live performance or film version.

So far in our examples, we have examined the ambition of Ozy-mandias and Sister Carrie in poetry and fiction, respectively; now let us look at how this subject is treated in drama. In Shakespeare's *Julius Caesar* (Act 3, Scene 2), Brutus and Antony speak before the public at the funeral of the murdered Caesar. Brutus, a thoughtful and logical politician, justifies the assassination of Caesar:

> If then that friend demand why Brutus rose against
> Caesar, this is my answer: Not that I lov'd Caesar less, but
> that I lov'd Rome more. Had you rather Caesar were living
> and die all slaves, than that Caesar were dead, to live all free
> men? As Caesar lov'd me, I weep for him; as he was fortu-
> nate, I rejoice at it; as he was valiant, I honour him; but —
> as he was ambitious, I slew him.

The crowd then applauds Brutus, until Antony speaks. In his elo-quent speech, Antony, seemingly overcome with grief, manipulates the emotions of the audience and persuades them that Caesar was not an ambitious tyrant but rather a compassionate leader. At the same time, he casts doubt on Brutus' honor:

> Friends, Romans, countrymen, lend me your ears;
> I come to bury Caesar, not to praise him.
> The evil that men do lives after them;
> The good is oft interred with their bones;
> So let it be with Caesar. The noble Brutus
> Hath told you that Caesar was ambitious.
> If it were so, it was a grievous fault;
> And grievously hath Caesar answer'd it.
> Here, under leave of Brutus and the rest —
> For Brutus is an honourable man;
> So are they all, all honourable men —
> Come I to speak in Caesar's funeral
> He was my friend, faithful and just to me:
> But Brutus says he was ambitious,
> And Brutus is an honourable man.
> He hath brought many captives home to Rome,
> Whose ransoms did the general coffers fill:
> Did this in Caesar seem ambitious?
> When that the poor have cried, Caesar hath wept:
> Ambition should be made of sterner stuff.

The contrasting styles of the speeches show us much about Shake-speare's attitude toward each of these men. Though it may take more than a single reading to perceive, Shakespeare's irony becomes apparent through Antony's choice of words.

What is nonfiction prose?   Nonfiction prose may have originally been written primarily to inform readers but becomes literature because of its universal and lasting appeal. Essays — personal opinion, familiar, persuasive, descriptive, expository — and such material as letters, diaries, journals, proclamations, and histories may be regarded as literature. Important characteristics of nonfiction prose are *style*, *theme*, *structure*, *tone*, and author's *persona* (the speaker or narrator of the work).

Again, let us examine ambition, this time in nonfiction prose. In *The Prince*, Niccolo Machiavelli, an Italian statesman and philosopher during the Renaissance, gives advice on how to preserve political power:

> A prince, moreover, who wishes to keep possession of a country that is separate and unlike his own, must make himself the chief and protector of the smaller neighboring powers. He must endeavor to weaken the most powerful of them, and must take care that by no chance a stranger enter that province who is equally powerful with himself; for strangers are never called in except by those whom an undue ambition or fear have rendered malcontents. It was thus in fact that the Ætolians called the Romans into Greece; and whatever other country the Romans entered, it was invariably at the request of the inhabitants.
>
> The way in which these things happen is generally thus: so soon as a powerful foreigner enters a province, all those of its inhabitants that are less powerful will give him their adhesion, being influenced thereto by their jealousy of him who has hitherto been their superior. So that, as regards these petty lords, the new prince need not be at any trouble to win them over to himself, as they will all most readily become incorporated with the state which he has there acquired. He has merely to see to it that they do not assume too much authority, or acquire too much power; for he will then be able by their favor, and by his own strength, very easily to humble those who are really powerful; so that he will in all respects remain the sole arbiter of that province. And he who does not manage this part well will quickly lose what he has acquired; and while he holds it, he will experience infinite difficulties and vexations. The Romans observed these points most carefully in the provinces which they conquered; they established colonies there, and sus-

tained the feebler chiefs without increasing their power, while they humbled the stronger, and permitted no powerful stranger to acquire any influence or credit there.

Many readers enjoy Machiavelli's direct, concise prose style; yet many are shocked that this matter-of-fact style is used to convey his seemingly ruthless and cunning approaches to government.

WHY READ LITERATURE?

We read literature because it gives us pleasure and because it gives us some form of truth — truth about ourselves or our world, about what is or what could be. How does literature accomplish this?

First, literature is art; reading it is an aesthetic experience. Although you may be taking a "Survey of . . ." or an "Introduction to . . ." course organized chronologically or by genre, you should realize that literature is more than history or a study of types. Literature is an artistic ordering of words, ideas, and emotions into a unified experience that interprets reality. The arrangement, the pattern of truth and experience found in art, is meant to be enjoyed. The author's skillful use of such tools as powerful language, plot turns, symbols, character development, and irony are meant to give readers pleasure.

Second, literature is "real" even though, paradoxically, the situations and characters it portrays may be fictive. The events in Nathaniel Hawthorne's short story "Rappaccini's Daughter" did not "really" happen. The characters are totally fictitious, and the very idea that a young woman could exhale poison sounds ludicrous and unbelievable. And even though archeologists have discovered a historical Troy, that geographical and cultural reality does not coincide with the reality presented in the *Iliad*. How then, can artists' recreations of reality seem as real as life itself, at times even more real? One answer is that in their creations, artists organize, simplify, and yet simultaneously perceive and evaluate life more fully than most of us who live it ever can.

We tend to be overwhelmed by the mass of impressions received every moment — lived life is a jumble which the artist, by focusing on just one small segment, can turn into a pattern of startling clarity. Observe the contemporary Canadian writer Margaret Atwood recreating a landcrab through a pattern of vivid images in her poem "Landcrab":

> Hermit, hard socket
> for a timid eye,

> you're a soft gut scuttling
> sideways, a blue skull,
> round bone on the prowl.
> Wolf of treeroots and gravelly holes,
> a mouth on stilts,
> the husk of a small demon.

You may have seen a landcrab too, but perhaps you saw it in a setting which provided such a complexity of sensory detail (the day was warm, you were hungry, you were with someone you loved), that you never really saw the crab until you read the poem. The poem, a work of imagination, creates the reality of the creature for the reader.

When Aristotle, the fourth-century B.C. Greek philosopher, writes in his *Poetics* that art is an imitation of the real, he implies that art suggests or gives an impression of truth:

> . . . the instinct of imitation is implanted in man from child-
> hood, one difference between him and other animals being
> that he is the most imitative of living creatures, and through
> imitation learns his earliest lessons. And no less universal
> is the pleasure he takes in seeing things imitated.

Aristotle observes, then, that art gives lessons and pleasure.

Third, then, literature teaches, and there is enjoyment in learning about ourselves and others. Reading James Joyce's short story "Araby" may help you recall and finally understand why the anticipation of childhood outings was many times more exciting than the actual outing.

We as readers also derive pleasure from contemplating ideas, particularly moral and ethical problems. Many writers offer no clear–cut solutions to the problems they raise. Their works provoke thought and challenge our assumptions. After reading Henrik Ibsen's play *The Doll House*, we are left contemplating Nora's decision to leave her husband and children. Mordecai Richler's short story "The Summer My Grandmother Was Supposed to Die" confronts us with the often painful social problems of caring for the elderly. Gwendolyn Brooks' poem "The Mother" forces us to examine the point of view of a woman who has had several abortions, a perspective perhaps too often ignored. And Henry David Thoreau's essay "Civil Disobedience" questions our views on obeying laws when those laws seem unjust. Contemplating ideas and reasoning through problems raised in literature challenge us to confront our own values and examine our own motives for behavior.

THE READING PROCESS

Aldous Huxley, a poet and fiction writer best remembered for his novel *Brave New World*, has written, "Every man who knows how to read has it in his power to magnify himself, to multiply the ways in which he exists, to make his life full, significant, and interesting." To gain this power of magnifying ourselves — of multiplying the ways in which we exist, we need to develop our reading skills. We need to know how to imagine to bring a selection to life — to make reading a significant and pleasurable experience. We need to know how to read beyond the literal level — to read between the lines, to infer, to interpret, and to evaluate what we read. And finally, we need to become aware of how we read — to understand our roles as active readers.

Reading is a dynamic process involving communication — an interaction between readers and the work of literature. As readers, we have roles to fulfill: we are "partners" in the reading experience, not just recipients or viewers.

When we make a "reading," or interpretation, of a work of literature, we engage in a process of composing or constructing meaning and value. Our readings are seldom static; instead, they are dynamic. Different readers produce different readings of the same work of literature. Your reading of Walt Whitman's "The Learn'd Astronomer" may be different from a classmate's reading of that poem; you may see it as an attack on science while your classmate sees it as an admonition to appreciate nature.

Furthermore, what the poem says to you during a first reading may change when you read the same work a week, a month, or a year later. Consider the student who reads Robert Frost's "Stopping by Woods on a Snowy Evening" and enjoys a poem that celebrates the beauty of nature. Yet after a second and more careful reading, she feels convinced that the poem is a dark meditation on death. Likewise, what a work says to one generation or culture may differ from what a work says to another. Your reading can also be influenced by your age and gender, political and religious affiliations, or national and ethnic heritage.

Let us also make a distinction between kinds of "readings." Basically, we read for two purposes: information and pleasure. Reading for information is reading for outcome. When the reading is over, we have learned something that makes us more knowledgeable, or we have learned some useful process. For example, reading directions on how we elect a president is useful reading. The reading produces a tangible outcome: the informed voter. Or perhaps you are curious about the pyramids and read several books and articles explaining why and how the pyramids were built. Although you may never build or even visit one, you are informed about them. Your curiosity has been satisfied and that can be a pleasurable experience.

Yet when we read for pleasure, we read to experience a semblance of reality and to have our feelings and attitudes stimulated. Rather than reading for a useful outcome after the reading, we read for the pleasure that is produced during the reading. We become engaged in or by the experience. We imagine the characters, respond to their conflicts, feel their emotions, sympathize with them, or hate them. We also infer their motivation, predict the outcome, and arrive at conclusions. These activities may also be continued after the reading as we recall the work or discuss it or write about it in a variety of ways, from a free response to a formal research paper. In other words, we gain pleasure from literature as we respond to it during the reading as well as after the reading.

It is true, however, that the distinction between informational and pleasurable reading is not always clear. Often there is a crossover between reading purposes. Quite unexpectedly you may find yourself receiving pleasure from the witty directions and descriptions in a cookbook such as Rombauer and Becker's *Joy of Cooking*. On the other hand what began as a pleasurable reading of a short story suddenly could become practical hands-on knowledge; novelist Richard Wright is said to have taught himself to hunt and fish from the superb details in Hemingway's Nick Adams stories.

Still, knowing your purpose for reading is part of the reading process because it influences both how you interact with the work during the process and what you receive after the process. In this chapter, we have been concerned with the pleasurable reading of imaginative literature (also known as aesthetic reading); however, the skills and abilities you develop for aesthetic reading will strengthen your reading skills in other subject areas as well.

As we have seen, reading involves making sense or making meaning as you read. The ability to make meaning (or multiple meanings) depends on several strategies (some of them occurring simultaneously) before and during the reading. Two helpful strategies are asking questions and rereading.

Reading is an imaginative and problem-solving activity that brings you closer to understanding and solutions. As you read, you will find yourself asking questions such as: What is the author saying to me here? What motivated this action? Could the poet be using a symbol here? What does the title imply? What else has the author written? One goal of this book is to promote question asking. Each chapter poses questions that will help you read and respond to literature. However, the ultimate goal is to help you become an independent reader — to enhance your own ability to imagine and make meanings and to ask questions and produce solutions. Our lists of possible questions are never complete — only suggestive.

Another reading strategy is rereading. As we have said, reading is a process of making meaning; this process often involves backtracking when a passage does not communicate. Perhaps the diction is difficult or the sentence structure unusual. Or perhaps there are not enough transitions to see how the writer has reached point B from point A.

Rereading or backtracking, though, is not done just to clarify or revise meaning. Many readers, struck by the beauty and significance of a passage, reread it to savor the pleasure it brings. The more a passage is read, the better it is known. Multiple readings of the same work enhance your ability to interact with the text.

BEFORE THE READING: ATTITUDES AND EXPECTATIONS

The first stage of the reading process involves your attitudes and expectations about reading. It also involves your prior knowledge of the author and genre and your personal response to the work's title.

Considering Attitudes

First, consider your attitude about the reading process. Are you reading for information or are you reading for pleasure (or both)? Are you reading because you want to read or merely because you have been given an assignment? Is the reading an enjoyable challenge — a valuable experience waiting to happen? Or is it a drudgery — a required chore waiting to be completed?

In a literature class, you are assigned imaginative reading as a course requirement. Your attitude can either enhance or hinder your reading. In other words, your interpretation is influenced by the way you feel about the reading assignment. The most effective readers know they may be changed or challenged by what they read and welcome the experience.

Building Expectations

Besides attitude, you bring your expectations, often based on prior knowledge of the author and genre and perhaps your personal response to the title, into the reading.

First, ask yourself what you know about the author. If you have been assigned Flannery O'Connor's short story "A Good Man Is Hard to Find," and recall reading another of her stories such as "Good Country People," you begin the reading with expectations. You remember that she is a Southern writer from a Catholic background and that she shocks her readers into recognizing spiritual truths. You know her characters typically experience a conflict, often violent, that drastically changes them. And you are familiar with her style of comic violence.

Your expectations are also influenced by the genre of the work. If you notice that a particular poem you are about to read, let's say Gerard Manley Hopkins' "God's Grandeur," is a sonnet, you will be expecting fourteen lines. You may also know that in some sonnets the first eight lines present a problem or situation while the last six offer a solution to the problem or a comment on the situation. Knowledge of genre, then, often establishes expectations which, when fulfilled, bring pleasure.

Analyzing the title (and subtitle, if there is one) is a good way to begin your reading. The title may have personal associations or may reveal important clues. Perhaps the title is a statement that reveals a truth to be dramatized in the work: "A Good Man Is Hard to Find." Perhaps the title reveals the importance of the setting in a work such as Ernest Hemingway's short story "A Clean, Well-Lighted Place." Perhaps the title indicates a possible symbol as in William Faulkner's short story "A Rose for Emily." Perhaps the title is a character's name as in Anton Chekhov's play *Uncle Vanya*. Sometimes, though, literature surprises us by deliberately not fulfilling our expectations. When we read Eliot's "The Love Song of J. Alfred Prufrock," we discover that what Prufrock has to "sing" is far from a love song; rather, it is more of a neurotic monologue in which he laments his total ineffectiveness as a lover. And Flannery O'Connor shows us that "Good Country People" are not always so good.

Besides the title, an epigraph can also help to establish expectations. An *epigraph* is a short quotation after the title but before the body of the work. For example, T. S. Eliot includes epigraphs before many of his poems. Preceding his poem "The Hollow Men" are the epigraphs, "Mistah Kurtz — he dead" and "A penny for the Old Guy."

"Mistah Kurtz" is an *allusion* (a reference to some person, place, thing, or event in history, myth, or literature) to Joseph Conrad's novel *Heart of Darkness* while "A penny for the Old Guy" is an allusion to Guy Fawkes' Day in England. Both Mistah Kurtz and Guy Fawkes are examples of the "lost, violent souls" portrayed in "The Hollow Men"; Guy Fawkes is remembered by burning his effigy — a hollow suit of clothes stuffed with straw. The epigraph is ironic, though, since both Kurtz and Fawkes were capable of exercising their own will and actions in contrast to the hollow men Eliot describes as incapable of choice. (Rereading epigraphs after you finish the work may suddenly clarify the meaning.)

In a literature class, your expectations may also be created by your instructor and your textbooks. Listen carefully to any comments your instructor makes about an assignment to be read. An instructor who says that Nathaniel Hawthorne uses many symbols prepares you to take physical objects in his stories for more than their literal meanings. Some instructors may require you to read for a specific element of literature. For example, you may be asked to read for point of view in Faulkner's "A Rose for Emily." Such specific reading requirements create expectations.

The introductions to reading selections in your anthology or text-book also create expectations. One anthology introduces Flannery O'Connor by mentioning her lack of religious sentimentality and the grotesque humor of her work, thus preparing readers for her tone.

DURING THE READING

Reading imaginative literature requires time. Part of the discipline of being a student requires scheduling enough time for a thoughtful and perceptive reading. Reading will be more pleasurable when there is time to think about a passage, to mull it over, to ask questions, to reread. So turn off the TV, unplug the phone, shut your door, and schedule enough time to read through the work.

During the reading, you may employ numerous strategies to help you make meaning and enjoy a work of literature. These strategies, used concurrently, include adjusting the reading pace, marking the text, responding in a journal or notebook, recognizing vocabulary and allusion, comprehending at the literal level, engaging the imagination, detecting point of view, inferring meaning, and recognizing and comprehending figurative language and symbols.

Adjusting Reading Pace

How fast should you read literature? The answer is that your
reading purpose determines your pace or reading rate. If you are reading a newspaper article to gather only the main ideas and a few details
of a current story, you can speed up your pace. But when reading
aesthetic literature, slow down your pace. First, skim the work and
note the number of pages. A short story is meant to be read in one
sitting. A novel or three-act play, however, will require more time.

Try reading a work at least twice. If you have time for two readings, your first reading can be a quick and intense one to grasp the
unity, gain an overall impression, and decide what is important to you.
Your second reading can then be slower and more "critical," as you
will pay more attention to detail and structural devices.

If you have a tendency to read too quickly to retain all significant
detail, two activities that may force you to slow down your reading
pace and make a thoughtful reading are marking the text and recording
responses. Both these activities occur during the actual reading.

Marking the Text

Highlight, circle, draw arrows, underline; in other words, mark
your text. In the margins or in your reading notes, you can ask questions, make inferences, predict outcomes, and highlight symbols, images, figurative devices. Marking your text will help you later as you
participate in class discussion or prepare for an essay or exam.

Note how one reader marked this passage from Nathaniel Hawthorne's short story "Young Goodman Brown":

Young Goodman Brown came forth at   *Symbolic names?*

time
sunset into the street at Salem village;

but put back his head, after crossing the

Salem witchcraft trials?
threshold, to exchange a parting kiss with

his young wife. And Faith, as the wife was

aptly named, thrust her own pretty head

into the street, letting the wind play

with the pink ribbons of her cap while she

called to Goodman Brown.

"Dearest heart," whispered she,

softly and rather sadly, when her lips

were close to his ear, "prithee put off

what journey?   *time*

your journey until <u>sunrise</u> and sleep in

your own bed tonight. A woman is troubled

what dreams?

with <u>such dreams</u> and such thoughts that

she's afeard of herself sometimes. Pray

tarry with me this night, dear husband, <u>of</u>

<u>all nights</u> of year."

what could this mean?

Also notice how one reader annotated William Blake's poem "Infant Sorrow":

Infant Sorrow   *who is sorry? Baby or parents?*

My mother <u>groan'd</u>! my father <u>wept</u>.   *strong verbs; dramatic opening; somber tone*

Into the <u>dangerous</u> world I leapt: *why dangerous?*

Helpless, naked, piping loud   *Is baby strong or weak?*

Like a fiend hid in a cloud.   *Unusual comparison to describe a newborn — is this why parents groaned and wept?*

Struggling in my father's hands,   *Seems as if baby is*
                                      strong — only gives in
Striving against my swadling bands,   *after a struggle —*

                                      Why does baby "think best"?
[Bound and weary] I thought best   *Because of dangerous world?*

To sulk upon my mother's breast.   *No name, no sex — could*
                                      be any baby.

Responding in a Journal or Notebook

You may also keep a response journal during the actual reading. Record first impressions. These first "fresh" impressions can never be recreated. As we have seen, with each new reading impressions will change. As you note the changes in your reactions, you can record your growth as an interpretive reader.

In a journal, write down passages that are significant to you and comment on them. You can interrupt your reading at key points to predict how the story or drama might end. The response journal can provide a valuable commentary on how you read. For example, after reading how Montresor lures Fortunato into the wine cellar in Poe's "The Cask of Amontillado," did you predict at that key point that Montresor would act out his revenge in such a ghastly manner?

Examine the following personal response made after a student finished reading William Blake's poem "Infant Sorrow":

I don't like this poem! The title made me think it was going to be about a trivial sorrow—mommy yells at baby or daddy doesn't bring any presents home. But instead it's about how tragic it is for a child (male, female?) to be born. That bothers me because I want to think that parents welcome their children. The instructor said Blake was a Romantic and I gathered from the introductory lecture that Romantics thought being a child was wonderful and the world would be a better place if we were all more child-like. But this child is a monster—I wonder if it is a literal monster, a deformed birth of some kind. Probably not, because the fiend is "hid in a

cloud" and that image seems to refer to the pale sweet flesh of
the baby.

Well, it is a strong poem and I guess I would have to say
it's an unusual treatment of a "blessed event!" (Note: the
birth is unattended—no doctor, no midwife, not even a friendly
neighbor or an older sibling—just the triangle of the father
and the mother and the child—is that unusual? Does it indicate
the economic position of the family?)

Now, the instructor suggested we question our own
responses. Why do I think this is an unusual treatment? Well,
I'd like to have a baby someday, but not this baby! That's an
interesting question—is it the baby who's at fault in this poem
or the parents or somebody or something else? How can something
be helpless and naked and also be a fiend? Why would a birth
make a father cry? Why does the baby think it best to give in,
even if temporarily?

I think I'd better look at Blake's poem ''Infant Joy'' in
<u>Songs</u> <u>of</u> <u>Innocence</u>. Maybe that will help me figure this one
out. One baby is wanted and the other isn't. Or is it that
simple? Is it the "dangerous world" that's the problem? Is this
baby going to grow up? Is it going to be allowed to grow up?
Is the mother going to die from the aftereffects of the
childbirth? Should I check and see if Blake was married and had
children? What about the infant mortality rate then? No birth
control? What economic condition is this baby born into? Is
that the difference between being wanted and not wanted?

Comment   This reader responds most strongly to the subject matter of the
poem, the tone, and the language. Although feeling that most births are welcomed, the student can visualize a cultural and economic situation in which a
birth is not desired. That leads to questioning who is responsible for the conflict
in the poem. Reading the companion poem is a sensible thought; the student
might also want to read the longer manuscript version of the poem in Blake's

Notebooks. The student could explore other historical and biographical data for a fuller response or a more formal paper.

A personal response to a longer work will differ from this example in that readers will note only those episodes, characters, or other aspects that affect them most strongly. The following questions could be used to guide a personal response:

1. What is my initial reaction to the work?
2. What does the work say to me?
3. How does it say it?
4. Which elements of the work are most responsible for my response?
5. What have I brought to the reading that affects my response?

Recording personal responses to the literature you read helps you center on your reading, helps you analyze why you react to a certain work as you do, gives you a basis for comparing your response to those of your classmates, and can provide the basis for more formal papers. The next chapter discusses reader-response journals and offers numerous examples of response strategies.

Recognizing Vocabulary and Allusions

Your reading comprehension also depends on your ability to define words and make sense of allusions. Reading builds and strengthens your vocabulary. As you read, mark any unfamiliar words. If you are unable to define the words in context or if the usual definition doesn't seem to fit the context, look them up in a dictionary and jot down brief definitions in the margins of the text. You may also wish to keep a separate list of new words that you encounter in your reading to enhance your personal vocabulary.

The better your vocabulary, the better reader you become. The process of reading requires that you "translate" what you read by defining words. The more accurate your definitions, the richer your reading.

Also, look up any unfamiliar allusions. When J. Alfred Prufrock says, "No, I am not Hamlet," he alludes to Shakespeare's Hamlet whose fatal flaw was vascillation — an inability to act quickly. So, ironically, although Prufrock cannot see himself as a tragic hero, Prufrock is Hamlet. (You will find more comments on defining words and understanding allusions in Chapter 7.)

Comprehending at the Literal Level

Understanding vocabulary and allusions helps you read at the literal level, interpreting for "face value," that is for the "facts" that are directly stated. Because the literal level is the fundamental level of comprehension, it is a good place to begin your reading. After (or even during) reading a work of literature ask yourself first, What happened? or What has the writer created? Base your response on the facts of the work.

For example, after reading Robert Frost's poem "Stopping by Woods on a Snowy Evening," you may say, "A traveler on his way home from a village stops for a moment during a cold and dark evening to look at the woods fill up with snow. His horse is puzzled at the change in the daily routine of driving home. The traveller decides he can pause no longer since he has many miles to go to reach his destination."

At the literal level, you may have experienced pleasurable recognition — you may have identified with the conflict between taking time to contemplate nature and fulfilling an obligation.

Engaging the Imagination

To imagine means to make images. Although we often speak of creating images in the mind's eye as we read, imagery is not restricted to the sense of sight. Images involve all the senses: seeing, touching, smelling, hearing, tasting. You need to use your imagination as you read for the work to become personally meaningful. As you read, recreate the work in the theater of your mind. Imaginative literature, whether a play, a short story, a novel, or a poem, can be seen as a performance. And as you read, you can become the director of the script.

Can you think of times when, having read a novel and envisioned it in your mind, you then saw the movie? Perhaps the movie version was quite different from your mental vision either in the setting or the characterizations. Movies, although requiring visual literacy — active viewing — do much of the imagining for you. When you read, the act of imagination is your responsibility.

How you imagine a work may be very different from how one of your classmates imagines the work since your imaginings are based on the personal experiences and knowledge you bring to the reading. Clearly, how you "see" a character or setting will be different from other readers' visions of that same character or setting.

Note, for example, the images in this passage from D. H. Lawrence's novel *Women in Love:*

> There was a long pause, whilst Ursula stitched and Gudrun went on with her sketch. The sisters were women, Ursula twenty-six, and Gudrun twenty-five. But both had the remote virgin look of modern girls, sisters of Artemis rather than of Hebe. Gudrun was very beautiful, passive, soft-skinned, soft-limbed. She wore a dress of dark-blue silky stuff, with ruches of blue and green linen lace in the neck and sleeves; and she had on emerald green stockings. Her look of confidence and diffidence contrasted with Ursula's sensitive expectancy. The provincial people, intimidated by Gudrun's perfect sang-froid and exclusive bareness of manner, said of her: "She is a smart woman."

Analyze your reading of the above passage. What images come to mind as you read the passage? How do you "see" Gudrun? What images help you see her? Look up the allusions to Artemis and Hebe. How do these allusions enhance character? Look up the term *sang-froid*. How does this term apply to Gudrun? Now compare your images of the two women with another reader's images. How do they differ? Why?

Detecting Point of View

As you read a work of literature, you will discover its point of view: who tells the story. Point of view becomes apparent early in a work. Although point of view will be discussed more thoroughly in Chapter 10, basically, a work is narrated either by someone in the work or by someone outside the work. In either case, the narrator may be deeply involved in the action or removed from it.

When you know the point of view, you can read the selection through the narrator's eyes as well as your own. For example, if you simply examine the events in William Faulkner's short story "A Rose for Emily," you may be horrified; however, if you read the events through the point of view of the narrator who represents the town in the story, you may sympathize with Miss Emily and have pity for her.

You may also find yourself asking: Can I trust the narrator? What if the narration is distorted? Suppose the narrator is drunk or insane? When a story is told by an unreliable narrator, use your powers of inference to determine what you think really happens. What one of Edgar Allan Poe's mad narrators tells you happened is often quite different from what you may infer "really" happened.

Many writers also experiment with narration. This experimentation may interfere with your reading until you recognize the narrative technique. Emily Dickinson, for example, wrote some poems from the point of view of someone who is dying or dead. You may find yourself asking, How can a dead person tell a story?, but you must make a leap of the imagination and accept the writer's narrative viewpoint. Having made such a leap, you can now ask, What's the point and effect of telling the poem in the voice of a dead person?

Reading Inferentially

As mentioned above, you may have to infer events in a story rather than depend on the narrator. When you read inferentially, you go beyond the literal level — you become sensitive to innuendo, suggestion, and implication. Since authors do not directly state all meaning in a work, become an effective reader — be open to what is left unsaid.

You may be asking: Why do writers write indirectly? Why do they not just state plainly what they have to tell? First, to state directly all meaning would bore many readers. But more importantly, suggestiveness is a powerful method of revealing information and engaging the reader. Suggestiveness creates interpretive literature. Connotative diction and symbolic action also make demands on the reader who must rely on insight, experience, and knowledge to draw conclusions, bridge gaps, and interpret the text.

Remember, though, that valid inferences must be based on facts; what you infer must be supported by the facts in the work itself. The facts in a piece of literature can be underlined; personal inferences are mental and cannot be underlined.

The student who infers that the speaker in "Stopping by Woods on a Snowy Evening" is Santa Claus presents an interesting interpretation; nevertheless, it is one that cannot be validated by the facts of the poem. However, the student who infers that the speaker possesses a death wish can indeed validate such an inference because the facts in the poem support this view.

When reading literature, you can make inferences:

1. from a single piece of information;
2. by relating two or more pieces of information within a single passage;
3. by relating two or more pieces of information from various parts of the entire work;
4. by bridging gaps; and
5. by predicting outcomes during the reading.

First, you can infer meaning from a single piece of information. In Poe's short story "Ligeia," the narrator asks, "Where were the souls of the haughty family of the bride, when, through thirst of gold, they permitted to pass the threshold of an apartment so bedecked, a maiden and a daughter so beloved?" From this single piece of information, the reader can infer that Rowena's parents knew how horrible the living conditions would be for their daughter. (We can also infer, from the tone of the passage, the narrator's hostility towards his new bride.)

Second, you can infer meaning by relating or connecting two or more pieces of information within a single passage. In Robert Browning's poem "My Last Duchess," the Duke informs his listener:

> Oh sir, she smiled, no doubt,
> When'er I passed her; but who passed without
> Much the same smile? This grew; I gave commands;
> Then all smiles stopped together. There she stands
> As if alive.

From this passage we realize that the Duchess was friendly with everyone, and that the Duke was jealous. When he "gave commands," her smiles stopped. From reading the last line "There she stands/As if alive," we infer that she is dead and that the Duke may even have had her murdered!

Third, you can infer meaning by relating two or more pieces of information from various parts of the entire work. At the beginning of Act II of Arthur Miller's play *Death of a Salesman*, Willie Loman asks his wife not to mend her stockings in front of him. We may wonder why he makes such a request. Later in the play, though, we (along with Willy's son) watch Willy give a box of new stockings to a secretary in a Boston hotel. When we read this action, we connect the two events. By making connections, we not only see the unity of the work, but we make an inference: Willy does not want to see his wife mend stockings because that action makes him feel guilty about his gifts to his mistress.

Fourth, you can infer what happens in literature by bridging gaps in time. An author may skip over ten years in a character's life between paragraphs. And you must be able to infer, based on the text, what happened to that character in those ten years. In Nathaniel Hawthorne's "Young Goodman Brown," the title character walks into a forest one evening and has an experience that profoundly affects him. He returns to his village the next morning a suspicious, sad man. In a matter of a few paragraphs, Hawthorne jumps over the intervening years to Brown's death as an old man:

> And when he had lived long, and was borne away to his grave a hoary corpse, followed by Faith, an aged woman, and children and grandchildren, a goodly procession, besides neighbors not a few, they carved no hopeful verse upon his tombstone, for his dying hour was gloom.

Yet from the details in this passage, the reader infers that the intervening years were primarily sad and gloomy for Brown.

Fifth, you can predict outcomes during the reading. Part of the pleasure of reading literature is wondering what will happen next. During the actual reading, we often pause to guess future action. Using evidence and foreshadowing, we make a "hypothesis" about the fate of a character or the end of the story. When we finish the work, our hypothesis is either confirmed or negated. Because we enjoy discovering whether or not our predictions are accurate, we do not want a story too easily "set up." Readers may even criticize a work as "too predictable." Emily Dickinson reminds us, "the riddle that we guess / We easily despise."

Recognizing and Comprehending Figurative Language

As your reading becomes more sophisticated, you will recognize the necessity of understanding literary devices such as figurative language or comparisons that are not literally true. Figurative language suggests meanings and often, just as does indirection, can make a truth more clear than if it were told literally.

Since figurative language will be treated more fully in Chapter 7, let's consider here as examples only two figures that you will encounter frequently during your reading: the metaphor and the simile.

A metaphor is a comparison most often using a form of the verb *to be*. The poet William Butler Yeats writes, "An aged man is but a paltry thing, / a tattered coat upon a stick," thus implying that an old man is a scarecrow in some ways.

A simile also compares; however, the comparison requires the use of *like* or *as*. Ben Johnson writes:

> A secret in his mouth is like
> a wild bird in a cage,
> whose door no sooner opens,
> than 'tis out.

The simile in this passage, because of the word *like*, is indirect; a secret escaping a mouth is not a bird escaping a cage but it is similar (simile).

Metaphor and simile, like all figurative language, are not reserved for poetry alone. Many prose writers incorporate these figurative devices into their works. Note for example, this description from Flannery O'Connor's short story "A Good Man Is Hard to Find": "Bailey didn't look up from his reading so she wheeled around . . . and faced the children's mother; a young woman in slacks, whose face was as broad and innocent as a cabbage and was tied around with a green handkerchief that had two points on the top like rabbit's ears." An unflattering image of Bailey's wife results from O'Connor's vivid similes.

Recognizing and Comprehending Symbols

Symbols — objects, people, settings, and actions that stand for something else — greatly influence your comprehension of literature. To be a careful reader you do not have to see symbols in everything you read nor do you have to go on "symbol hunts," but you should be aware that an object which recurs throughout a work may very well be symbolic.

For example, many readers think that Robert Frost's famous line "miles to go before I sleep" is symbolic because it is repeated twice at the end of the poem. The first time we read the line, we may take it literally: the speaker has a long way to travel before he can climb into bed. But the second time we read it, we may think, Does the poet mean something more than the evening journey? Could "miles" mean life with its multiple responsibilities, and could "sleep" mean death?

CHAPTER REVIEW

In this chapter the term *literature* has been defined as that written work which has lasting appeal and which is highly regarded and widely accepted by its readers. This book will consider as literature poetry, fiction, drama, and nonfiction prose.

We read literature because it gives us pleasure and truth. Literature is art, and reading it is an aesthetic experience. In particular, we can derive pleasure from contemplating ideas and problems raised in the literature.

Reading literature is a dynamic process involving an interaction between the reader and the work itself. As readers we are "partners" in the reading experience; we produce meaning and receive pleasure as we bring our own experiences and knowledge into the reading process.

As a process, reading literature involves skills practiced before and during the reading. Before the reading, we should consider our attitudes and expectations towards the work. The genre, the title, epigraphs, instructors' comments, and introductions to reading selections help build our expectations.

During the reading process, we can adjust our reading pace, mark the text, respond in a journal or notebook, recognize vocabulary and allusions, comprehend at the literal level, engage our imaginations, detect point of view, read inferentially, and recognize and comprehend figurative language and symbols. These skills can be learned and refined to make us stronger, more thoughtful readers.

CHAPTER 2

Responding through Journal Writing

THE PURPOSE FOR KEEPING A JOURNAL

*K*eeping a journal is one productive way of responding to literature. Your instructor may require a journal, or you may decide to keep one to invent and record ideas about literature.

Many professional writers like Henry David Thoreau, Nathaniel Hawthorne, F. Scott Fitzgerald, and Sylvia Plath kept journals to record their thoughts, impressions, observations, and experiences. Ideas and observations first jotted down in their journals often became material for their literature. Hawthorne, for example, kept a notebook of ideas that foreshadowed the major themes of his stories. In one passage he wrote, "The unpardonable sin might consist in a want of love and reverence for the Human Soul; in consequence of which, the investigator pried into its dark depths, not with a hope or purpose of making it better, but from a cold philosophical curiosity, content that it should be wicked in whatever kind or degree, and only desiring to study it out." This entry eventually provided the theme for his story "Ethan Brand," a tale of the consequences of a lime burner's search for the unpardonable sin.

The journal can also be an excellent tool of discovery for student writers. Journals foster your ability to observe and record your observations. With continued practice in seeing, you develop a greater awareness of yourself, your vision, and your world. In your journal you have a chance to be real — you do not have to present a mask as you may do in front of people. Your journal offers you the opportunity to write down intuitions and hunches, to define problems, to express powerful emotions, and to expand sensitivity and perception. You have time to reflect and meditate. You have the opportunity to sharpen your senses.

THE LITERATURE JOURNAL

In some classes, the journal provides an opportunity to write about your personal life, class lectures, reading and writing assignments, class discussions, or current events. Although you may do some or all of these in your literature journal, your primary journal goal is to respond to the reading and writing assignments in your class.

Your literature journal can become a companion to your textbook or anthology. Keep your journal next to your textbook as you read an introductory explanation, a poem, a drama, or a prose work. As you read, record observations and reactions in your journal. Consider the following examples:

> Henry James' short story "The Beast in the Jungle" bored me to tears! However, Mark Twain's "The Man That Corrupted Hadleyburg" appealed to me. I like Twain's plot twists.

Comment   Record immediate and "gut" reactions to a reading assignment. Often these immediate reactions will be in the form of "likes" and "dislikes." These reactions will help you review before a class discussion.

•   •   •

> Emily Dickinson's poetry is difficult to read. She uses words in strange ways. Some of her poems are like word puzzles. "After Great Pain" is a good example. I can't figure this one out.

Comment   Record problems and frustrations you had with the literature. You can present these problems for class discussion and clarification.

•   •   •

I really like Francis Bacon's essays. Especially "Of Studies." His sentences are well constructed: "Reading maketh a full man; conference a ready man; and writing an exact man."

Comment   Record and respond to passages that speak to you because of their style or meaningful content.

•   •   •

I know someone just like J. Alfred Prufrock. Self-absorbed, fearful, unable to act on desires. They are both pathetic.

Comment   Many instructors like to begin a class session by asking a general question such as, "What is your reaction to T. S. Eliot's 'The Love Song of J. Alfred Prufrock'?" Your journal can provide you with accurate and immediate reactions. You may even wish to read a passage from your journal to your instructor or class.

•   •   •

This course began with poems by Emily Dickinson and ended with poems by Sylvia Plath. Interesting! I see some similarities—especially in their treatments of death. Possible essay topic here!

Comment   The journal is a source of ideas for essays. When you are given a writing assignment, you can search for a topic in your journal. Also, some instructors have students select one or two journal entries and develop, revise, and polish them into an essay.

•   •   •

Wow! Langston Hughes' essay "Salvation" was powerful! I could see myself in that essay. Reminds me of the days when my grandmother forced me to attend revival meetings.

Comment   In your journal you can relate literature to your personal life and draw connections to current events.

I never stop being amazed at Madame Bovary's inability to correctly interpret the events in her life. Now she wants to have an affair with a scoundrel. I bet she has that affair, and I bet it will be a complete disaster for her.

Comment   You can predict and then follow character development, themes, plot turns, conflicts, symbols.

·   ·   ·

I've never really considered the book of Ruth as a short story. But all the elements are there—plot, character, setting, and conflict. The author tells a good tale—well written.

Comment   You can comment on the author's style.

·   ·   ·

Dear Virginia Woolf,

Could I come for tea this afternoon? I'm having some problems with <u>To the Lighthouse</u>. Could you shed some light on your style—"stream of consciousness"? Sometimes I get the feeling that your book just rambles on like random thoughts and impressions.

Comment   You can be divergent and creative with your responses. For example, write a letter from one character to another. Write a letter to the author. Clip newspaper articles that relate to the literature you read.

Writing in the Journal

Here is some more specific advice about keeping a literature journal:

> 1. *Identify.* Number, date, and title your entry. The title may simply be the name of the work of literature, or you may invent a clever, perceptive title of your own.

#16, October 2, Zora Neal Hurston's prose

#25, January 25, A Letter to F. Scott Fitzgerald

#8, March 13, Reactions to Chaucer's "The Wife of Bath"

2. *Predict.* Examine the work's title (and epigraph, if there is one). Read the first few paragraphs (the exposition) or the first stanza of a poem. Write down what you think is happening or what you think will happen.

> OK. I've read the first paragraphs of Poe's "The Fall of the House of Usher." I'm ready for gloom—lots of it. All those gloomy adjectives! He sure has set the tone.

3. *Evaluate.* After finishing a work, respond to your predictions and expectations. Were they accurate? Why or why not? In what ways did the literature surprise you?

> I never thought that Edward Albee's "The Zoo Story" would have such a tragic ending! I did not feel prepared for the violence. I did note, though, that conflict between Jerry and Peter did build pretty fast.

4. *React.* React emotionally and subjectively to content and style. Try to make sense of your reactions. Why do you feel the way you do?

> I enjoyed Coleridge's "The Rime of the Ancient Mariner." The story had a magical—hypnotic effect on me. I think because of the sound pattern.

5. *Associate.* Associate, relate, or connect the work with anything from your experience, from current events, or from other reading.

> I'm surprised at how timely Gerard Manley Hopkins' poem "God's Grandeur" is. He could have written it yesterday. We are using up the world's resources—and yet God replenishes the earth daily.

6. *Analyze.* What images, words, phrases, motifs, or symbols stick in your mind after finishing the work?

> I still can't forget that final scene in
> Faulkner's "A Rose for Emily." Emily kept that body all
> those years—she just can't let go of the people she
> loves. She tried to keep her father's body too.

7. *Backtrack.* After finishing a class discussion, lecture, or film, respond to the literature again. How did the classroom experience confirm or change ideas that you developed during your first reading?

> I was surprised at the class reaction to
> Hawthorne's "My Kinsman, Major Molineux." I thought
> Robin was a pretty nice guy. A lot of students disliked
> him. Some classmates even thought Robin was sort of
> evil—he used people for his advantage.

8. *Reread.* Reread the literature and make journal responses based on your second reading. You will be surprised at what you "see" during your second reading!

> Second readings on Poe stories are helpful. You
> really see how crazy his characters are. Also, after
> reading "The Cask of Amontillado" twice, I can detect
> the irony.

Sample Journal Entries

You may wish to start your journal with some responses about your class, your instructor, and your text. Many students like to start the journal with a response about keeping a journal.

Note one student's first reaction to her literature class:

#1, January 18: First Day of Class

> I think I'm going to enjoy this class. I hope so, anyway.
> I enjoy reading. Especially short stories. I read several

stories by Flannery O'Connor. Really enjoyed her style! I hope
I can survive the writing assignments. I don't know how to
write an essay about literature. But the instructor seems fair
enough—even gave lists of course objectives, reading and
writing assignments, and due dates. At least I know what to
expect. The first reading assignment is Emily Dickinson. I
remember reading her in high school—and I remember that I
didn't understand one word I read! I hope this instructor
explains them! Edgar Allan Poe comes next. Goody! I like a
good, spooky story.

Comment   This journal entry records some of the student's initial reactions
to the class. She also feels free to write about both her likes and dislikes. Note
her comments about past experiences in literature classes.

One way to begin writing in your journal is to start with "likes" and
"dislikes." After reading a piece of literature, begin your entry with "I like . . ."
or "I dislike . . ." Give three reasons for your opinions.

Here is a journal entry on Stephen Crane's short story "The Open
Boat":

#12, February 2: Reactions to "The Open Boat"

I liked this one! Couldn't stand that story by Sarah Orne
Jewett—too honey—coated for me. Read like a soap opera. Now
this one—"The Open Boat"—appeals to me. I like the way those
men battle the waves. Those waves are always pushing them back
each time they try to reach the shore. Just like life! I also
like the correspondent's change in attitude by the end of the
story. He's no longer cynical—but has learned the importance
of the "brotherhood"—how survival sometimes depends on how
much we help each other through rough times. I also liked
Stephen Crane's macho style.

Comment   Note that this student gives very specific reasons for his "likes."
Note too that his response is very informal, almost chatty. He is very candid in

his comments about Sarah Orne Jewett. He is not afraid to comment about a piece of literature he does not like.

Journal entries can serve as reminders of what happens in a work — a plot or story summary. Writing a summary shows that you can follow the events and conflicts in the story. Read, for example, this student's summary of "The Open Boat":

#18, February 5, "The Open Boat"

"The Open Boat" is about four men in a boat—a lifeboat. They were on a larger boat but it sank. These men are trying to get to the shore but the waves keep pushing them back. Eventually they are swamped and have to swim to shore. One of the men dies.

Comment   This journal entry is a brief plot synopsis. It offers no evaluation, only summary.

However, many instructors will want your entries to reveal more interpretation and evaluation than is possible in a summary. Compare the above entry with another student's journal entry.

#18, February 6, "The Open Boat"

I think this story is "heavy duty." I liked the class notes on realism and naturalism. I think I see life "naturalistically." I often feel like a victim of fate—a plaything of nature. I often feel "out of control." And those waves just keep on coming!

"The Open Boat"—Loved it!

Men out of control.

Much irony—deadpan humor even. Narrator is cruel!

Each character gets a quick, precise description.

Those waves are symbols for obstacles in life.

I bet some of the men won't make it to shore—the
correspondent and the captain—I bet they die!

These men are out of control! Things are bad enough and
then that shark comes I like the way the correspondent cusses
into the water. Nice detail!

Wow! The oiler died! And he was the strongest of them all!
What irony. More irony. I think Stephen Crane likes irony. Now
that's a good topic for a paper: Irony in "The Open Boat."

Comment   Note that this reader's entry begins with some general comments
about class notes and feelings about her own life. Her use of slang such as
"heavy duty" is fine for a journal. Some of her response to the story is in the
form of a list. Note, too, that her list is fragmented and offers a running
commentary on the story. She also uses sentence fragments as she jots down
ideas.

Sometimes an instructor will attempt to focus a journal entry by
requiring a response to a specific question. An instructor might ask for
a response to tone, symbols, or themes in a particular work. These
journal responses often provide content for later writing assignments
about literature. For example, one instructor asked students to read
"The Open Boat" and write a journal response on the theme or meaning of the work. Here is one response to this assignment:

#12, January 28, Theme in "The Open Boat"

Absurdity! We're all in an open boat. We're all out of
control. Sounds bleak—but it's the truth. You are born and you
die! And in the middle you combat each wave that comes your way
until eventually you are swamped. The key to the theme is the
"subtle brotherhood of man" mentioned in the story. This is
what the characters learn. New vision to help them survive. New
vision helps them become "interpreters." I like this story.
It's serious—I'm a serious person. I don't like froth.

Later in class, the instructor asked students to write a paragraph
about the theme in "The Open Boat," using ideas developed in the

journal. Here is the student's paragraph based on her journal entry above:

Theme in "The Open Boat"

Stephen Crane enlightens his readers to the absolute absurdity of existence and offers a pathetic response to combat this realization in his short story "The Open Boat." We are all in an open boat. We spend our lives battling circumstances beyond our control. We get over one life-threatening wave, sliding back to what we think is safety only to face another bigger and meaner wave. Why? The irony of existence is that people walk around in the dark—not knowing that their destiny is staring them boldly in the face. They ignore it! What they should know is that there are two points to existence—you are born and then you die. That's it! What happens in between doesn't really matter because we are all being drawn to the same destiny—death. Hence, nothing matters. In the face of death, everything is absurd. We must eventually realize this and develop a conviction to fight it. Stephen Crane in "The Open Boat" suggests the concept of "subtle brotherhood." If there is any meaning to be extracted out of all this meaninglessness called life, it is brotherhood. This meaning is the characters' "new vision." They experience the epiphany of realizing the absolute absurdity of existence, find a way to combat it, and now consider themselves "interpreters" of life.

In your journal, respond to literature that speaks powerfully to you. Try to locate the source of the power. One student was impressed with Langston Hughes' poem "A Dream Deferred." Note his entry:

#16, March 5, "A Dream Deferred"

I never thought I'd enjoy a poem this much. "A Dream Deferred" really speaks to me as it would to any member of the black race. I want to read more poems like this. Hughes speaks

for the black people or for any people who have to defer their
dreams.

I see now where the play Raisin in the Sun got its name.
What I particularly like about this poem is the way Hughes asks
questions and follows up each question with a simile. "Does it
[deferred dream] dry up like a raisin in the sun?" His imagery
is vivid—"fester like a sore," "stink like rotten meat." The
last line of the poem is explosive.

Comment   This response offers reasons why the poem speaks to him. The
student also incorporates the language of the class (simile and imagery) into
his entry.

Sometimes a reading assignment will be difficult, full of ambiguity
and complexity. When you encounter a difficult reading assignment,
describe your difficulties in your journal. Note the following reader's
problems with Gerard Manley Hopkins' poem "God's Grandeur":

#25, April 25, "God's Grandeur"

This poem is a tough one! A challenge! At first I was
really confused about the meaning—and I'm still not sure I
understand it! The first few times I read it, I got caught up
in the sound effects of the poem. I read this one aloud.
(Imagine me reading a poem aloud!) But the poem really has
sound! (I like that "ooze of oil.") Actually the sound sort of
distracts me from the meaning.

I think Hopkins is writing about how man has used up (or is
using up) our natural resources. Also, man does not pay much
attention to God's care for us.

But in the second stanza, I feel that Hopkins says that
God still cares for us in spite of all the rotten things we do.

Comment   Although she finds the poem to be a tough one, a challenge, her
journal entry reveals that her basic interpretation is sound. She also pinpoints
a very important aspect of the poem — its sound effects.

The journal is also a good place to record your experiences as a result of class reading assignments. One student read *Oedipus Rex* and recounted the plot to his family. His journal response records their reactions:

#3, January 27, Oedipus Rex

    Wow! Had to jot this down. During dinner, I explained to my parents and sister what happens in Oedipus Rex. None of them had read it. (Now I know where the Oedipus complex comes from. I read about it in psychology last semester.) Well—at dinner I watched my parents' faces as I summarized the story. For once Dad listened to me and not the television set. And even my little sister stopped playing with her string beans. Boy did their eyes bulge out. Then Dad asked, Is that what you're learning in college? Hah! Then my mom asked what I learned from the story. I told her what we discussed in class—about pride and the relentless search for the truth.

Some instructors will make journal assignments designed to stretch the imagination. For example, one instructor asked students to read the textbook's introductory chapter on Emily Dickinson and write a journal response that relates her to our age and time. Note what one student writes in response to this journal assignment:

#1, January 18, Emily Dickinson

    Emily Dickinson has a great deal in common with comedian Woody Allen. Both Emily and Woody are intrigued with death as a theme. They also enjoy depression, loneliness, and the like. Emily was slightly more reclusive than Woody although both avoid publicity. The two writers also share the problem of having editors revise and correct their work. Finally, Emily and Woody tell others of such desperate problems that the reader/viewer can't help but feel his own pale in comparison. Perhaps if Woody were to retreat to his room for thirty or forty years, his work would last as long as Emily's has.

Creative Projects

The journal also provides an opportunity for creative expression and experimentation. Creative journal projects call for abstract thinking. You may need to make some unusual leaps of the imagination to complete a project. Consider the following creative project assignment: You are Emily Dickinson's next-door neighbor. Write a letter about Emily Dickinson to your cousin in Salem.

Here is how one student responded to the journal project:

```
#15, September 17, Letter to Cousin in Salem

    Now the task has fallen upon me to write a letter to tell
about the death of Emily Dickinson. How shall I go about it?
She was a unique person whom I met more than thirty years ago.
Her poetry seemed simple—spoken from the heart. Now she is
dead. How shall I tell of her death?




                                            May 21, 1886


Dear Julian,

    I have been bothered about something that has occurred
here in Amherst, and no one seems to want to believe my account
of what happened. For my sanity's sake—you are my last hope.
Please read this letter—and believe that what you read—is
true!

    You will recall that in previous letters I have mentioned
the rather peculiar little lady who lives (or lived) next door
to me—Emily Dickinson, by name. Well, I have been told that she
died on May 15, about a week ago. May 15 is a day that I shall
never forget, and when I relate my tale, you will understand
why.
```

I was tending my roses in the front garden that afternoon as I do most days during the spring. And while about my tasks, I heard the sound of horses' hooves coming down the street. I wondered who it might be, and looking down the street, my eyes beheld a most astonishing sight! A carriage was approaching—a carriage so white that it appeared almost translucent. The wheels, shiny and gold, seemed to float above, rather than roll along the pavement. Two beautiful, stately, white horses drew the carriage up the street and stopped in front of the Dickinson house.

There was somebody in the carriage, but as I had never seen him before, I do not know who it was. Miss Emily must have known him though, and she must have been expecting him. When the carriage halted, I saw the door of the house open, and Miss Emily, looking vibrantly healthy, came out and walked towards the waiting carriage. She paused once, and I noticed how lovely she looked all dressed in white. Her gown was gossamer, her tippet only tule. She almost looked like a bride. After a moment's hesitation, she glided out to the carrige, climbed in and seated herself next to the very civil stranger. He must have been a long awaited friend or perhaps her secret lover!

The horses' heads never strayed once from their forward-looking position. When Emily had been comfortably seated, the horses sprang forward as if by some internal signal. The wheels turned and as I watched, carriage, horses, Emily, and the stranger simply disappeared in one blinding glow of light!

I was later told that Emily had died that day. How can that be?

Write me soon and tell me what you think!

Your cousin,

Betty

Comment   This journal entry is creative, fresh, original, and thoughtful. The response is experimental and shows insight into both Emily Dickinson's life and her poem "Because I Could Not Stop for Death."

Imitation and Parody

Two more methods of creatively responding to a work are imitation and parody. Imitation, sincere flattery or not, is also a respected literary form in its own right and can be a useful tool for literary interpretation. An *imitation* adopts as much of the original writer's style and subject matter as possible in an attempt to recreate the flavor of the original; therefore, it is easiest to imitate a writer with a unique style. For possible journal entries consider a series of short essays in the style of Sir Francis Bacon, a "Canterbury Tale" à la Chaucer, or perhaps a diary entry in the vein of Virginia Woolf.

Imitation that exaggerates the qualities it imitates or inappropriately matches style to content, is *parody*, another ancient literary form. It is similar to cartooning or caricature in visual art. Parodies center on an unusual feature of an author's style — for example, Gertrude Stein's syntax in *Tender Buttons* — and then exaggerate that feature. Parodies may also imitate a style in a fairly straightforward manner, without exaggeration, but treat a wholly inappropriate subject. You might, for example, write a parody of Jonathan Swift's essay "A Modest Proposal" in your journal. Calling hers "A Modest Disposal," one student parodied Swift by writing a satire on twentieth-century methods of dealing with pollution.

More Creative Ideas

Here is a list of other creative projects that you can use or adapt for journal entries or other assignments:

1. *Diary*. Write diary entries from the point of view of an author or character. For example, write a page from the diary of Emily Grierson in Faulkner's "A Rose for Emily." Or produce several entries from Ann Bradstreet's diary written on her voyage to America.

2. *Long-lost short story*. Write a short story using a specific author's style. For example, write Edgar Allan Poe's last work (which you found,

no doubt, in an old desk in New England.) You may wish to update the story by making reference to the present.

3. *The Evening News*. Write an evening news script for an event narrated in a novel, poem, or play. Imagine a news story covering the plight of King Lear. Perhaps "perform" the news story (in evening news style) for your class.

4. *I Met. . . .* Write a letter in which you recount a meeting with an author or a character from a work of literature. Suppose you met Willie Loman from Arthur Miller's play *Death of a Salesman*. Include details that you observed during that meeting. Base your letter on information from the original work.

5. *Eulogy*. Write a funeral oration or eulogy for a character or an author. Perhaps you attended Walt Whitman's funeral or spoke at J. Alfred Prufrock's funeral.

6. *Psychological case report*. You are a psychiatrist. A character from one of Lovecraft's tales (or perhaps Lovecraft himself) has come to you for help. After your first session with the character or author, you must write a report for your files or for a magazine such as *Psychology Today*.

7. *Interview with a character or author*. Interview someone like Thoreau and use quotations from his writing to answer your questions.

8. *Scenario*. Write a scenario for a video. Your scenario must be so detailed that the director and camera technicians will have no problems in filming. Find appropriate music and locations for your project.

9. *Newspaper account*. Write a newspaper account of an event in a work of literature or an author's life. Include a picture. For example, write a feature article on author Flannery O'Connor. Or perhaps write an article on the grandmother in O'Connor's tale "A Good Man Is Hard to Find."

10. *Reply*. A variation of the personal response is a reply to a work. The reply is a particularly good response when a work seems so biased or prejudiced or slanted that your initial reaction is vehement opposition. For example, suppose you're a young woman and you've just read Robert Herrick's "To the Virgins, to Make Much of Time." The whole premise of the poem, that the only worthwhile fate for a woman is marriage, irritates you. What can you do? Present your point of view, the angle the author, for whatever purpose, has neglected. Write an answering poem to Herrick, perhaps entitled "To the Poet, I'm Not Worried" or "To the Young Men, to Be Less Concerned about the Courtship Game."

CHAPTER REVIEW

The journal can be a valuable tool for discovering and recording ideas. A literature response journal gives you the opportunity to react to literature in a variety of ways. You can record observations, problems, questions, frustrations, or meaningful passages. In addition, you may comment on an author's style, characters, themes, plot turns, conflicts, and symbols. Other journal entries could include predictions, evaluations, associations, reactions, analyses, or backtracking. The journal is also a good place for creative projects such as letters, imitations, and parodies. Responding in a journal can sharpen your powers of observation and original thinking. Journal entries can also provide valuable insights for class discussions and more formal writing assignments.

CHAPTER 3

Responding through Creative Activities

THE NATURE OF CREATIVITY

When physicist Albert Einstein was a teenager, he imagined himself in flight riding a beam of white light across the universe. What a magical image! Einstein in flight! This wild image may have been the beginning of his theory of relativity. His theory, though, was in the creating stage for quite some time. $E = MC^2$ didn't just suddenly appear to him. It was the product of imagination and years of creative incubation.

Creativity is a process we are all capable of performing. And often the result of the process is a product — whether a work of art, an understanding of a piece of music, a scientific formula, a recipe, or an essay for a literature class. Other rewards of the creative process are knowledge, insight, and self-satisfaction.

Before we examine some specific creating activities that will help you produce ideas for essays in your literature class, here are some qualities you can develop.

Creative People Have a Sense of Daring

Being creative means launching out in new directions. This launching demands courage. Psychologist Rollo May, in his book *The Courage to Create*, identifies imagination as the vital human capacity to "consider diverse possibilities, to cast off mooring ropes, taking one's chances that there will be new mooring posts in the vastness ahead."

Taking a literature class demands some daring on your part. When you interpret a work of literature, make some bold guesses about the author's intentions. Present what was meaningful and valuable to you to your class and instructor. Remember, too, that other readers of literature and literary responses are always looking for fresh ways of seeing and understanding the works you study together. If you have found a new way of interpreting Hawthorne's "Young Goodman Brown," perhaps an interpretation based on symbols and setting, then write out your ideas, develop them, let them cool, and then come back to them. If you can support your interpretation, share these findings.

Creative People Tolerate Ambiguity

Creative people have learned to be open to multiple interpretations. Ambiguity teases the mind and makes us think. When we tolerate ambiguity, we learn to see divergently rather than in either/or or right/wrong dichotomies. Either/or thinking limits possibilities, and right/wrong thinking is inappropriate when interpreting literature.

Perhaps you have seen the famous picture of the rabbit and the duck.

At first you may be looking at a picture of a rabbit. Then, without warning, you see a duck or vice versa. You become aware of two creatures lurking in the lines. And, at any one moment, you can perceive either animal, but not both. And yet both are there. Tolerate the ambiguity — recognize the possibility of both.

In an American literature class, you may read Hawthorne's "Rappaccini's Daughter." During class lecture and discussion, you may hear three different interpretations of the story, each backed with proof. Which one is correct? Perhaps they all are or perhaps they each leave unanswered questions.

Creative People Develop Imagery

Thinking in images — not just words — is another characteristic of creative people. In fact, creating often begins where language ends. What is a dream or a fantasy? When we dream or fantasize, we often do so in pictures, sounds, and smells.

Take, for example, the creative process of Emily Dickinson. In an effort to understand death, she personifies it, gives it human characteristics. By putting a face on death, she can encounter death and deal with "him" as she writes, "Because I could not stop for Death — / He kindly stopped for me."

The ability to image is an important skill to develop in a literature class. As you read, try to see the characters and their conflicts. Try to see the setting and watch the action.

CREATING ACTIVITIES

Creating activities are examples of private writing. Private writing can be a powerful tool for the discovery of ideas eventually presented to the public. Five creating activities that will help you discover and rediscover ideas are brainstorming, listing, making inquiries, cubing, freewriting, and responding to questions.

Brainstorming

One way to generate ideas about a piece of literature is to talk about it with other people and to listen to their ideas and record what is useful to you. Sometimes an informal discussion will produce ideas that had not occurred to you. When you brainstorm, you tap the ideas of others. And often, other people's ideas will lead you to ideas of your own.

Here are some guidelines for brainstorming:

1. Freely call out ideas on the work
2. Do not criticize any ideas you hear, however silly they may seem to you.
3. Write down information that seems useful to you.
4. Evaluate the information later.

Here is part of a recorded brainstorming session held in one professor's class. The students were asked to read Ernest Hemingway's short story "A Clean, Well-Lighted Place" and to come to class prepared for an informal discussion designed to generate ideas for a class paper.

Randy: Well, at least this one was short — a real short short story!

Sue: It may have been short, but I had to read it several times. I think there's a lot going on there. There's a lot of meaning there — about encountering darkness.

George: Yeah — there were some pretty heavy symbols in that story — I think. Like the light and darkness.

Instructor: What do you think the light and darkness mean?

George: Well, the light could be knowledge — maybe self–knowledge.

Terri: But light can mean other things. You know — you've heard of "divine light."

Instructor: And the darkness?

Terri: Darkness can be the lack of light. Or the lack of truths for guidance.

Jenny: But those characters lived by light.

George: Yeah — but it was electric light. Electric light is not real light. It's man–made light.

Instructor: In other words, then, you find the setting symbolic?

Frank: The light and dark are symbolic, but so are the cafe and the bar. One is clean and well lighted. The bar is dirty.

Jenny: The characters — well the main character, that is, is looking for a clean place. He doesn't like the bar.

Frank: But he still goes there, doesn't he?

Jenny: He goes there, but he doesn't like it — it's dirty. He wants to be in a place where there is cleanliness and light — like his own cafe.

Frank: But his cafe is closed late at night, past two, that is. What he should really do is just go home.

[Several students started talking all at once in reaction to Frank's comment.]

Billy: He can't go home because he's lonely.

Frank: A lot of people are lonely and stay up late at night. They're just like this waiter — they can't sleep. They're not married and no one is at home.

Randy: Did you notice that he sleeps during the day and works at night?

Jenny: Yes — he sleeps during the day to avoid the truth about himself.

Instructor: What truth is that?

Jenny: That he's really a lost and confused person.

Randy: I don't think he's lost and confused. He knows what he's doing — he runs that late-night cafe for people like the old man who tried to commit suicide.

Jenny: He may run the cafe at night — but he's lost. He's a spiritually lost person.

During this brainstorming session, students made notes about the story. Later they evaluated their notes, crossing out what was not significant, and then examined them for possible paper topics. One student, for example, became interested in the symbolic setting. She had written down several ideas produced during the final interchange. Although she remained practically silent during the brainstorm, she "participated" by listening and synthesizing.

Listing

You have undoubtedly made many lists in your life. Whether it was a shopping list, a laundry list, a vacation agenda, or a list of Saturday chores, your list helped you get organized. As you wrote it, you probably discovered additional things to do. A list, then, is another creating activity that can help you discover and rediscover ideas.

Here are a few guidelines for using lists as a creating activity:

1. Put the topic at the top of the page to keep you on target.
2. Set a time limit, perhaps five minutes.
3. Simply list words and phrases that come to your mind.
4. Feel free to jump from thought to thought.
5. Judge your list only after it is finished.

One instructor asked students to make a list of qualities that described the character Anton Rossicky in Willa Cather's short story "Neighbor Rossicky." Here is one such list:

Characteristics of Rossicky

1. bad heart
2. sixty-five years old
3. "gleam of amusement in his eyes"
4. reflective quality
5. easy manner
6. contented disposition
7. affectionate toward family
8. finds happiness in family life
9. loves his land
10. worries about his daughter-in-law
11. has a comfortable farm
12. generous, warm-hearted
13. thinks of the graveyard as "homelike"
14. at one time he loved the city life
15. grew to hate city life, prefers the country
16. the city cemented him in, he felt unnatural in the city
17. felt concerned about his daughter-in-law and his son Rudolph
18. makes the best out of hard times (see Fourth of July picnic)
19. is not scared of dying, for he has lived a good life
20. wants his children to stay in the country
21. his life is complete and beautiful

After examining his list, the student decided that the thesis of his character analysis would be "Because Rossicky's life had been complete and beautiful, he did not fear death." The list provided him not only with the thesis but with the details for the supporting paragraphs of his essay.

Making Inquiries

As you read a work of literature, make inquiries. When an event puzzles you or when a reference is unclear, respond with a question. As you read, you develop a list of questions that can be used to generate class discussions and can serve as topics for essays, particularly the problem/solution essay. Having asked a question, you can research the answer.

Here are some guidelines for making inquiries:

1. Put a title at the top of your page.
2. Ask questions on your second reading of a work. (Remember to read the work through once for an overall impression of its unity or totality.)
3. Write down questions or problems you have as you read.
4. Try to answer the questions after you finish your list.
5. If you cannot answer the questions yourself, research the answers or bring the problems to class for discussion.

As one student read T. S. Eliot's poem "The Love Song of J. Alfred Prufrock," she asked the following questions:

1. Where, exactly, is Prufrock going to "visit"?
2. Where is the "room" where the women are? Who are these women? Why does he want to visit them?
3. What is the purpose of the yellow fog?
4. Why is Prufrock so paranoid?
5. Why does he want to become a pair of ragged claws?
6. What is the purpose of the allusion to *Hamlet*?
7. Who is the eternal footman?
8. Why do the mermaids not sing to him?
9. Is this poem a comedy or tragedy?
10. Does Eliot see himself as a "Prufrock"?

As she answered these questions and analyzed her answers, she decided that her thesis would be "Although there are some comic elements in 'The Love Song of J. Alfred Prufrock,' essentially the poem is the tragedy of a man afraid to live naturally."

Cubing

Cubing (from the word *cube*) is an activity that permits you to view a topic from six points of view.

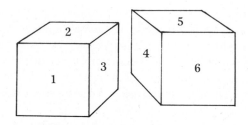

This activity causes you to see a topic in ways you may never have considered. You will be surprised at how fresh vision helps you create ideas. Here are the six sides of a cube for discovering ideas about literature: (1) What did you like about the selection? (2) What did you dislike? (3) What do you associate with the work? (4) How can this work be "useful"? (5) What is one of the author's purposes? (6) To what can I compare and/or contrast this piece?

Here are a few guidelines to follow when you cube:

1. Put the topic at the top of your page.
2. Give yourself a time limit for each side of the cube (perhaps two to five minutes per side).
3. Don't worry about your mechanics, grammar, or sentence structure, but do try to write down your ideas in complete sentences. Complete sentences more easily reveal full thoughts.
4. Keep writing! Don't let the pen stop until it is time to move to another side of the cube.
5. Judge your cube later, not during the activity.

Here is a cube on Ernest Hemingway's story "The Snows of Kilimanjaro."

1. What did you like about the story?

I liked the setting and the symbols, but that's about all!
Actually the setting is a symbol. The mountain is a goal that

Harry must reach—but he could never reach it. He didn't even try! Perhaps he reached it in his imagination or on his deathbed—I'm still not sure about the ending. The leopard was symbolic (I like symbols—they make me think!). At least the leopard tried to reach the top of the mountain—Harry didn't even try. Even though it was kinda weird, I liked that hyena's laugh at the end of the story. That nasty animal seemed to be laughing at Harry's death.

2. What did you dislike?

I could sure go on about this question. I absolutely hate the way Harry treats his wife. I understand that Hemingway treats women pretty badly in his stories. Well, this story is a good example. He is cruel, mean, nasty, and unappreciative of his wife. If he dislikes her so much, he should never have married her. He only used her—used her money—and became a lazy writer. This story had a sickening tone—very unpleasant. I did not like reading about the gangrene in his leg. The whole story was sick—Harry's rotten life, the cruel way he treats his wife, and his early death. An unpleasant story. I really didn't like this story—and yet the guy sitting next to me loves it! I think most women do not like reading Hemingway, but men like him.

3. Associate the work. (What does the work make you think of?)

This story makes me think of sickness. Harry is sick—a really sick man. Hey, I think I've discovered an idea. His physical sickness correlates with his personal sickness—his spiritual sickness. He (Harry) is a sick writer and a sick husband. (Hemingway might be a bit sick himself!). Sickness is at the core of this story. I could sure write about that.

4. How can the work be "useful"?

Actually I don't have much use for this story. Hah! And
the teacher says that it is one of Hemingway's greatest short
stories! What is great about it? How can I "use" this story?
Let's see. Well, I know I never want to be like Harry. He sold
himself out as a writer to marry Helen. He lived off her money
and used her. I have seen people in this story that I do not
like. I don't ever want to be like them. The story does make me
think though. Like I said earlier, the story makes me think
about symbols—the setting—the snow, the leopard, the gangrene.
Reading the story makes me think—I suppose that's useful!

5. What is one of the author's purposes?

I know what this question asks—what is the theme! Like the
teacher said, what idea does the author dramatize? Ugh! Theme—
theme—theme—theme. This story dramatizes . . . let's see—
When you sell yourself out for easy money, you cease to be
productive—you might as well die because in a way you're
already dead. This might be the theme. I'll think about this
later.

6. To what can I compare and/or contrast the work?

This story is like . . . a journey that never really gets
started. Those characters are at the foot of the mountain—
waiting to start their lives over—but nothing happens. They
can't start over—they're too far gone.

This story is like a funeral—an obituary! Harry's death—
his obituary. Through the flashbacks we see why he (like his
leg) is such a rotten person.

Although this student's cube is very informal, it is a rich source of
ideas. The very act of cubing has made her think critically. She even-

tually decided to write on Harry's physical sickness as a symbol of his spiritual sickness.

Freewriting

Another creating activity is freewriting. As the word implies, you "write freely" to discover ideas. The very act of freewriting clarifies ideas and produces new ideas. It allows a writer to jump from one idea to another. You may begin a paragraph whenever you wish. You might even discover that once you start freewriting, you will end up with a rough draft of an essay! Follow these guidelines for freewriting on a literature topic:

1. Write the topic at the top of the page to keep you on target.
2. Write "freely" about your topic.
3. Set a time limit if you wish.
4. Don't let your pen stop.
5. Evaluate your ideas after, not during, the activity.

Here is one student's freewriting in response to Mary Wilkins Freeman's story "A New England Nun":

My favorite story so far in this course. After reading this story twice, I can really see how it's put together! All the parts fit! When Joe enters the house, Louisa's canary flutters wildly. That bird represents Louisa's feelings. In a sense, she (Louisa) is a caged bird. But she likes being caged. Louisa likes her solitary life. Joe is a threat to her way of life.

When Louisa hears Joe and Lily talking, Louisa finds her way to free herself from her engagement to Joe. Louisa would have hated life with Joe and his mother. Louisa is a very independent lady!

Louisa is also very particular! I enjoyed watching her put on all those aprons—three of them! And she is very particular about how the objects are arranged in her house. When Joe rearranges her books, she gets sort of nervous and must place

```
the books back to the way they were! Joe can't understand her
desire for perfect order.
      Louisa also swept the rug after Joe left her house! I know
what that means—she wants Joe out!
```

This freewriting is the beginning of a character analysis of Louisa. Through the freewriting, the student has explored some of Louisa's characteristics and motivations. Notice, too, the specific examples that she has used to illustrate ideas. Her freewriting led to an essay on the paradox of Louisa's life — freedom and independence within a very rigid and structured life.

Responding to Questions

Responding to a list of questions can also generate ideas. Two important questions you can respond to are, What has the author revealed about life? and How has the author revealed it?

A list of specific questions that you can apply to literature makes you answer in detail and makes you think about the elements of literature as they apply to a specific work. Note the following lists of questions for each of the four literary genres: fiction, poetry, drama, and nonfiction prose. If some of the literary terminology is unfamiliar to you, use the index and glossary. Keep in mind, too, that these lists are only a beginning. You will undoubtedly invent many questions of your own to generate ideas.

Questions to Ask about Fiction

1. What is the setting? (Where in time and place?) What words describe the atmosphere?
2. How does the setting relate to character and theme?
3. What are the characters like?
4. Do the characters change? If so, how?
5. How is each character revealed?
6. How do the characters interact?
7. What conflicts does the plot present?
8. Who is the main character and who (or what) opposes him or her?
9. How are the conflicts resolved?
10. Who tells the story and why has the author chosen this form of narration?

11. What is the tone and how is it established?
12. What does the work say about its subject and how is this theme communicated?
13. What is the value of this story to you?

Questions to Ask about Poetry

1. What is the apparent subject of the poem?
2. Why did the poet write it?
3. What does the poem say to you?
4. What sound devices does the poet use?
5. What is the structure of the poem?
6. What images are there? Are they literal or figurative (metaphor, simile, etc.)?
7. What diction does the poet employ (concrete, abstract, connotative, denotative, etc.)?
8. Is there deliberate ambiguity and complexity?
9. What is the tone of the poem?
10. Do you detect any irony in the poem? If so, explain.
11. What symbols do you find?
12. Is there a speaker? Who is it? What is he or she like?
13. What is the value of the poem to you?

Questions to Ask about Drama

1. What is the story of the play?
2. Is the play a tragedy or comedy, or is it an example of another type of drama?
3. How many acts are there? What is the main action of each act?
4. What are the conflicts? Are there both major and minor conflicts? How are they resolved?
5. Where is the climax of the play?
6. Were you prepared for any plot twists? Was there foreshadowing?
7. Who are the main characters? What are their relationships?
8. Is all the action motivated?
9. What is the theme of the play? How do you know? How was the theme dramatized?
10. What is the setting? Is it symbolic?
11. What is the atmosphere of the play? Does the atmosphere play an important part in the production?
12. Of what literary movement is the play an example? How do you know?
13. What is the value of the drama to you?

Questions to Ask about Nonfiction Prose

1. What is the work about?
2. Is there a specific purpose for the work? What is it?
3. What is the thesis? Is it explicit or implicit?
4. How is the thesis proved or supported?
5. What is the author's persona?
6. How is the work structured?
7. For what audience is the work intended? How can you tell?
8. What kind of language does the author use (formal, informal, figurative, literal, slang, jargon, foreign terms, etc.)?
9. What types of sentences does the author use? Does the style seem suited to the purpose?
10. What is the tone of the work? How is the tone created?
11. Are there any shifts in tone?
12. What is the value of this nonfiction prose to you?

CHAPTER REVIEW

Creativity is a quality that can be developed. Creative people have a sense of daring, tolerate ambiguity, and develop their ability to imagine. Specific creating activities can help you generate ideas and create opportunities for discovery. Techniques such as brainstorming, listing, freewriting, cubing, making inquiries, and answering questions produce private responses you can evaluate and develop.

PART II

ADDITIONAL RESPONSES TO LITERATURE

CHAPTER 4

Analyzing
and Synthesizing

ANALYSIS

To analyze a work of literature means to separate or break down the work into its smallest component parts in order to discover what they are, how they function, and how they relate to the whole. A *literary analysis* can also be called a *close reading.* It is an effective tool for solving a literary problem because dividing a work into its various parts and then examining the parts one by one clarifies their functions and interrelationships. Thus, analysis can lead to interpretation (or a synthesis of the parts to produce meaning). Finally, since it is impossible to cover all the aspects of a work in the short papers commonly written for a literature class, literary analysis helps you concentrate on just one element of the work.

What are some elements of a literary work you can analyze? You may want to look ahead at the chapters and sections in Part III in which such components as structure, plot, point of view, words, images, sound, theme, symbols, irony, characterization, and speakers are treated in detail. Any of these elements would be a suitable subject for an analytical essay. You will also find questions to help you analyze specific elements in a literary work.

Let us follow a typical analytical essay assignment from personal response to final draft:

The Assignment

Write a multi-paragraph essay analyzing a major character in one of the short stories studied so far in our class. As you make your analysis, particularly note the main conflict this character faces. Does the character resolve the conflict? To prove your assertions, be sure to include quotations from the primary source. Your audience is the instructor and the class.

Personal Response to the Character Anson Hunter in F. Scott Fitzgerald's "The Rich Boy"

There's no doubt in my mind that a lot of Anson's problems are due to his alcoholism. I've seen and been around alcoholics and I know what they're like. I've read some materials, too, published by the AAA and know how to spot an alcoholic. Believe me—Anson Hunter is one!

I noticed, too, that Fitzgerald also mentioned Anson's "superiority" several times. Anson's feelings of superiority are definitely one of his problems. His superiority is what holds him back from intimacy with his women. Both Paula and Dolly are victims of his superiority. I was furious with the way he treated Paula! And I bet the girl with the red tam at the end of the story is his next victim!

I think I'll write about Anson's superiority and the effect it has on the two women in his life since that's what interests me.

Scratch Outline for Character Analysis

    I. Anson's superiority
        A. As a youth

B. In school

C. With women

II. Paula Legendre

    A. His love for her

    B. Discovery of her wealth

    C. The end of their relationship

    D. Effect of her

III. Dolly Karger

    A. His attraction to her

    B. The end of their relationship

    C. Effect on her

Rough Draft with Revision Markings

Anson Hunter's Superiority

In F. Scott Fitzgerald's short story "The

Rich Boy," the protagonist, Anson Hunter, seeks ~~∅~~

yet fails to achieve intimacy with women. He

almost marries Paula Legendre but cannot commit

himself/ *to her.* ~~Furthermore,~~ *next* he has an affair with Dolly

Karger but is unable to give himself *to her* ~~in~~ love.

Although Anson is a complex character, his

inability to achieve intimacy can be narrowed down

to one cause. Because of his superiority, Anson

Hunter ~~cannot gain intimacy with his women. And in~~ *Wordy/comb.*

~~his attempts to seek relationships, he~~ nearly

destroys the women who try to love him.

    Anson has ~~always suffered from~~ a̶n̶ *cultivated* ~~inferiority~~ *superiority* *all his life.*

complex/ The narrator reveals, "Anson's first

sense of superiority came when he realized the

half-grudging American deference that was paid to

him in the Connecticut village" (2297). When

Anson play*s* ~~ed~~ with other children, he refuse*s* ~~d~~ to

struggle for pr(e)sc(e)dence *sp* over them, and when it

is ~~was~~ not given freely to him, he withdr*aws* ~~ew~~ from

their company. Anson also ~~felt~~ *feels* superior in school.

use pres. tns!

The narrator adds, "Nevertheless, his very

superiority kept him from being a success in

college—the independence was mistaken for

egotism, and the refusal to accept Yale standards

with the proper awe seemed to belittle all those

who had" (2297). ~~Even~~ *a* after college, ~~when~~ he ~~took~~ *moves*

to *where his superior attitude is welcomed*

~~a job in~~ New York, ~~he kept his superior attitude~~. *if not encouraged.*

"Anson accepted without reservation the world

of high finance and high extravagance, of divorce

and dissipation, of snobbery and of privilege" *unrelated ideas* ↑ *use transition*

sense of

(2297). With his superiority deeply rooted in

his character, Anson attempts to establish

relationships with women. *NOTE: make sure quote proves assertion*

trans   The results of his relationships with women

are

~~were~~ disastrous for Anson as well as Paula

New topic sentence

Legendre and Dolly Karger. (When he finished college,

attempts a relationship

he ~~fell in love~~ with Paula Legendre.

attitude

His superior~~ity~~, however, breaks up their

relationship, saddens Paula, and brings to surface

his childish and "rich boy" nature. ~~At first~~

feels   *finds*

Anson ~~felt~~ happy with Paula until he ~~found~~ out

is

that she ~~was~~ worth nearly a million dollars. From

the moment of that revelation, the relationship

is   *gets*

~~was~~ doomed. Once, when Anson ~~got~~ drunk on a date

with Paula, he apologized the next day; however,

Anson "made no promises, showed no humility, only

delivered a few serious comments on life which

brought him off with rather a moral superiority at

the end" (2299). After three years of the~~(ir)~~

relationship, Anson ~~could~~ *can* never make the

oommitmont to marry hor. Eventually, the saddened

Paula ~~left~~ *leaves* him, and he, in remorse, would

"suddenly bend his head into his hands and cry   *ADD CONTENT*

like a child" (2301). *(more information needed here to prove their affair was a disaster for Paula.)*

After his disastrous relationship with Paula,

Anson next ~~met~~ *eets* and attempt~~ed~~ *s* a relationship with

Dolly Karger. From the beginning of their affair,

though, Anson ~~could~~ *can* not fall in love with her; his *sense of*

superiority once again ~~interfered.~~ *looks down upon Dolly and* He even ~~told~~ *tells*

~~Dolly~~ *her* quite frequently that he ~~didn't~~ *doesn't* love her.

"She meant nothing to him—but at her pathetic

ruse everything stubborn and self-indulgent in him

came to the surface. It was a presumption from a

mental inferior and it could not be overlooked"

(2304). When Anson end~~ed~~ *s* the affair, "Dolly

Karger, lying awake and staring at the ceiling,

never again believed in anything at all" (2305).

Like his affair with Paula, ~~his~~ *this* affair ~~with Dolly~~

end~~ed~~ *s* in disaster *for Dolly.*

show that he doesn't love her. *ADD CONTENT*

Anson Hunter, then, is unable to establish

intimate relationships that last *because* his superiority

complex. ~~interferes with his attempts to create~~

~~intimacy.~~ ~~And~~ *W*ith each attempt, he nearly

destroys those women who love him. He ruins his

relationship with Paula Legendre and nearly

dev*as*tates Dolly Karger. At the end of the story,

the reader is
~~we are~~ left wondering what destruction he will

bring to the girl in the red tam. That her fate

will be
~~is~~ no better than Paula's or Dolly's is certain,

for Anson is a static character. He has learned no

lessons. Although he has become cynical from his

feels
experiences, he ~~is~~ just as superior at the end of

the story as he was when he was a ''rich boy.''

In fact, that is just what he is and always will be—a "rich boy."
As the narrator notes at the end of the story,

''Perhaps . . . there would always be women in the

world who would spend their brightest, freshest,

rarest hours to nurse and protect that superiority

he cherished in his heart'' (2313).

Work Cited

Fitzgerald, F. Scott. ''The Rich Boy.'' <u>American</u> <u>Literature:</u> <u>The</u>

<u>Makers</u> <u>and</u> <u>the</u> <u>Making</u>. 2 vols. Ed. Cleanth Brooks et al.
New York: St. Martin's, 1973. 2:2297—2313.

Final Draft

Anson Hunter's Superiority

In F. Scott Fitzgerald's short story "The Rich Boy," the
protagonist, Anson Hunter, seeks yet fails to achieve intimacy
with women. He almost marries Paula Legendre but cannot commit
himself to her. Next, he has an affair with Dolly Karger but
is unable to give himself to her in love. Although Anson is a
complex character, his inability to achieve intimacy can be
narrowed down to one cause. Because of his superiority, Anson
Hunter nearly destroys the women who try to love him.

Anson has cultivated a superiority complex all his life.
The narrator reveals, "Anson's first sense of superiority came
when he realized the half—grudging American deference that was
paid to him in the Connecticut village" (2297). When Anson
plays with other children, he refuses to struggle for
precedence over them, and when it is not given freely to him,
he withdraws from their company. Anson also feels superior at
school. The narrator adds, "Nevertheless, his very superiority
kept him from being a success in college—the independence was
mistaken for egotism, and the refusal to accept Yale standards
with the proper awe seemed to belittle all those who had"
(2297). After college, he moves to New York where his superior
attitude is welcomed, if not encouraged: "Anson accepted
without reservation the world of high finance and high
extravagance, of divorce and dissipation, of snobbery and of
privilege" (2297). By the time Anson has his first love affair,
the narrator has firmly established him [Anson] as having a
superiority complex.

As the story moves from the exposition into the rising action, the reader wonders what effect Anson's superiority will have on the women who try to love him. Unfortunately, the results of his relationships with women are disastrous for Anson as well as Paula Legendre and Dolly Karger.

When he finishes college, he falls in love with Paula Legendre. His superior attitude, however, breaks up their relationship, saddens Paula, and brings to surface his childish and "rich boy" nature. Anson feels happy with Paula until he finds out that she is worth nearly a million dollars. From the moment of that revelation, the relationship is doomed. Once, when Anson gets drunk on a date with Paula, he apologizes the next day; however, Anson "made no promises, showed no humility, only delivered a few serious comments on life which brought him off with rather a moral superiority at the end" (2299). After three years of their relationship, Anson can never make the commitment to marry her. Eventually, the saddened Paula leaves him, and he, in remorse would "suddenly bend his head into his hands and cry like a child" (2301). Paula, on a rebound, "immediately" marries Lowell Thayer, and the marriage ends in divorce. Only years later can Paula find true happiness with a man.

After his disastrous relationship with Paula, Anson next meets and attempts a relationship with Dolly Karger. From the beginning of their affair, though, Anson cannot fall in love with her; his sense of superiority once again interferes. "She meant nothing to him—but at her pathetic ruse everything stubborn and self—indulgent in him came to the surface. It was a presumption from a mental inferior and it could not be overlooked" (2304). The affair, though, was doomed from the beginning due to his "realization that naturally fast girls were not worth sparing" (2305). He looks down upon her and often tells her that he does not love her. One night, he stares

at her with "abomination" and tells her, "I don't love you and
you'd better wait for somebody that loves you. I don't love you
a bit" (2310). When Anson ends the affair, "Dolly Karger, lying
awake at night and staring at the ceiling, never again believed
in anything at all" (2312). Like his affair with Paula, this
affair ends in disaster for Dolly.

Anson Hunter, then, is unable to establish intimate
relationships that last due to his superiority complex. With
each attempt at a relationship, he nearly destroys those women
who try to love him. He ruins his relationship with Paula
Legendre and nearly devastates Dolly Karger. At the end of the
story, the reader is left wondering what destruction he will
bring to the girl in the red tam. That her fate will be no
better than Paula's or Dolly's is certain, for Anson is a
static character. He has learned no lessons. Although he has
become cynical from his experiences, he feels just as superior
at the end of the story as he was when he was a "rich boy." In
fact, that is just what he is and always will be—a "rich boy."
The narrator notes as the story concludes, "Perhaps . . .
there would always be women in the world who would spend their
brightest, freshest, rarest hours to nurse and protect that
superiority he cherished in his heart" (2313).

Work Cited

Fitzgerald, F. Scott. "The Rich Boy." American Literature: The
    Makers and the Making. 2 vols. Ed. Cleanth Brooks et al.
    New York: St. Martin's, 1973. 2:2297–2313.

Comment   Note that in the final draft, the student, while incorporating the
suggestions made by the instructor on the rough draft, remains faithful to his
original response to the story. The final draft develops that response and supports it with solid evidence from the story.

SUMMARY

A *summary*, a brief recapitulation of a work, can become a useful part of most writing-about-literature projects. As one method of analyzing literature, it also involves a personal response.

Part of this personal response to the work will be deciding how long your summary should be. Will you summarize a novel in a few sentences? If so (and this is obviously analysis), which subplots, episodes, or characters will you include or leave out? You may generalize and omit some details, but which? Which details are important to the plot or message or effect of the work? Determining your purpose and choosing your audience for the summary will help you reach a decision on length. Give the chosen audience as much knowledge of the work as is possible and necessary.

One method of summarizing is simply to jot down two or three sentences as soon as you finish reading the passage, answering questions such as: What is the work about? What happens in the work? Why does it happen? What are the important features of the work? What is the writer trying to do? Then reread the work or passage and try to state the summary as one sentence. Try to be objective and represent the author's view rather than your own; still, as noted above, even your omissions reflect your point of view.

Student Summaries

Students asked to summarize the William Blake poem "Infant Sorrow" printed in Chapter 1 have produced the following summaries. Note no two summaries are alike. One student suggests:

"Infant Sorrow," told from the point of view of a newborn child, describes its birth as dangerous and probably unwelcome, the world as hostile, and itself as sullen and devilish.

But another student summarizes the poem this way:

The birth of the child in "Infant Sorrow" is a catastrophe rather than a blessing because the world it is born into is dangerous.

And still another student offers this summary:

Contrary to how most of us regard a newborn child, the speaker of "Infant Sorrow" is a personality in its own right, able to struggle and resist, and thus fit for life in a "dangerous" world.

For more information on how to write summaries, consult Chapter 6.

PARAPHRASE

Another way to analyze a short work or a passage from a longer work is to *paraphrase* it, or to restate it in your own words. Use whatever language comes most naturally. You will first have to define any unfamiliar words because you can't paraphrase if you don't understand what you have read; paraphrasing helps clarify a passage or work. Since you will probably discover it takes more of your words to restate the work or passage, a paraphrase will be at least as long as the original and probably longer. It should follow the organization or structure of the original. A student working with the marked text of Blake's poem "Infant Sorrow" paraphrased the poem as follows:

Student paraphrase

A mother and a father are very sad at the birth of their child who comes suddenly into a frightening environment. The baby is weak and unclothed but can cry shrilly and resembles a devil disguised as something soft. The baby fights the father and the bindings before finally submitting and sullenly resting in the mother's arms.

Comment   As this rather prosaic paraphrase shows, paraphrasing is an excellent way to train yourself to notice style; the paraphrase seems pale and feeble compared to Blake's poem. No synonym can reproduce exactly the feeling of the original, and that, of course, is exactly the essence of poetry — the right word in the right place.

EXPLICATION

Paraphrasing is closely related to another method of analysis, explication. An *explication* should examine all parts of a work in relation to the whole. Because of the detail of a complete explication, this method of examination is best suited for brief poems or short passages of poetry or prose. In an explication, analyze what happens in the passage line by line, calling attention to every important detail such as symbols, sound effects, motifs, and figurative devices.

Working from a personal response, a paraphrase, and a summary of Blake's "Infant Sorrow," a student asked to write a close analysis of that poem has produced the following essay:

Infant Sorrow: A Different View of Birth

In this deceptively simple, brief poem from the volume
Songs of Experience, William Blake reverses the usual
expectation of joy at the birth of a child. Indeed, the poem is
a companion piece to "Infant Joy" from Songs of Innocence, but
it can be usefully analyzed on its own. The birth experience in
this poem is presented from the point of view of the newborn
infant. While the speaker never directly says whether his or
her birth was planned or desired, the diction and tone of the
poem make clear that this birth is not a happy occasion for
either parents or child.

First, the title itself is ambiguous. Is "infant" being
used as an adjective to modify the noun "sorrow" so that we
expect a sentimental little poem about a very young child
mourning a broken toy or a parent's frown? Or, more darkly, and
more likely after we read the poem, is the agony caused by the
child itself rather than being the sorrow of a baby over a
trifle?

The identity of the speaker is clear almost from the
first sentence: "my mother" and "my father" indicate that the
speaker is a child, and the second and third lines indicate
the age of the child. But the child is unnamed and even unsexed.

Thus, Blake implies the universality of his contention: the birth of a child is not always a joyous occasion. The reaction of the parents to the birth is clearly and vividly described by two strong verbs: "groan'd" and "wept" in the two shortest, and most dramatic, simple sentences in the poem. While it is true that many women groan in the stress of labor and that a father might naturally weep at the sufferings of his wife, in this situation the pain seems to be caused more by the arrival of the infant than by the pain of the birthing itself.

The second line supports this interpretation because the infant is born into a "dangerous world." Why dangerous? "Dangerous" means risky, hazardous, perilous; it also means likely to cause physical injury. Is the world dangerous simply because it lacks the security and comfort the newborn has a right to expect, or is Blake implying that the parents will eliminate the baby if they dare? Later in the poem the baby struggles in his father's hands as though fearing him.

And how is the infant equipped for this world? The third line begins with the strong adjective "Helpless" which, by interrupting the regular pattern established in the first two lines, acquires extra emphasis. This strong adjective is followed by another just as evocative, "naked." Both of these adjectives would seem to indicate that the newborn is poorly equipped for the dangerous world, yet the second line has stated that the babe "leapt" into this world. "To leap" is to move or act suddenly, to spring through the air, and we even use it to mean a leap into the unknown, implying courage and strength, rather than passive helplessness. The colon after "Into the dangerous world I leapt" shows that the two following lines restate or define the sentence. Thus, the strength implied by the verb "leapt" is supported by the description in the third line of the baby as "piping loud." No mewling infant, this. He has, as the folk expression states, a "full set of pipes."

The fourth line, the closure of the first stanza, makes clear the position of this baby in this home. No angel from God "trailing clouds of glory" as Wordsworth romanticizes the newborn in "Ode: Intimations of Immortality," this infant is "Like a fiend hid in a cloud." A cloud can obscure, darken, or cause gloom, trouble, suspicion, and disgrace, while a fiend is a monster, a diabolically cruel or wicked person. The cuddly pale flesh of this newborn cloaks a malevolent intent; this cloud of flesh hides a devil from hell rather than an angel from God.

The second stanza begins with three modifying phrases and reinforces the image of this devil baby who struggles in his "father's hands" in line 5 and "strives against" the conventional swaddling which restricts free movement and would indeed be resented by one who "leapt" into the world. Only after being "bound and weary" from the struggle, as described in line 7, does the infant subside onto its "mother's breast" in line 8. But this is a temporary lull, not a graceful surrender to the necessity of being swaddled and nursed. Blake describes the baby, not as resting peacefully or happily, but sulking, holding itself aloof from even the mother who would nurse and succor it, just as it earlier struggled against the father.

Thus, the poem "Infant Sorrow" makes it clear from connotation, tone, and sentence structure that the birth of a child, normally celebrated in literature and life as a "blessed event," is sometimes something altogether different, perhaps even a curse for both parents and child.

Work Cited

Blake, William. Complete Writings. Ed. Geoffrey Keynes. London: Oxford UP, 1972. 217.

Comment   This close reading, although by no means exhaustive, has thoroughly explored the language, structure, and tone of the poem. Through this analysis, the writer has reached a tentative conclusion about the poem's meaning.

SYNTHESIS — INTERPRETATION

The purpose of literary analysis is the revelation of meaning, to show how the analyzed details work together to create meaning. Analysis is not the end but a means to an end. After you have examined a work and discovered how its smallest parts function and how each relates to the whole, what then? Succeeding where "all the King's horsemen and all the King's men" failed with Humpty Dumpty, the next step is putting the work whole again, perhaps the most pleasurable part of literary analysis. But now, based on your knowledge of its separate parts, you can make a statement about the work and its total effect. To say that Blake's poem "Infant Sorrow" contains strong, dramatic verbs and participles is incomplete; use that analysis to illustrate an interpretation — for example, that the poet thus suggests that the newborn is a forceful individual.

The following essay on a passage from a sermon by Jonathan Edwards demonstrates both a close analysis of the diction and rhetorical structure of the passage and a synthesis, an explanation of the integration of form and meaning the writer found in the work. (Since the text is a short passage from a longer work, the analysis begins with an identification of the subject matter of the whole work, the location of the passage in the work, and a statement about the importance of this passage to the entire work. For the reader's convenience, the lines of the passage are numbered.)

STUDENT ESSAY

A Sermon You Couldn't Sleep Through:
Jonathan Edwards' "Sinners in the Hands of an Angry God"

1	O sinner! consider the fearful danger you are in;
2	it is a great furnace of wrath, a wide and bottomless
3	pit, full of the fire of wrath, that you are held over
4	in the hand of that God, whose wrath is provoked and
5	incensed as much against you, as against many of the

6   damned in hell; you hang by a slender thread, with the
7   flames of divine wrath flashing about it and ready every
8   moment to singe it and burn it asunder; and you have
9   no interest in any Mediator and nothing to lay hold of to
10   save yourself, nothing to keep off the flames of wrath,
11   nothing of your own, nothing that you ever have done,
12   nothing that you can do to induce God to spare you one
13   moment. (102)

This passage from one of the best known sermons in American history was designed by its author, the Puritan Jonathan Edwards, to awaken his congregation to a sense of its sinfulness. This particular passage is striking for its tone of unrelenting terror and its vivid imagery. The theme of the sermon is that only God can save men, that any human effort is futile.

The passage comes from the "application" portion of the sermon which follows a lengthy exegesis on a passage from Deuteronomy, "Their foot shall slide in due time." Edwards has explained in the exposition that God alone can prevent men from going to hell, that all men stand at all times in immediate threat of death despite any human actions, and that no one who has not accepted God through Christ has any hope whatsoever. In the application portion of the sermon, he has begun by saying that the purpose of the sermon is to convert unbelievers. This particular passage is one of many illustrations of the terrible plight of the unconverted; yet, it also serves as a microcosm of the entire sermon as an examination of its structure will show.

One of the first things to notice about the passage is that, despite its length, it is really only one complex-compound sentence which begins with the direct address, "O sinner!" (The uncapitalized "consider" lets us know that, despite the exclamation point after sinner, the phrase is to be considered part of the long sentence.) Such an address was

bound to awaken anyone in the congregation who had dared nod
off and, indeed, still has the power of awakening interest.

The three semicolons in lines 1, 6, and 8 indicate the
four main divisions of thought: the sinner is admonished to
consider his danger (1), hell is vividly described (2—6), the
precarious situation of the sinner is described (6—8), and
then he is convinced that nothing he can do will avert God's
wrath (8—13). Thus, this passage does summarize the whole
sermon.

The first line with its imperative direct address and the
term "consider" sets the tone of the passage by immediately
mentioning "fearful danger." The "f" will be repeated six
times in words such as "furnace," "fire," and "flames,"
linking the pattern of images of hell. The second and third
lines make the abstract "fearful danger" concrete: the danger
is a "furnace of wrath" and a "bottomless pit, full of the fire
of wrath." "Wrath" (and the context makes it clear that this is
God's wrath) is a repeated motif in the passage; the very word
itself is repeated five times. "Pit" shocks us with its
succinctness; although "abyss" is a possible synonym, its
somewhat melodious sound would be entirely wrong; "pit" is
exactly right.

Now where in this imagery is the person addressed, the
sinner? In the hand of God. Now doesn't that sound pleasant and
comforting? Not in Edwards' world view. God is not supporting
and sustaining the sinner with His hands; rather, He is
dangling the poor unfortunate over the pit and furnace as
though by a "slender thread" (6), and He is as "provoked" and
"incensed" against him as against the poor unfortunates
already in hell (4—6). There is almost a pun in his use of the
word "incensed," which in many religions means the burning of
aromatic substances as part of a sacred ceremony; but in

Edwards' use it definitely means enraged or inflamed with wrath.

In lines 6—8, the image of the sinner dangling from the hand of God as though by a thread ready at any moment to be burned in two is concretely and vividly expressed. The final section (8—13) stresses the utter hopelessness of the unconverted sinner with a fivefold repetition of the word "nothing." Like hammer blows nailing a coffin shut, the word echoes through the passage; the sinner has "nothing" within himself now, nor has he ever had, nor will he by himself ever be able to forestall the wrath of God for even "one moment." True, the "Mediator" is mentioned but only negatively; the unconverted sinner has "no interest" in such a person. Repetition here, as in the Old Testament, is an important rhetorical device for sustaining the tone of the passage. "Wrath" is repeated five times, "nothing" is repeated five times, and "flames" is repeated four times with five related words, "furnace," "hell," "flash," "singe," and "burn." If there is any color in this bleak passage, it is the color of wrath, hell—fire, and damnation, not the green of hope or resurrection.

We know from contemporary accounts that Edwards was a very successful evangelist; however, even if we did not have that testimony, our own senses could tell us that sermons with passages such as this would be a powerful tool for converting unbelievers.

Work Cited

Edwards, Jonathan. "Sinners in the Hands of an Angry God." American Literature: The Makers and the Making. 2 vols. Ed. Cleanth Brooks et al. New York: St. Martin's, 1973. 1:97—105.

Comment   This essay delves deeply into the language of the passage, using the analysis of diction to support an interpretation of the work as a synthesis of meaning and form.

To conclude, we have seen in this chapter that the purpose of literary analysis is to read a work closely and then describe its parts so that other readers can see the work more precisely and accurately. Careful observation, thoroughness, and an objective tone are the hallmarks of literary analysis; yet, as the last paragraph of the essay above shows, it is difficult to write a wholly neutral analysis. The last paragraph reflects a judgment. The next chapter will examine in detail how to use the results of a careful analysis to write an argumentative paper, one which supports a personal opinion on the merits or flaws of a particular work.

CHAPTER REVIEW

Literary analysis is a method of breaking down or separating a work into its component parts. Some useful methods of analysis are summary, paraphrase, and explication. A summary is a brief recapitulation of the work. A paraphrase is a personal restatement of a short poem or prose passage using about the same number of words as the original. A close word-by-word and line-by-line reading of a work is an explication, which can be used to elucidate a brief work or short passage from a long work. However, most analysis ends with a synthesis, an explanation and interpretation of the whole work as revealed by a careful study of its individual parts.

CHAPTER 5

Arguing about Literature

WRITING AN ARGUMENT

*E*ssays written for a literature class, although based on personal response, summary, and analysis, usually go beyond those activities to argumentation. After you have analyzed and interpreted a literary work, you are ready to argue for your interpretation, to argue about issues in the text, to evaluate the work, or to present and solve a problem in the text. This chapter examines three types of argumentative essays common in literature classes: (1) an evaluation of a literary text, (2) an argument for your reading versus someone else's, and (3) an argument for or against an issue in the text.

A successful argumentative essay is based on an objective analysis of the text or passage, clear definitions of key words, supportive illustrations, and an appropriate and convincing organization. You should offer a thesis, enforce your judgments with quotations and specific evidence, and anticipate and refute any opposing arguments while avoiding weakening your own arguments by oversimplification or distorting evidence.

The sections below offer suggestions on how to move toward argumentative essays from the personal responses, summaries, and analyses discussed in the previous two chapters. For convenience they use

two of the same literary works referred to in those chapters, the passage from Edwards' sermon "Sinners in the Hands of an Angry God"
and Blake's poem "Infant Sorrow."

Argument 1: An Evaluation of a Literary Work

At first glance, it may not be apparent how an evaluation of a work
differs from an initial personal response to a text — "This play bored
me to tears." "I can relate to this poem." "This short story is exciting!"
"What planet does this author come from?" However, as discussed in
the previous chapters, as a reader you can move on from your initial
responses to questioning what qualities or aspects of the work cause
those reactions: "This short story excites me because the writer has
vividly described the rising tension in the relationship between the
couple." You can also consider those factors in your own background
that may have contributed to your responses: "I responded to this story
because my best friend is involved in a similar relationship." In other
words, you analyze your responses to a work, and you analyze the
work itself. To evaluate a text, turn your personal opinion into a critical
opinion by supporting it with an analysis of the text and by basing
your judgment or evaluation on standards that other readers also agree
are important.

We will discuss those standards after these two suggestions. First,
try to avoid writing on topics or works about which you feel absolutely
neutral. You can describe, you can summarize, you can analyze with
complete objectivity — but you can't argue as successfully as you can if
you write about a work that has caused you to react. As you prepare to
write an argumentative essay, ask yourself how much you care about
what happened to the characters in the work, whether the repetition
of a refrain bored you, or whether you found the work long on description and short on action. Choose works or authors to which you do
respond strongly, either positively or negatively, and select from within
that group the response that seem easiest to support and prove.

Second, it is difficult to argue for or against a response based solely
on taste or personal preference. If you prefer images drawn from science rather than images drawn from nature, then you may prefer the
poetry of Donne to the poetry of Keats; but you will have difficulty
persuading some audiences that Donne is a better poet than Keats.
Granting both poets their merit and talent, write instead on the qualities you like in Donne's poetry, perhaps contemporary science as revealed in two or three of his poems.

Since many writers and works will be found in most anthologies, no matter when the texts were published, standard criteria for evaluating literary works upon which most readers, despite age or culture or background, agree, and upon which all readers can base their judgment, must exist. After you have responded to a work, checking your response against the following criteria (or similar ones, perhaps even criteria you develop as a critical community in your early class meetings) may assure you that your evaluation is on solid ground — that you are, in fact, evaluating the work, rather than just expressing your personal preference.

A work of literature is generally regarded as excellent if it is consistent, true, and pleasurable, and if it uses language effectively.

1. *Consistent.* A good literary work is unified and harmonious. Sudden reversals are foreshadowed; endings are logical rather than surprising or tricky. Characters do not suddenly change behavior or motivation; metrical systems in poetry, once established, are not whimsically changed. The world view reflected in the work is consistent. Everything fits; and although there is sufficient detail, there is no unnecessary repetition.

2. *True.* Even though the world and people portrayed may be fictional, they "ring true"; they seem alive and real. Because the work reflects and comments on human life, the reader becomes involved in the imaginary world. In nonfiction, given the writer's purposes and circumstances and given the audience to whom the work is addressed, the message seems appropriate.

3. *Pleasurable.* After finishing a work, readers are satisfied that the work was worth their effort and time. And, perhaps more to the point, they want to reread the work. The pleasure they derive may change with each rereading and it may be different from reader to reader, but it will always be present. The work becomes part of its readers.

4. *Effective language.* The tools of the writer, the words, are carefully chosen; the style fits the message; the dialogue fits the characters. Within the constraints of appropriateness, the language is clear, natural, and comprehensible.

If your evaluation of a work, positive or negative, is based on a careful reading of the work and on these or similar criteria which you have explicitly defined, you should be able to defend your evaluation.

As noted in the previous chapter, it is often difficult to keep a subjective evaluation out of an objective analysis. The last paragraph of the essay on Edwards' sermon becomes an argument for the value of the text when it calls the sermon "a powerful tool for converting unbelievers." However, the essay is still primarily an analysis rather than an argument. How do you develop an evaluative argument?

Recall the student essay in Chapter 4 which analyzes one aspect of Blake's "Infant Sorrow." Suppose that you have been asked to evaluate "Infant Sorrow" as a lyric poem. First, read and respond to both the poem and the description of lyric poetry. Establish and define the criteria upon which you will then base your evaluation — effective language? tone? truth? Then analyze the poem to see exactly how these elements operate. Prepare to write your argument by developing a thesis such as "'Infant Sorrow' is a successful lyric because. . . ." Anticipate and refute objections to your evaluation by stating and defining your standards of evaluation early and clearly and by illustrating each point with quotations from the poem. Organize your points effectively; comparing and contrasting the poem to the established criteria would be one method for structuring the essay. Moving from your weakest argument to your strongest helps you build your essay to a strong conclusion.

Argument 2: My Reading versus Someone Else's

As noted previously, no two students are likely to produce identical summaries of even a single work because a summary also represents a personal response. The answer to either the question "What is the most important aspect of the work?" or "What is the work about?" depends upon the reader's response to the work. As you can clearly see below, each student response given in Chapter 4 could be developed into a different argument.

> Reading #1: "Infant Sorrow," told from the point of view of a newborn child, describes its birth as dangerous and probably unwelcome, the world as hostile, and itself as sullen and devilish.

> Argument based on Reading #1: Blake seems very anti–Romantic in "Infant Sorrow" because he portrays a newborn child as a "fiend."

> Reading #2: The birth of the child in "Infant Sorrow" is a catastrophe rather than a blessing because the world it is born into is dangerous.

Argument based on Reading #2: It is not the newborn child that is responsible for the conflict between child and parents in "Infant Sorrow," but the "dangerous world" into which the child is born.

Reading #3: Contrary to how most of us regard a newborn child, the speaker of "Infant Sorrow" is a personality in its own right, able to struggle and resist, and thus fit for life in a "dangerous" world.

Argument based on Reading #3: In portraying the newborn child in "Infant Sorrow" as a powerful, forceful, active personality, Blake anticipates a modern scientific view of the capabilities of the newborn.

Class discussion or a brainstorming session can provide a valuable forum for exposing and discussing these different personal responses. But which of these interpretations or arguments is "correct"? All of them could be successfully argued, as could many others. As long as your point of view is based on careful reading and analysis, do not abandon it simply because it is different from those of other students. If you think your interpretation is supported by the details of the work, feel free to argue your response.

Examine again the sample essay on "Infant Sorrow" reproduced in Chapter 4. Does it seem that you could not possibly argue for a different reading, that this reading is definitive? It isn't. For example, one could successfully argue that the writer misinterprets some of the language of the poem to support her contention, that, in fact, the writer has misread poetically precise, descriptive language which does not, as the writer contends, describe a mysterious or supernatural birth, but rather just an ordinary birth. For instance, the verbs "groan'd" and "wept" are simple descriptive terms for the labor of childbirth, and "leapt" is unusual, not because it describes a superhuman act of strength, but because it is a remarkably precise description of the sudden expulsion of the baby at the conclusion of labor. Of course, the baby is born helpless and naked; the shrill cry of the newborn is aptly described in "piping loud." Again, the "struggling" and the "striving" of this newborn are not unusual as anyone who has tried to bathe a slippery baby will acknowledge.

But do you see a flaw in this second interpretation also? This argument ignores the key phrase, "like a fiend hid in a cloud." So, there's a point for a third essay. Is that phrase a flaw in an otherwise unremarkable poem about the pains of childbirth, or is it the key to the interpretation of the poem? Again, no single essay on any single work can be definitive; if this were so, professional journals would have to cease publication! There is always room for one more contribution to literary interpretation.

However, when arguing for your reading or evaluation against someone else's, avoid oversimplification and sweeping generalizations based on insufficient evidence: "Blake is an unskillful poet because he always writes such short lines." (He varies the length of his lines; you could possibly argue a statement such as "Blake's short lines in "Infant Sorrow" make it impossible for the poem to carry the weight of the message.") Or, "Edwards' sermon would not appeal to a modern congregation." (How can you be certain of this? Revise such an assertion to something such as "Edwards' sermon provides a valuable tool for understanding the mood of the Great Awakening.")

Argument 3: An Argument about Some Issue in the Text

An argument about an issue in the text begins with a question, possibly one that has occurred to you during your reading such as "Why is the speaker in 'Infant Sorrow' the baby rather than the mother or father?" However, the question may be based on a problem that your instructor points out ("Based on our reading of the Romantic poets thus far, can we generalize about their attitudes toward children?") or one that develops through class discussion ("What are the techniques by which Edwards develops an extensive sermon based on just one short Bible verse?")

The first and third questions are examples of an *intrinsic* issue, that is, a problem based in the work itself — its language, its structure, its art, its ideas, or its content. The second question relies on reading besides the text itself; such issues are called *extrinsic*. Extrinsic issues may involve subject matter such as biography, history, or psychology, or, as in the second question, movements, influences, or genres.

An excellent source of material for writing about issues is your journal, especially if you have continually questioned works as you read them. To return to our sample texts, let us see how a student could develop an argument based on a personal response. Recall that one student's initial response to "Infant Sorrow" presented the main conflict in the poem, the conflict between child and parents, as caused by the world rather than by either the child or the parents. To answer the question, Why does Blake present such a conflict? that student might read some background material on child labor in Blake's England and discover that conditions were horrible indeed; no wonder Blake describes the world as "dangerous." A baby would have to be strong and vigorous to survive in such a world, even if that meant struggling against its own parents.

Examining a different issue entirely, another student may want to compare and contrast "Infant Joy" and "Infant Sorrow" to demonstrate how Blake achieves their quite different tones through metrics, language, and speaker.

Still a third student might read the longer, manuscript version of the poem in Blake's *Notebook*, discuss the deletions, and argue that Blake revised the poem to eliminate a religious issue and restrict the conflict of the poem to an economic issue.

What other issues or problems in a text could be argued? As noted above, you can argue issues of style: What stylistic qualities moved the audiences of Edwards' sermons?

You can argue issues of ideas: Do you agree with Blake's concepts of childhood? How would you solve the problems he implies? What was Edwards' concept of salvation? How is it presented in his sermons?

You can argue issues based on either the writer's or the work's background: In what way is "Infant Sorrow" a Romantic poem? What typical characteristics of oral literature do Edwards' sermons exemplify?

As we have seen, you can argue issues based on genre: How does "Infant Sorrow" fit the definition of a lyric? From reading Edwards' sermon, what would you say is the typical structure of a Puritan sermon?

To write an essay arguing an issue you must come up with a convincing solution supported by relevant materials from the text itself. For questions which will help you formulate your own intrinsic problems in a text and for examples of essays which argue intrinsic issues, see Chapters 6, 7, 8, 9, and 10. For questions which produce arguments based on extrinsic issues and samples of student paragraphs exemplifying these issues, see Chapter 11.

CHAPTER REVIEW

The most common essay you will write for a literature class is the argumentative essay, which asks you to support your opinion, interpretation, or evaluation of a literary work with a careful analysis, clear definitions, well-chosen examples, and effective organization. One type of argumentative essay evaluates a text, developing a personal opinion into a critical opinion by analyzing the text and by using standard criteria. A second argumentative essay argues for your reading against someone else's, and a third argues about an intrinsic or extrinsic issue or problem in the text.

PART III

DISCOVERING AND RESPONDING TO ELEMENTS OF LITERATURE

CHAPTER 6

Structure

ANALYZING STRUCTURE

*D*iscovering the structure underlying a work of literature is a logical place to begin a critical analysis. A study of structure involves thinking about what happens in a work, why it happens, and how it happens. When you've discovered the what, the why, and the how, you are ready to interpret the happenings or analyze the theme, experience, and effect of the work. By analyzing structure — examining and then synthesizing the parts — you gain a sense of the work's organization and unity. Understanding form and its relationship to meaning will help you perceive the total potential of a literary work.

Literature Is Organized

When you have discovered the structure of a work, you will understand its organization. In narrative literature (literature that tells a story), most events have definite causes. Action is motivated, the parts are connected, and there is an orderly sequence of purposeful actions. We detect (and often expect) a logical pattern of reasoned movement. These patterns or sequences of action are like webs writers have spun to support their artistic intentions and to let you discover what is meaningful.

An artist's intention, however, may be to present an unbalanced, chaotic, or absurd world where events do not have causes, where actions are not motivated, and where the parts do not connect. Many modern writers break with conventional structural techniques to reflect the complexities of contemporary life. Others seek to transform traditional structures and experiment with language, ideas, and form. As a consequence, much modern literature simply cannot be pigeonholed into predictable structures.

Many modern dramatists such as Samuel Beckett and Edward Albee have written plays lacking conventional plots. Some readers and viewers of Beckett's *Waiting for Godot* may complain, "Nothing happens!" They experience a succession of scenes in which two tramps, Vladimir and Estragon, merely wait for Godot, a mysterious character who never arrives. These readers complaining of finding no plot may find little or no meaning. However, other readers who believe the play is about the act of waiting itself find that the seemingly unrelated succession of scenes showing characters "marking time" reinforces that theme. Some readers may even say the structure is the theme.

Literature Is Unified

Structure includes not only organization but also unity. All the parts connect and work together to define and give form to the emotions and ideas expressed in the work. The most predominant unifying forces are the work's theme, emotion, and intention which limit as well as propel movement.

Many writers have commented on the importance of unity. For example, in his "Theory of Composition," Edgar Allan Poe writes, "In the whole composition there should be no word written, of which the tendency, direct or indirect, is not to the one preestablished design." Similarly, Aristotle felt that in classical drama, all incidents should be necessary and interrelated. In his *Poetics*, Aristotle writes that the actions should be "so closely connected that the transposal or withdrawal of any one of them will disjoint and dislocate the whole."

As said earlier, however, these theories on unity do not apply uniformly to all modern literature. Modern writers experiment with language and ideas as they continually search for new ways to structure and unify their works.

Story and Plot

The structure of fiction is most visible through story and plot. The novelist E. M. Forster analyzes the difference between the two:

> A plot is also a narrative of events, the emphasis falling on causality. "The king died and then the queen died," is a story. "The king died and then the queen died of grief" is a plot. The time sequence is preserved, but the sense of causality overshadows it.

The *story* is the set of events often appearing in chronological order. The *plot*, though, involves the sequence of events or incidents and the reasons those incidents occur. Plot does not necessarily include physical action; the plot of a story may occur in the mind of a character — mental action. Perhaps you have read stories in which little or nothing seems to "happen." In Henry James' "The Beast in the Jungle," readers are far more aware of John Marcher's state of mind than his overt actions.

Whether the action is physical or mental, the very essence of plot is conflict. Analyzing the plot in a work of fiction will help you discover the conflict. And since theme, experience, and effect arise out of conflict, your interpretation of a work will evolve from your analysis and synthesis of plot.

You may analyze plot by examining its traditional elements, designated by some writers and critics as *exposition, rising action (conflict), climax,* and *denouement.*

The Exposition

The *exposition* or early part of the work may provide background, introduce us to the setting and characters, create atmosphere, begin the conflict, or even hint at the theme. Examine how Poe sets the dreary mood in his exposition to "The Fall of the House of Usher":

> During the whole of a dull, dark, and soundless day in the autumn of the year, when the clouds hung oppressively low in the heavens, I had been passing alone, on horseback, through a singularly dreary tract of country; and at length found myself, as the shades of the evening drew on, within view of the melancholy House of Usher.

One method of exposition in drama is the *prologue*, a short speech introducing a play, as seen in Shakespeare's *Romeo and Juliet*. The Chorus enters and indicates the story yet to unfold:

> From forth the fatal loins of these two foes
> A pair of star-crossed lovers take their life,
> Whose misadventured pitious overthrows
> Doth with their death bury their parents' strife.

Another method of exposition in drama is a speech by the narrator or one of the play's characters. In Tennessee Williams' *The Glass Menagerie*, Tom Wingfield enters dressed in a sailor's uniform. He comments on the setting, the characters, the importance of memory, and his role as the narrator. The play is then told through flashbacks shaped by his memory.

Yet another method of exposition is the opening dialogue and action between characters. In the exposition of Edward Albee's *Who's Afraid of Virginia Woolf*, George and Martha return home at two in the morning after a faculty party. After arguing about the title of a movie, Martha criticizes George as stupid and ineffectual. George retaliates by reminding Martha of her age and drinking habits. The exposition prepares the reader for the rest of the play, a night of matrimonial battle.

The Rising Action

The rising action defines the *conflict* — the clash of internal or external forces. Such conflicts are the heart of the action. This conflict creates tension or even anxiety in the reader over what will happen and may give rise to theme or meaning in the work. Traditionally, conflict has been classified as (1) human vs. human, (2) one vs. oneself, (3) human vs. nature or environment, and (4) human vs. God, the gods, or fate. A character might face several of these conflicts simultaneously.

Elisa Allen in John Steinbeck's "The Chrysanthemums" is in conflict with her environment: an isolated and lonely farm; she is in conflict with her husband: a simple man who does not understand her passions; and she is in conflict with herself: a woman torn by her duties as a farmwife and her desire to live a romantic life with someone who understands her.

Rising action is also known as the *complication*. Often, the plot of a play consists of a series of complications building to a climax. In drama, as in fiction, the appearance of a new character may be the beginning of a complication, just as in the real world people may enter and bring their problems into our lives. In Tennessee Williams' *A Streetcar Named Desire*, Stanley and Stella seem to live an uneventful life until Stella's sister Blanche arrives and disrupts their existence.

The Climax

Our word *climax* comes from the Greek word *klimax*, meaning *ladder*. When events in a story are climactic, they build or rise to a moment of high intensity or crisis. The rising action eventually reaches a peak, a crisis, or a point of no return. In Shakespeare's *Othello*, the climax occurs when Iago persuades Othello that Desdemona is faithless. Othello, who has been obsessed with the possibility of her infidelity, becomes enraged with jealousy.

In Alice Munro's short story "Boys and Girls," the crisis occurs when the young girl narrator frees the horse Flora instead of following her father's instructions. By closing the gate she would have condemned Flora to slaughter, but even as she frees the horse, the girl knows she has disassociated herself from her father's world. Readers see her inner dilemma resulting in action as she says:

> And when my father found out about it he was not going to trust me any more; he would know that I was not entirely on his side. I was on Flora's side, and that made me no use to anybody, not even to her. Just the same, I did not regret it; when she came running at me and I held the gate open, that was the only thing I could do.

Some climaxes are *epiphanies* — moments of insight, revelation, or illumination. For the writer James Joyce, an epiphany was the moment when "the relation of parts . . . its soul, its whatness leaps to us from the vestment of its appearance." Many of Joyce's characters in his collection of stories entitled *Dubliners* experience epiphanies. In "The Dead," when Greta's husband learns of her long-past passionate love for a young boy she once knew, he realizes his own inadequacies as a husband. In Ibsen's play *The Doll House*, Nora eventually realizes she has been repressed by a man unworthy of her. In her newly awakened state, she makes a decision for herself — she leaves her husband.

The climax of a play may be a *reversal* or a point in the structure when the protagonist's fortunes change. In Sophocles' *Oedipus Rex*, Oedipus experiences a reversal when he realizes his fate was to kill his father and marry his mother. In tragedy, this reversal may be followed with a moment of truth or a *recognition*. Oedipus blinds himself after learning he has fulfilled his fate. But by being blind, he now understands that at last he has gained insight into who he is.

The Falling Action (Denouement)

The *denouement*, from the French word meaning *unknotting*, is the final resolution of conflict. In Alice Munro's story mentioned above, when the father discovers what his daughter has done, he replies with resignation, "She's only a girl." The narrator then accepts her father's dismissal by commenting, "I didn't protest."

In Williams' *A Streetcar Named Desire*, Stanley's poker friends are playing as usual in the denouement even though Blanche, now insane, is waiting for the asylum administrators to take her away. Stanley and Stella merely return to their somewhat sordid lives once Blanche is gone.

Some modern dramas, however, lack a denouement; modern dramatists tend to structure the climax near the very end of the play. The playwright may choose to leave the conflict unresolved to reflect life in which conflict does not end but continues. Although the lack of resolution may leave an audience unsettled, the dramatic effect is powerful. In *The Normal Heart*, Larry Kramer sees little or no immediate resolution of the problems affecting AIDS patients.

Other Plot Devices

Foreshadowing is a structural device that can build suspense and tension and also provide credibility for future events in the story. Since readers expect most works of art to be organized and express unity, surprise endings often disrupt the story's pattern and may cause displeasure. Many readers are surprised to discover that the oiler dies at the end of Stephen Crane's "The Open Boat"; however, the author provides some foreshadowing early in the story when he writes, "his oar was ready to snap." Rereading a story would obviously help you detect foreshadowing since during the second reading you would be well aware of the story's outcome. Foreshadowing that is subtle and unobtrusive is one hallmark of good fiction.

In some stories, the foreshadowing is extensive. In William Faulkner's "A Rose for Emily," the narrator has actually prepared the reader for the shocking ending — the discovery of not only Homer Barron's rotted corpse in the upstairs bedroom but also the strand of gray hair next to the corpse. Throughout the story, the narrator refers to "the smell" around Emily's house and to the gradual graying of her hair over the years.

As is true in fiction, foreshadowing can be an important structural element in drama. Foreshadowing builds suspense and tension as the reader anticipates actions and is, in a way, "set up" for any reversals. Dramatists can prepare readers to accept certain unpleasant events with foreshadowing. In *Death of a Salesman*, Miller prepares the reader for Willie's suicide by revealing that he has concealed a rubber hose near the gas water heater. Yet much modern drama does not include foreshadowing. In Eugene O'Neil's *Desire Under the Elms*, the reader is unprepared for the sexual tension that immediately arises when Eben meets his father's pretty new wife. Modern dramatists may want to reflect the shock of modern life by surprising the reader with rapid turns of events and unexpected action.

Another common literary device is *flashback*. A flashback stops the chronological order of events to present an incident or incidents from the past. What we learn from the flashback is crucial for our understanding of subsequent events. In Ernest Hemingway's "The Snows of Kilimanjaro," the protagonist, Henry, has flashbacks to his youth which help him and the reader understand his disappointing life.

WRITING ABOUT STRUCTURE

Plot Summaries

As mentioned in Chapter 5, summarizing the story is one useful way of writing about structure in fiction. A story summary (also called a plot synopsis) is an accurate retelling of what happens in a short story or novel. A summary is short so it usually concentrates only on significant action.

A summary or synopsis can be used in a variety of ways, but the summary is most helpful as a component of a larger writing project such as an analytical essay, a critical review, or a research paper. Just how much you summarize depends on your audience. Remember, readers do not like to be told what they already know. If the audience has already read the work you are analyzing, you will want to keep your summary very brief because it will serve merely as a reminder of the plot line. Other times, if your audience will not have read the work you are analyzing, a thorough but concise summary is crucial for your reader to understand your analysis.

The one-sentence and the paragraph summary are appropriate for either reading tests or plot reminders in larger essays. But before attempting to write either, make sure you have read the work carefully enough to outline the significant action. If you own your book, you should mark your text, noting major divisions and crucial actions. Determine which events are most important, and if you are reading for plot, not just story, decide not only what happens, but also why and how it happens.

The One-Sentence Summary

The one-sentence summary encapsulates the major action of a work in one concise and precise sentence. These one-sentence summaries may summarize the entire work or just a part of the work, a chapter, for example. Note the following examples:

> Story summary: In Shirley Jackson's "The Lottery," Tessie Hutchinson is stoned to death by her townspeople.

> Plot summary: In Shirley Jackson's "The Lottery," Tessie Hutchinson is stoned to death by her townspeople, who blindly act out a ritual sacrifice.

The Summary Paragraph

The summary paragraph allows you to examine the structure of the plot. The events you describe should be presented in chronological order (even if the story includes flashback). Remember to be accurate and brief. Identify the significant incidents and condense them into a few sentences. Eliminate specific details and concentrate on major occurrences. Examine this paragraph plot summary of Gabriel Garcia Márquez's "A Very Old Man with Enormous Wings":

> Subtitled "A Tale for Children," Gabriel Garcia Márquez's short story has a very simple plot. In an unnamed village somewhere by the sea in an unnamed Latin American country, Pelayo and Elisenda discover, after three days of rain, a very

old man with enormous wings lying in the courtyard of their house. Because he speaks an unfamiliar language they decide that he is a sailor, but other villagers think he is an angel. Since their sick child recovers soon after his arrival, they do not kill the winged man but instead imprison him in their chicken coop. The villagers at first throng to see this anomaly, and Pelayo and Elisenda become rich by charging admission to all who would see him, whether as mystery, miracle, or freak. The old man bears the visits and various indignities with stoicism. However, when he fails to perform any real miracles, he soon loses his novelty and, when a spider woman comes to town in a traveling show, is deserted entirely by the crowds. He stays on in the chicken coop for several years until one winter he becomes very ill and moults. They are afraid that he will die; however, he recovers, and that spring his feathers grow back. One sunny day he simply and suddenly escapes and flies away.

Comment   This summary paragraph identifies the major events in the story. They are presented in chronological order and are accurate and brief. This summary makes no attempt at interpretation; instead, it concentrates only on major action.

Plot Analysis

An essay on plot is usually a plot analysis. Few readers want to be told only what happens; they want to know why it happens and how it happens. As we have just seen, a story summary or plot synopsis tells what happens. A plot analysis tells why and how those actions occur.

An essay would probably not just recount the events of a story because an essay analyzing plot requires interpretation and argument. Your essay then becomes your attempt to persuade the reader that your views are valid. A reader may disagree with your view of exactly where the climax occurs or your explanation of character motivation, so a plot analysis requires proof and justification.

Writing the Essay on Structure in Fiction

If you are asked to write about structure in fiction, first examine your writing task and decide what the project calls for you to do. Will the summary be just one part of a larger writing project? If so, should it be given all at once, perhaps at the beginning of the essay? Or should you intermingle summary and analysis throughout the essay? Who is your audience? Just how much summary does the audience need?

Does the assignment ask for a plot analysis? Does the assignment ask for you to analyze other structural devices? A structural analysis involves far more than mere summary. You must explain how the different structural elements combine to produce unity of action and effect.

After you have an understanding of the assignment, try some creating techniques to discover ideas. You may want to start by writing in your journal. You may also want to answer some or all of the questions that follow:

1. Is the story developed chronologically or through flashbacks?
2. What information do you find in the exposition?
3. What are the major conflicts?
4. Where does the climax occur? How do you know?
5. Are the conflicts resolved? Why or why not?
6. Does the plot contain a denouement?
7. Does the work have a surprise ending?
8. Do you detect any foreshadowing?
9. Do you notice any unusual plot twists?
10. Is all action justified and motivated?
11. Is the plot based on cause and effect relationships?
12. Do you notice any unusual treatment in the plot such as a dream sequence?
13. Does the story conclude with a happy or unhappy ending? Why?
14. Do you detect any loose threads?
15. Does anything distract from the unity of the story?
16. Is the story believable?
17. Do you detect any special forms or patterns in the work (such as a ritual or an initiation)?
18. Are the events vivid and memorable?

Once you decide what you want to say about structure, decide how to organize your ideas. If you are writing an analysis, you might organize it around the major divisions of the work or around one or more of the structural devices.

Student Essay on Structure in Fiction

Conflict in Hemingway's "The Short Happy Life

of Francis Macomber"

Hemingway's short story "The Short Happy Life of Francis Macomber" is the story of Francis and Margot Macomber's big game safari in Africa with their hunter and guide, Robert Wilson. It is a hunting story, the story of Francis conquering fear, and yet it is also the story of a shallow and superficial marriage, a union which has held together only because "Margot was too beautiful for Macomber to divorce her and Macomber had too much money for Margot to ever leave him" (52). These two subjects, the hunt and the marriage, provide the two main conflicts of the story: the first, the internal conflict in Macomber between his desire to prove his manhood by shooting big game and his fear of death; and the second, the external conflict between Macomber and his wife over who has the power in their marriage.

The hunting conflict is quickly revealed in the exposition as we soon learn that Francis has "just shown himself, very publicly, to be a coward" (40). Later we are given all the details of the hunt, beginning with Macomber's fear the night before the hunt when he hears the lion roar outside the tent. Our suspense is aroused as the tension quickly mounts through the preparation for the hunt. Wilson and Margot are excited; Macomber is almost sick to his stomach. The tension continues through the search for the lion, Macomber's poor shooting which only wounds the lion, the tracking of the lion into the bush, and Macomber's flight when the lion charges.

However, the next day the rising action peaks quite differently as Macomber successfully and bravely kills buffalo, providing the turning point or climax for the hunting conflict. He feels a "drunken elation" because "in his life he had never felt so good" (56, 57). He has conquered his fear and earned the respect of Wilson.

However, there is still the conflict between Margot and Francis to be resolved since his initiation into courage and manhood does not please her. Before, she was able to manipulate him; his cowardice even gave her the right to humiliate him by sleeping with Wilson, the "real man." When, however, Francis gains courage, Margot recognizes the change in him, and she is "very afraid of something" (60). That something is Francis, now fully a man for the first time in his life. Both realize that their marriage will have to change. How will the conflict be resolved? In Hemingway's world, the resolution comes with a bullet to the brain. Margot "accidentally" shoots Francis when a wounded buffalo charges at him. After this climax, the story ends quickly.

Francis successfully resolves his conflict with fear, but the resolution of the marital conflict has been taken out of his hands by Margot.

Work Cited

Ernest Hemingway. "The Short, Happy Life of Francis Macomber."
     The Norton Introduction to Fiction. 3rd ed. Ed. Jerome
     Beaty. New York: Norton, 1985. 39–62.

Comment   This essay analyzes structure by identifying major actions and conflicts and commenting on them. The plot is followed chronologically, and the writer examines conflicts arising out of both the hunt and the marriage. The student correctly uses key terms such as conflict, exposition, rising action, climax, and resolution.

Structure

Writing about Structure in Poetry

Because both fiction and drama are narrative, they usually have a plot line or sequence of related incidents. Some poetry, including epics, ballads, and others, is also narrative and contains exposition, rising action, climax, and denouement.

Of course, not all poetry tells a story; yet, as we have seen, all poetry has structure. Although there is no "plot," let's say, in William Carlos Williams' "The Red Wheelbarrow," there is still perceivable form.

Various structural devices can give poetry form. Form may grow out of the arrangement of lines, stanzas, sounds, ideas, or images. Poets may use figurative devices or rhythm and rhyme to create structural patterns. (These devices are explained in Chapter 7.) You may discover the arrangement of parts as one key to a poem's structural unity as well as its meaning.

As we have seen, one way to write about structure is to summarize the work. You can easily summarize a narrative poem by recounting its "plot" as you would with narrative fiction or drama. But what about summarizing a nonnarrative poem? Some readers believe it is impossible to adequately summarize or paraphrase a nonnarrative poem because a poem means more than it says and its essential meaning would be lost in such an attempt. No doubt these readers would agree with poet Archibald MacLeish that "a poem should not mean / But be."

However, writing a summary of a narrative or nonnarrative poem is one way for you to actively "engage" the poem. To get started, simply ask yourself: What happens in this poem? or What experience is presented? You may then want to answer the following questions as a creating technique to generate ideas for writing about structure in poetry:

1. Is the poem narrative or nonnarrative?
2. If the poem is narrative, is it a traditional type such as a ballad or monologue? (Consult the glossary for the conventions of the particular type of poem.)
3. If the poem is nonnarrative, is it structured by the conventions of a fixed form such as the sonnet or ode? (Again, consult the glossary for these structural conventions.)
4. If the poem you are analyzing is not a fixed form, can you discover an original structure in the work?
5. Does the poem contain structural devices such as repeated images, ideas, or stanza patterns?

6. How do the structural devices unify the poem and give it form and meaning?

7. Does the poem contain any devices such as metaphor or simile (explained in Chapter 7) that help structure the poem?

Answer these questions and carefully analyze your responses. What have you discovered about the structure of the poem (or poems) you have been reading? How is the structure tied to the meaning or experience you have defined? State your idea about the poem's structure in one or two sentences and develop key points to support your discovery.

Students in a literature class were asked to discover the structure in one of Emily Dickinson's death poems. Here is how one student responded.

Student Essay on Structure in Poetry

The Death of Reason: Structure in Dickinson's "I Felt a Funeral
in My Brain"

Emily Dickinson structures her poem "I Felt a Funeral in My Brain" around a Protestant funeral service. The service in the poem, however, is not quite a typical funeral. Although the mourners have come to pay their respects, no one has died. Although a coffin has been prepared, there is no corpse. These two examples present a paradox until it becomes clear that the speaker's sanity, not her body, has died. Dickinson uses the structure of a funeral service to symbolize the slow death of reason. Each four-line stanza presents a different part of the service from mourning to burial or, rather, from an attempt to control her sanity to a total breakdown of mind and senses.

In the first stanza, the speaker informs us, "I felt a Funeral, in my Brain" (1). Since the funeral is a mental one, the "mourners" who keep "treading-treading" (3) are possibly thoughts. These thoughts represent her last effort to control her sanity. These thoughts keep treading "till it seemed /

that sense was breaking through—" (4). A mental breakdown has not yet occurred.

In the second stanza, all of the mourners are seated so the service may begin. The service is "like a drum" (6) which keeps "beating—beating" (7) until the speaker thinks, "My Mind was going numb—" (8). The repetition of "treading" and "beating" emphasize her growing madness and help structure the poem. The funeral service, perhaps an oration of confused and painful thoughts, paralyzes her ability to think and reason.

In the third stanza, the funeral service has ended, and her coffin is about to be carried out of the church. She "heard them lift a Box / And creak across my Soul" (9–10). At first she hears the mourners' "Boots of lead" (11), and soon, "Space [silence]—began to toll—" (12). The "Space" represents the silence in her mind as she is no longer able to reason or feel.

In the fourth stanza, Dickinson employs several figures of speech to dramatize the next part of the funeral service. As the speaker is being carried to the cemetery, the knell of silence overpowers her. The image of deafening silence is an example of an oxymoron, the combination of incongruous terms. The stanza also presents a metaphor that emphasizes the silence in her mind. All the "Heavens were a Bell" (13) and "Being, but an Ear" (14).

In the fifth and final stanza, the speaker has arrived at her gravesite. But as her coffin is being lowered into the ground, something startling and appalling occurs. The bottom of the coffin breaks loose. "And then a Plank in Reason, broke / And I dropped down and down—" (17). At this point in the service, the speaker has experienced a complete loss of reason. The speaker "hit a World at every plunge, / And Finished knowing—then (20). The speaker has by now experienced a death of the senses. She has gone insane!

Work Cited

Emily Dickinson. "I Felt a Funeral in My Brain." Literature:
    The Power of Language. Ed. Thomas McLaughlin. New York:
    Harcourt, 1989. 194.

Comment   The student reflects the structure of the poem in the structure of his essay. As he analyzes the parts of a Protestant funeral service, he follows the poem stanza by stanza, connecting the metaphorical service with the growing insanity of the poem's speaker. Notice, too, how he mentions poetic devices such as repetition, metaphor, and oxymoron as structural devices.

Writing about Structure in Nonfiction Prose

Of course, some of the literature we read is nonfiction prose which may take a variety of forms depending on the author's purpose, audience, tone, and subject matter. You have undoubtedly read essays, proclamations, declarations, sermons, letters, travel accounts, speeches, autobiographies, biographies, or histories embodying structures preset by tradition or invented to suit the author's and readers' needs.

As you know, expository essays may use a variety of structural arrangements involving classification, comparison, contrast, process, definition, or cause and effect. Although very few nonacademic essays are "pure" examples of a specific pattern, many do have a dominant mode of organization developed through a variety of expository modes. Argumentative essays may be arranged inductively or deductively with any number of concessions and refutations.

Certainly one common feature of nonfiction prose is the presence of a beginning, middle, and end. In a sense, nonfiction prose also contains an exposition, development, a climactic moment, and a conclusion. Works such as Thomas Jefferson's political document "The Declaration of Independence," Martin Luther King's "Letter from Birmingham Jail," and Jonathan Swift's satire "A Modest Proposal" are arguments and therefore are structured with assertions and evidence. Their structures are also governed by inductive and deductive patterns that build to climactic moments and then logically conclude. Beryl Markham's autobiography *West with the Night* also builds to a climactic moment through the use of a narrative structure.

Before writing about structure in nonfiction prose, find out if the selection you are analyzing is an example of a pre-set or traditional form. If it is, you may want to research the form itself. Once you know the conventional features of a particular type of nonfiction prose, you can analyze how an author uses or ignores them. Here are some questions to ask about form in nonfiction prose:

1. Does the work reflect an established prose pattern (like a sermon)?
2. What are the elements of that traditional form?
3. Is the primary purpose of the nonfiction prose descriptive, narrative, expository, or argumentative?
4. Has the author invented a structure to suit the purpose? What are the parts of that structure?
5. Where do you sense the beginning, middle, and end in the work?
6. Does the work have a climactic moment? If so, how did the author build to that moment?
7. What is the purpose of the conclusion in the work?

Review your responses to these questions to discover how the structure relates to the author's purpose. In particular, note how the structure supports and enhances the message. State your idea about structure in one or two sentences and then list the main points you would use to support your discovery. For example, students in an American literature survey course have been assigned to write an essay on the structure in Puritan sermons or Federalist political documents. Several students in the class are struck by the argument in Thomas Jefferson's "The Declaration of Independence." The author of the following essay analyzes the deductive argument in the document.

Student Essay on Structure in Nonfiction Prose

```
     Structure in "The Declaration of Independence"

 Aside from being one of the most important documents in
American history, "The Declaration of Independence" is a
brilliant study in persuasive argumentation. When writing the
document, Thomas Jefferson argues deductively. He structures
his argument around a major premise, minor premise, and
conclusion. By constructing his document in such a fashion,
```

Jefferson carefully guides his audience through the reasons
leading up to the declaration and then presenting the
American people as victims who have no choice but to be free
of the Crown.

The introduction (or preamble) of the document states
that it has become a necessity, not just merely a wish or
desire, for Americans to dissolve their political ties with the
British government. Jefferson supports this necessity by citing
the "Laws of Nature and of Nature's God" (481) as entitling
Americans to certain "self—evident" truths (481). By use of
this term "self—evident," Jefferson assures readers that these
truths are obvious and apply to all people. He states that
". . . all men are created equal, that they are endowed by
their Creator with certain unalienable Rights, that among
these are Life, Liberty, and the pursuit of Happiness" (481).
Jefferson then identifies the purpose of government as an
institution formed by the consent of the people to secure the
preceding rights. When a government serves to destroy these
rights, Jefferson asserts that it is the people's right to
abolish or change the government. But in anticipation of a
counterargument, he cites that governments should not be
changed for short—lived or frivolous causes. Thus he assures
readers that the causes for the break have been weighed heavily
and are significant. In addition, he makes plain that it is
not only the right, but the duty of the people to eradicate a
government which impinges on these unalienable rights, thereby
giving his cause not only a moral but a legal obligation.
Jefferson's major premise, then, is that a tyrannized country
has the right to form a new government.

Next, Jefferson defines a tyrant. He supports this key
definition by citing fifteen crimes committed by the Crown. In
presenting this information, Jefferson repeats the phrase "he

has" prior to each offense. This repetition reinforces the strong impression of frequent, recurring injustices that the king imposed on the American people. In addition, by candidly presenting the facts, Jefferson allows the facts to speak for themselves; he does not need to resort to a purely emotional appeal. Then, he presents the American response to each one of these injustices. He states that the country has petitioned repeatedly for a means of seeking a remedy. Moreover, he states that Americans have done this "in the most Humble terms" (483), representing themselves as unpretentious and modest. Yet, in response to the pleas of the Americans, the British government has answered by committing further injustices. Such injustices further support Jefferson's definition of a tyrant and the claim that dissolving the country's tie to England is necessary. Jefferson's minor premise in his deductive argument is that America is indeed a tyrannized country.

Finally, Jefferson concludes with a declaration. He appeals to the "Supreme Judge of the world for the rectitude of our intentions" (483), which indicates the moral integrity by which the Americans have reached their decision. Jefferson then simply states that the American colonies are now—and have the right to be—free and independent of the British Crown.

The structure of Jefferson's argument leads to a logical conclusion. A tyrannized country has the right to form a new government; America is a tyrannized country; therefore, America has the right to form a new government. He supports all his claims with facts and persuades his readers in a candid, precise manner. He employs negative terms such as "tyrant" to represent the Crown, and positive terms such as "humble" to represent the Americans. Thus, Jefferson enhances his argument with his style. Jefferson makes independence appear to be the only rational solution to the problem of tyranny.

Work Cited

Thomas Jefferson. "The Declaration of Independence." The

Informed Argument. Ed. Robert K. Miller. New York:

Haɪ ᴄᴏᴜɪ ᴛ, 1900. 401-04.

Comment   This student has noted the deductive argument in Jefferson's "Declaration" and structures her own analysis around his argument. This analysis requires familiarity with the parts of a deductive argument: major premise, minor premise, and conclusion. Each paragraph offers abundant support for her analysis. Note too how the author relates Jefferson's structure to the "Declaration's" purpose.

CHAPTER REVIEW

A work of literature is organized and unified. The parts should work together in a pattern or shape appropriate for the author's intent. Many works of literature follow the conventions of established literary genres. Many modern writers, however, may ignore traditional structures to experiment with a new form reflecting the complexities of modern life. Your discovery of form and its relationship to meaning and purpose in the work may help create a satisfying literary experience.

CHAPTER 7

Language

LITERAL AND FIGURATIVE LANGUAGE

*L*anguage can be used literally or figuratively; literal language tells the apparent truth while figurative language tells the apparent truth as well as the indirect truth. Emily Dickinson suggests that poets tell the truth "slant" because "success in circuit lies." Historians may describe the revolutions of 1848 in literal language; the poet Matthew Arnold figuratively describes the same period in "Dover Beach":

> . . . we are here as on a darkling plain
> Swept with confused alarms of struggle and flight,
> Where ignorant armies clash by night.

Both literal and figurative language have the power to portray reality.

DICTION — DENOTATION AND CONNOTATION

Although you may immediately associate figurative language with literature, obviously there is a need for analyzing literal language in literature, too. Basic communication requires that we agree in general on the *denotations* of words, the explicit meanings recorded in dictionaries.

Sometimes a search for precise denotation may require the use of a specialized dictionary such as the *OED* (*Oxford English Dictionary*), which traces the changing meanings of words. Since denotation expresses a consensus of use among speakers, meaning may change from generation to generation or century to century. "Fond" once meant "foolish," "idiotic," and even "imbecilic," before its usage was softened to "loving." If you know only the present denotation, you may not understand Thomas Carlyle's perjorative description of someone as "writing from the abundance of his own fond ineptitude. . . ."

Try to form the habit of defining unfamiliar words as you read, for if you skip over them, you may miss some of the impact of the work. In literature each word counts. For example, among other details, the narrator of "Rip Van Winkle" tells us that Rip's wife is a "termagant." A "termagant" is a quarrelsome, scolding, overbearing woman — a shrew. This definition not only helps characterize Dame Van Winkle but also lets readers understand Rip's motivation for fleeing his spouse.

As you can see, denotation is relative rather than absolute; meaning depends on context. While a first step in analyzing language is to read with a good dictionary handy, the second step is to test possible denotations in context and then select a suitable meaning based on your interpretation. Dorothy Parker has titled a witty little poem on suicide "Résumé." After reading the poem, decide whether by "résumé" she means a "list of personal and professional qualifications" or a "summary."

> Razors pain you;
> Rivers are damp;
> Acids stain you;
> And drugs cause cramp.
> Guns aren't lawful;
> Nooses give;
> Gas smells awful;
> You might as well live.

As writers and readers we must also discover the *connotations* of words, their implicit meanings based on our emotional responses to them. Connotation conveys subtle attitudes and moods and suggests shades of meaning denotation cannot. For instance, a thesaurus may list many synonyms for *season* including "span," "duration," "quarter," "time," "spell," "space," "interval," and "lunation," but these words do not convey identical emotional associations. Which would you use to refer to a semester of school? To the period spent waiting for a loved one to return home? When poet Alfred Tennyson says that his eagle stands "ringed with the azure world," the connotation of "azure" seems more poetically appropriate than its synonym "blue." Whereas azure can mean the sky or the heavens, blue can connote an emotional state of depression as well as a color and could destroy the triumphal mood of the poem.

Writing about Diction

To analyze *diction* (a writer's choice of words) in a literary work, determine the nature of the words used and the writer's purpose for his or her choices by asking questions such as the following:

1. What are some of the key words in the work?
2. Does the author predominantly use general or specific, concrete or abstract terms?
3. Are any common words used in an unfamiliar sense? Why?
4. Does the author use *dialect* (language which distinguishes its speakers either geographically or socially), slang, *jargon* (language specific to a particular discipline or field) or *euphemism* (language which substitutes a vague or mild word for one thought to be offensive or too harsh)? For what purpose?
5. Most importantly, how does the diction affect the tone and meaning of the work? (One method of discovering the importance of word choice is to substitute a synonym for a key word and notice whether the substitution changes meaning.)

After answering as many of these questions as seem relevant to your particular selection, synthesize your answers to reach an assertion or conclusion about how word choice affects the work. For example, after studying Huck Finn's colloquial speech in Mark Twain's novel, you may decide that dialect is one of the book's strengths, for, while remaining realistic with the limited vocabulary of his protagonist, Twain also manages to convey the poetry of the boy's response to nature. Then you might develop a thesis such as "Huck Finn's dialect, although limited and provincial, nevertheless permits a sensitive and lyrical description of nature." You could then prove this thesis with quotations from the novel.

For an example of how you might write about diction, look at the following student essay on a brief poem by Ezra Pound. Notice that the student has used the questions above as a basis for analysis.

Student Essay on Diction

Going Nowhere: Ezra Pound's "In a Station of the Metro"

The apparition of these faces in the crowd;
Petals on a wet, black bough.

Through denotation and connotation Ezra Pound conveys
a remarkable portrait of the fragility and instability of
mankind in only fourteen words.

Key words are usually nouns or verbs; this poem has no
verbs and only five nouns: "apparition," "faces," "crowd,"
"petals" and "bough." (However, three of the nouns often
function as verbs; the possibilities of "to appear," "to face,"
and "to crowd" also reverberate in the poem.) The poet is at
once spectator and participant in the scene he describes; the
faces are "these faces," but they are also an "apparition." The
use of the word "apparition" instead of the milder and more
pleasant "presence" or "illusion" or "shadow" both distances
the poet and conveys a certain uneasiness about this distance
because "apparition" also connotes "startling."

The last two words are related in a pattern of nature: the
phrase "petals on a bough" refers to springtime. These two nouns
could not be reversed without drastically changing the tone
and meaning of the poem. "A wet, black bough with petals" would
give a heaviness or stability to the scene, while putting
"petals" first repeats the pattern of "apparition" in the
first line, underscoring the fragility and the unsteadiness
the poet intends. The words "wet" and "black" also reinforce
this pattern of fragility because petals are usually stripped
off boughs by spring rains. We are also reminded of the
expression "bowed down"; a bough is bowed down with petals or
fruit, but people or crowds are usually bowed down by worries,
burdens, or grief.

Through the connotative aspects of his carefully chosen
words, Pound gives the reader a brief image of the lack of form
or reality of the subway passengers; except for their faces,
they are shapeless wraiths, and even their faces are as fragile
and transitory as petals clinging to the bough from which they
must eventually fall.

Work Cited

Pound, Ezra. "In a Station of the Metro." Literature: The Power
    of Language. Thomas Mc Laughlin. San Diego: Harcourt,
    1988. 41.

Comment   As a classroom exercise using a standard desk dictionary, this
essay manages to say a great deal about this fourteen-word poem. The writer
uses both the denotative and connotative implications of the key words to
understand how such a brief poem can convey such a significant message. As
part of the analysis, the writer tries replacing key words with synonyms and
even reversing the order of some words, effective methods for understanding
the power of a poem.

ALLUSIONS

You will also find that some writers rely on *allusions*, references to
persons, places, or things outside the immediate world of the work, for
added depth and richness. You will find the meanings of such allusions
in dictionaries, histories, the Bible, or art and mythology books; however, even more helpful is a carefully annotated edition of the work
explaining difficult or obscure allusions with notes and commentary. If
the text you are using is not annotated, look in the library for the
definitive edition of the work, which may be annotated. The allusions
to events such as the lashing of the Quaker woman and the burning of
the Indian village in the exposition of Nathaniel Hawthorne's "Young
Goodman Brown" help us understand Hawthorne's ambiguous attitude toward the Puritans, who in their religious extremism could be
guilty of flagrant intolerance. The tone achieved by the background of
such events prepares us for the narrator's suggestion that at least some
Puritans may have been in league with the devil.

A list of allusions to emphasize the stature of the event, the situation, or the character being described is called a *catalog*. Catalogs of ships, ancestors, gods, or warriors are typical of the epic and are also used as a unifying device in free verse. Note Walt Whitman's catalog of deities in *Song of Myself*:

> Taking myself the exact dimensions of Jehovah,
> Lithographing Kronos, Zeus his son, and Hercules his
>   grandson,
> Buying drafts of Osiris, Isis, Belus, Brahma, Buddha.

An *apostrophe* may also contain an allusion. An apostrophe addresses a person or quality not present in the world of the work as though it were present and could answer. For example, in his "Ode to the West Wind," Percy Shelley asks: "O wind, / If Winter comes, can Spring be far behind?" This apostrophe to the wind is simple, but Poe's apostrophe, "Helen, thy beauty is to me / Like those Nicéan barks of yore," alludes to classical mythology. If an apostrophe puzzles you, again, refer to an annotated text, a specialized dictionary, or other reference help.

Correctly interpreting allusions can lead you to a deeper understanding of the work and can increase your appreciation of the experience it creates. You will, however, want to know more than the specific referents for the allusions in a work; you will also want to ask why the author chose them. Why does a twentieth-century work like *The Waste Land* allude to an obscure legend of the Fisher King to such an extent that the poet, T. S. Eliot, provides explanatory notes? You may speculate that the Fisher King quest symbolizes the quest of the reader; like the knight, the reader must ask "why?" If you do not involve yourself with the poem this closely, it may remain a collection of abstract fragments rather than a single illusion of life and experience.

Writing about Allusions

After you have researched the allusions in a work, respond to questions such as these:

1. From what fields of specialized knowledge or historical periods are the allusions drawn? How do you know?
2. Are there allusions to other literary works? Which ones? Why? For comparison or contrast? Definition? Irony?
3. How do the allusions help delineate the world of the work?

4. Are the allusions primarily used to convey character? Setting? Atmosphere? Tone? Imagery?
5. Are there catalogs of allusions? If so, what is their effect?

The student essay below explores the use of allusion in Edgar Allan Poe's "To Helen."

Student Essay on Allusion

The Way Home: Classical Allusions in Poe's "To Helen"

The first time I read Edgar Allan Poe's poem "To Helen," I had no earthly idea how or what the poem meant. My problem, I soon discovered, was that I was looking for an "earthly idea." I should have looked beyond the earth—into the heavens of classical mythology. There, in the tales of Mount Olympus, lies the key to the poem's meaning. For a "weary, way-worn wanderer," the way "home" to a secure interpretation depends on an analysis of Poe's classical allusions.

The first stanza contains four classical allusions:

Helen, thy beauty is to me   1

    Like those Nicéan barks of yore,   2

That gently, o'er a perfumed sea,   3

    The weary, way-worn wanderer bore   4

    To his own native shore.   5

The allusion to Helen is a reference to Helen of Troy, daughter of Zeus and Leda, and wife to Menelaus, King of Sparta. According to myth, Helen was the most beautiful woman of classical Greece (<u>Oxford</u> 196). The speaker apostrophizes, or consults, Helen with an extended simile, comparing her remarkable beauty to the "Nicéan barks of yore." The word "Nicéan" is possibly derived from the word "Nike," the Greek goddess of victory (<u>Oxford</u> 987). Hence, the "Nicéan barks" are sailing vessels returning victoriously home. "The weary, way-worn wanderer" may be an allusion to the Greek god Dionysus

returning to Olympus after his travels (Oxford 147). However,
the "wanderer" may also be an allusion to Odysseus, who,
after leaving Ithaca to fight in the Trojan War, wandered for
twenty years before returning home (Oxford 290–2). Helen's
beauty, then, is like a vessel that transports a "wanderer"
safely home.

The second stanza also contains numerous classical
allusions:

On desperate seas long wont to roam,	6
Thy hyacinth hair, thy classic face,	7
Thy Naiad airs have brought me home	8
To the glory that was Greece,	9
And the grandeur that was Rome.	10

As the speaker continues his apostrophe to Helen, he alludes
to her "hyacinth hair." Hyacinth hair is probably a lustrous
dark red, a reference, perhaps, to the story of Hyacinthus,
Apollo's dear friend, whose fatal head wound bled a deep
crimson blood (Oxford 217). Helen possesses a "classical
face," a face that exemplifies ancient Greek or Roman
qualities. She also possesses "Naiad airs." In mythology, the
Naiads were water nymphs who lived in rivers, lakes, and
streams, giving them life (Oxford 284). Helen's beauty,
composed of these qualities, not only takes the wanderer to his
"native shore," but also transports the speaker to "the glory
that was Greece, / And the grandeur that was Rome" (Poe 9–10).

In the third and final stanza, further classical
allusions unify the poem and reveal a possible theme:

Lo! In yon brilliant window—niche	11
How statue—like I see thee stand,	12
The agate lamp within thy hand!	13
Ah, Psyche, from the regions which	14
Are Holy—Land!	15

In this stanza, the speaker actually sees Helen, standing "statue—like," holding an agate lamp, and, bathed in its light, he now alludes to her as "Psyche." According to the myth, Psyche awakened Cupid by spilling oil from her lamp on him. The word "psyche" is also a Greek word for "soul" (Oxford 352). Perhaps, then Psyche (or Helen) has awakened or illuminated in the speaker some inner or spiritual truth. If "Psyche" alludes to Helen, then Greece is a sacred land. If "Psyche" is an allusion to the soul, then "Holy—Land" is a sacred region within the speaker.

"To Helen," then, says that beauty can transport a "wanderer" not only to a safe shore but also back in time and place. Beauty can also deliver the "wanderer" into some deep, inner region where truths become illuminated.

Works Cited

The Oxford Companion to Classical Literature. Comp. Sir Paul
    Harvey. Oxford: Oxford UP, 1984.
Poe, Edgar Allan. "To Helen." The Harper American Literature.
    2 vols. Ed. Donald McQuade et al. New York: Harper, 1987.
    1:1638—9.

Comment   This essay demonstrates how a careful analysis of the allusions in a seemingly difficult poem can lead to interpretation, understanding, and pleasure. Using a standard reference work, the student explores possible meanings for each less obvious allusion, tests those meanings against the context, and develops an interpretation which satisfies him. Notice the student briefly uses "I." The first person can be abused in writing about literature — the repetition of "I think" or "I feel" or "It is my opinion" is boring and unnecessary — but its use in the first paragraph of this essay provides the author the opportunity for a rather charming and clever introduction.

IMAGERY — DESCRIPTIVE LANGUAGE

Writers use descriptive detail to present images or pictures so that readers can share their vision. In his introduction to *The Nigger of the Narcissus,* Joseph Conrad writes: "My task . . . is, by the power of the written word to make you hear, to make you feel — it is, before all, to make you *see*. That . . . is everything." Images recreate the author's reality in literature just as stone or metal recreates the artist's reality in sculpture. Part of the enchantment of Jonathan Swift's *Gulliver's Travels* for readers of all ages is the extraordinary verisimilitude or appearance of reality he achieves through remarkably detailed descriptions. We clearly see the boys and girls who play hide-and-seek in Gulliver's hair, Gulliver towing fifty Blefuscudian men-of-war across the channel, a horse sewing with a needle held in her hoof, and Gulliver being wedged in a marrow bone by the Brobdingnagian Queen's malicious dwarf.

Imagery can be literal or figurative. Swift's worlds are pretend; he wants readers to imagine that they see, feel, hear, smell, and even taste what he "images," to pretend his created worlds actually exist. As you read other works, let literal images sweep you into their worlds. Imagery lets you see the delightful feast that Porphyro in Keats' "The Eve of St. Agnes" has prepared for his lover Madeline, ". . . a heap / Of candied apple, quince, and plum, . . . / And lucent syrops, tinct with cinnamon." And it invites you to taste the "jellies soother than the creamy curd," and smell the "spiced dainties." Through imagery, you hear Porphyro take up the "hollow lute" and play "La belle dame sans merci" and feel the fear of the suddenly awakened Madeline.

To analyze descriptive imagery, ask questions like the following:

1. To which senses do the images appeal?
2. From whose point of view do you experience the images?
3. What emotions do the images evoke, both individually and collectively?
4. Do the images capture the experience (situation, emotion, setting, character) for you? How?
5. If the image is a familiar one (a lover as a flower), does the writer make it fresh?

FIGURES OF SPEECH: METAPHOR, SIMILE, PERSONIFICATION, ANALOGY, METONOMY

Moving beyond literal comparisons, writers may use figurative ones or "figures of speech" to create even more powerful images that surprise readers with their unexpected precision. When the tenth-century Chinese poet Li Yu writes, "My heart's a river flushed with spring that must forever eastwards flow," he does not intend for you to envision his heart as a real river flooded with spring snow melt or even muddy and clogged with debris. Rather, he wants you to see that, figuratively, his heart, like the east-flowing river, longs to return home so intensely that this feeling floods and "flushes" his entire being.

Images can be presented figuratively through metaphor, simile, personification, analogy, or metonomy. As defined in Chapter 1, similes explicitly suggest a comparison and are often called "direct," "stated," or "explicit," while metaphors imply identity rather than likeness. When William Wordsworth says in his "Ode: Intimations of Immortality" that "Our birth is but a sleep and a forgetting," he is using a metaphor; he uses a simile in "Sonnet Composed upon Westminster Bridge" when he writes, "This City now doth, like a garment, wear / The beauty of the morning."

This last image is also a *personification* because it gives the city, an inanimate object, a human-like quality, the ability to "wear" a garment. Poets express the depth of their feelings when they humanize something. The eleventh-century Chinese poet Huang T'ing Chien personifies spring as a young man when he questions: "Where has spring gone, where's he gone?" and then commands: "Call him back."

An *analogy* is an extended comparison, carrying out the comparison through several prose sentences or lines of verse. In the "Westminster Bridge" sonnet quoted above, Wordsworth continues the comparison of the city to a great "majestic" figure seen in the early morning when "the very houses seem asleep; / And all that mighty heart is lying still!"

Unlike the previously discussed figures of speech, *metonomy* does not compare one thing to another; rather it uses one aspect of an object or figure to represent the complexity of the whole; for example, in the familiar saying, "The pen is mightier than the sword," "pen" is a metonomy for the writer or the act of writing while "sword" represents a warrior or the act of war.

Writing about Figures of Speech

When analyzing figures of speech, first try to recreate the writer's vision and then ask why he or she has chosen this mode of expression. What is the total effect or meaning produced by the images? Here are some questions to ask about figures of speech:

1. What is being compared to what?
2. How does the comparison or representation function in the work?

3. How would the effect change if alternative images were substituted?

4. Is there a pattern to the figures of speech?

The following student work is a response to an assignment on finding a pattern of imagery, diction, and tone in a short poem, a pattern sometimes called the "controlling image" of the work. This student has chosen Psalm 13 in the New Jerusalem Bible translation; the poem is printed below with annotations, followed by the student's brief personal response, and then the essay itself.

Student Essay Process on Figures of Speech

Poem with annotations:

1 How long, Yahweh, will you forget me? For ever? *direct and personal for something sung written*

repetition How long will you turn away your face from me? *to God*

parent and child

2 How long must I nurse rebellion in my soul, *odd verb*

sorrow in my heart day and night?

3 How long is the enemy to domineer over me? *bully*

Look down, answer me, Yahweh my God!

Give light to my eyes or I shall fall *imperative; peremptory*

into the sleep of death. *nice line reminds me of that helmsman in the Odyssey (Iliad?)*

4 Or my foe will boast, 'I have overpowered him,' *personifies the enemy*

and my enemy have the joy of seeing me stumble.

↓ sudden shift in tone from complaint to praise

5 As for me, I trust in your faithful love, Yahweh.

6 Let my heart delight in your saving help, *parallelism and*

let me sing to Yahweh for his generosity to me, *repetition again*

let me sing to the name of Yahweh the Most High!

Personal response #1:

This poem sounds to me like an angry kid complaining to his parent that nobody loves him anymore. At least it does until the end when the writer changes his tune and says that maybe things aren't so bad after all. I guess you could call that trust. Well, in the end, most kids do trust their parents; after all, who else have they got.

The poem sure does break into two parts, the first one complaining, the second one praising.

Some of the language and sentence structure is even childish—"How long will you forget me? Forever?" There are some verbal paradoxes—"nurse" rebellion and sorrow?

Personal response #2:

Well, we just covered this psalm in class today and I found out some things that help me understand it better. It seems that most psalms are either psalms of celebration or psalms of appeal, called laments. No problem figuring out which one this one is! A lament could be written for the whole nation, a sort of communal appeal, or for an individual. This one seems pretty personal to me. No one knows who wrote it or when or even what specific event the poet may have been bemoaning. However, the trusting ending can be explained by the history of Israel; whoever the psalmist is, he knows that God has saved Israel and individual Israelites before.

Final essay:

Psalm 13: An Affirmation of Trust

The controlling image of Psalm 13, an individual lament, is that of parent and child. The psalmist is the child, rudely challenging the father in the apostrophe to Yahweh in verse 1:

"How long, Yahweh, will you forget me? Forever?" The challenge
then becomes a complaint against the parent who would "turn
away your face from me," the typical gesture of an angry
parent. The parent—child image is reinforced by the use of the
verb "nurse" in verse 2 even though it is the psalmist who will
"nurse," and, paradoxically, not the child to his bosom, but
"rebellion in my soul" and "sorrow in my heart." However, the
psalmist is once again the child in verse 3 with the image of
the enemy who bullies him or lords it ("domineer") over him.

Twice more in the next lines is the image of child and
parent reinforced: first in the metaphorical "fall into the
sleep of death" (verse 3) as a child whose sleep is deep and as
the psalmist himself will do if Yahweh does not answer him, and
second, in the image of the psalmist who "stumbles" in front
of his enemies (verse 4), much as a toddler learning to walk
lurches around. In the second stanza the psalmist reiterates
his "trust" in the "faithful love," "saving help," and
"generosity" of Yahweh (verses 5—6), all nouns which support
the parent—child relationship.

Although parallelism and repetition are characteristic of
all Hebrew poetry, they certainly function in this poem to
reinforce the idea of the speaker as a child. Just as a child
repeats a hundred times during a journey, "How long before we
get there?," so does the psalmist begin the poem with a
fourfold repetition of "How long . . . ?" (verses 1—3). His
"how long's" introduce the three actors in the poem: Yahweh,
the speaker and the enemy. The parallel imperative verbs (the
imperative mood is also typical of children) which begin the
third verse—"look down, answer me"—also spatially place Yahweh
above the speaker, again parent to child.

The last two verses of the psalm show an abrupt reversal
in tone and content as the psalmist, reassured somehow, maybe
just by airing his complaint, ends by singing Yahweh's praises

and promises that he will continue to do so because he "trusts" the "faithful love" of Yahweh. But perhaps the controlling image still explains the mystery of this ending. For what else can children do when faced with the inexplicable and unfathomable actions and words of their parents except, in the end, trust and praise them?

Work Cited

Psalm 13. The New Jerusalem Bible. New York: Doubleday, 1985.

Comment   This essay covers what the student has found to be the controlling image pattern of the poem — the speaker or psalmist as a child and Yahweh as a parent. She develops that thesis with a careful examination of diction, figures of speech, tone, and even sentence structure. The concluding sentence offers the strongest support for her thesis as she uses the shift in the last two verses to confirm the parent-child imagery she has seen in the poem. You may also notice that the informal language of the personal responses, appropriate when writing for yourself, has become more formal in the final essay.

IRONIC FIGURES OF SPEECH: UNDERSTATEMENT, HYPERBOLE, LITOTES, PARADOX, PUNS, MALAPROPISM

When the narrator of Stephen Crane's "The Open Boat" describes the shipwrecked men as having, in the "excitement of clambering about the deck of a foundering ship . . . forgotten to eat heartily," you understand that Crane uses the words "excitement" and "forgotten" to deliberately understate the men's desperate plight. *Understatement* is one method of using words *ironically* to convey the opposite of their literal meaning. Irony can make works *ambiguous* or capable of multiple meanings, and thus add depth, texture, and richness which may enhance your reading enjoyment.

Another method of creating irony is *hyperbole* or overstatement, obviously the opposite of understatement. Even ordinary speech uses hyperbole in metaphors or similes such as, "He was as ugly as sin" or "I have a mountain of books to read for exams." When Alexander Pope in *The Rape of the Lock* describes the heroine Belinda as having two graceful locks of hair "to the destruction of mankind," obviously he overstates the case. But if you take him literally, you may be confused and irritated rather than humorously prepared for the "epic" battle which results from the snipping of one of these locks.

Litotes is a form of irony resulting when a writer denies the opposite of what he intends to assert. Litotes is also typical of daily conversation: in response to "How are you doing?" you might say "Not bad," meaning "good." *Beowulf* is replete with litotes: "They felt no sorrow, no misery of men." (They were happy in their sleep.) "[Grendel] wanted no peace with any of the men of the Danish host." (He wanted to continue devouring them.)

A *paradox* is a statement or situation which may seem contradictory, unbelievable, or even absurd but on closer inspection proves to be true. Since many see life itself as paradoxical, you may say that literature is an attempt to make that paradox more palatable by treating it aesthetically. If you wonder why the innocent suffer, read Job and discover one answer; read *Oedipus Rex* and discover another. A paradox stated briefly and poetically is an *oxymoron*, the combination of two terms which seem at first to be contradictory. "A fine madness," "darkness visible," and "cold fire" are all oxymorons.

A *pun* can also convey irony and is usually, but not always, used for comic purposes. A pun is a play on words, using a word which sounds like another, but which means something else. Hamlet in Shakespeare's play is fond of punning; he uses it to relieve feelings he cannot state directly. When Claudius asks why "the clouds still hang on you" when he continues to mourn his father whom Claudius has murdered, Hamlet replies, "Not so, my lord; I am too much i' the sun." He puns on the meaning of "sun"; he is literally too much in the presence of the king, the "sun" of the court because Claudius is keeping too close a watch on him, but he also mourns because he is a good "son." When his mother berates him for excessive mourning because death is "common," he seemingly agrees that "Aye, madam, it is common," but he sarcastically refers to her behavior in remarrying so quickly, an act more suitable for a commoner than royalty. Hamlet's punning indicates a quickness of wit and intelligence not always shared by others in the drama but readily appreciated by the audience.

On the other hand, puns also may be used ironically by the author to reveal truths not known to the character. When the narrator of Poe's "The Tell-Tale Heart" tells us he must murder the old man to rid himself of his "Evil Eye," he may also mean his own "evil I." If so, he is successful, for the murder leads to the narrator's undoing.

Another form of word play, the *malapropism*, is used to mock the user. A malapropism is the ridiculous misuse of words similar in sound but far different in meaning. It derives its name from the character Mrs. Malaprop in Sheridan's play *The Rivals*. Malapropisms indicate characters overreaching their limitations, attempting a vocabulary for which education and wit have not prepared them, characters who may say, like Mrs. Malaprop, "I am the pineapple of success."

Writing about Ironic Language

Begin an assignment on ironic language by responding to questions such as the following:

1. Do hyperbole or understatement function to present tone? Character? Situation? Theme?
2. Do any apparent contradictions presented in the work prove, on closer inspection, to be true? In what sense?
3. What is the emotional force of the dominant figures of speech?
4. Are any figures of speech used for comic effect? Why?

This student essay is a response to an assignment requiring a short, informal essay on ironic language in a brief but key passage from a short story. The student has chosen the last passage of Flannery O'Connor's story "A Good Man Is Hard to Find."

Student Essay on Irony and Ambiguity

Literal Meaning Is Hard to Find

"She would of been a good woman," The Misfit
said, "if it had been somebody there to shoot her
every minute of her life."

"Some fun!" Bobby Lee said.

"Shut up, Bobby Lee," The Misfit said. "It's
no real pleasure in life."

This story of a homicidal maniac who murders a family of
six when they accidentally stray into his path is full of
irony—irony of situation, understatement, and overstatement.

In the last passage are several examples of language used
ironically, i.e., words which mean the opposite of their
literal meaning. First, the Misfit refers to the grandmother,
who has caused the whole catastrophe, when he says she would
have been a good woman if someone had been standing over her
ready to shoot her all her life. This statement has several
layers of meaning. On the surface, it simply means that she
talks too much. But that's also ironic because it's seldom that
talking too much causes one's murder. On another level, the
grandmother, after being shown throughout the story as a
stupid, shallow, selfish woman, has just displayed a moment of
true, unselfish concern for someone else when she responds to
the Misfit as though he were one of her own children. So, in
one sense, the Misfit is saying that if she had been faced with
the threat of death every day, she might have lived as a better
woman. Yet, this too is ironic because all through the story
the woman has professed her Christian beliefs (848, 849), and
Christians are always supposed to live as though they could die
at any moment. Finally, this statement is ironic because the
grandmother's last—minute maternal response, the response
which causes the Misfit to see her as having had the potential
to be a "good woman," is also the response which causes the
Misfit to shoot her "three times through the chest" (850).

Next, Bobby Lee says, "Some fun!" Literally, he means it
since he is so far from the ordinary human standard of values
that he can use the word "fun" to refer to killing a father, a
mother, their three small children, and the grandmother.
However, the reader recoils in disgust from the phrase.
Surprisingly enough, though, so does the Misfit. He tells Bobby
Lee to "shut up" because "it's no real pleasure in life." But
here irony is displayed once more as the reader can't be
certain what literal meaning is intended in this
understatement. What's no real pleasure—murdering helpless

families or being escaped convicts on the run or life itself?
Or all three? The Misfit hasn't been shown to relish the act of
murder; in fact, although he orders the deaths of the family
members, the grandmother is the only one he actually kills
himself. We haven't seen that the men's lives on the run are
any pleasure although apparently Bobby Lee thinks so. And
finally we haven't seen that the family enjoys much pleasure
either. Maybe this last sentence is actually a moral from the
author to the reader; there's no real pleasure in life, so
don't feel bad about this unremarkable family's remarkably
miserable end.

Work Cited

O'Connor, Flannery. "A Good Man Is Hard to Find." Literature:
The Power of Language. Thomas Mc Laughlin. San Diego:
Harcourt, 1988. 838–50.

Comment   This student uses a careful treatment of ironic language to reach
a tentative conclusion about one of the themes of the story. Her willingness to
explore several possible ironic meanings for such common words as "good,"
"fun," and "pleasure" leads to an enhanced appreciation of the complexity of
the story.

THE SOUNDS
OF LANGUAGE

The sounds of language also contribute to the structure, the sense,
and the feeling you perceive in a literary work. You may be accustomed
to thinking of the sounds of words, their musical effect, as important
only in poetry, but sound effects are important in all literature.

RHYTHM

In part, sound effects depend on repetition, one form of which is
rhythm. The regular recurrence of stresses, accented and unaccented
syllables, and pauses linking words into larger units is the rhythm of

language, which is essential in poetry but also typical of good prose. In poetry, the repetition often forms a regular pattern of *stressed*, or accented, syllables and words (those naturally emphasized by the voice when a work is read aloud) and *unstressed* syllables and words (those the voice does not linger on); in prose, however, the pattern is irregular. Note the rhythms of the following examples, the first from Milton's sonnet "How Soon Hath Time" and the second from his *Aeropagitica*, a pamphlet defending a free press. The diagonal mark (´) indicates a strong or stressed syllable; (˘) a weak or unstressed syllable.

> How soon hath Time, the subtle thief of youth,
> Stoln on his wing my three and twentieth year!
> My hasting days fly on with full career,
> But my late spring no bud or blossom show'th.

> Lords and commons of England, consider what nation
> it is whereof ye are, and whereof ye are the governors:
> a nation not slow and dull, but of a quick, ingenious
> and piercing spirit, acute to invent, subtle and sinewy
> to discourse, not beneath the reach of any point, the
> highest that human capacity can soar to.

Although the second passage is well-written prose, both balanced and rhythmic, it obviously does not display the regularity of the poem. Indeed, because the prose does not have a perceivable pattern, there's no real point in attempting to *scan* it (mark the stressed and unstressed syllables and words); these markings only demonstrate the difference between the rhythm of prose and poetry even written by the same author. In reading aloud or speaking, our voices rise and fall with certain words or groups of words as we emphasize content and meaning. Thus, stress is not just a matter of accented syllables within a word, but also reflects the meaning of the word within the line of poetry or within the phrase or sentence of prose. Clearly, then, not all readers will scan the same work in the same way.

Rhythm in literature should reinforce and emphasize organization, meaning, and key words and phrases. As Alexander Pope says in *An Essay on Criticism*: "The sound must seem an echo to the sense." You can see the stresses in the first line of Milton's sonnet quoted above fall on "soon," "Time," "subt(le)," "thief," and "youth," a combination from which you could almost guess the meaning of the line without the intervening unaccented words. The primary stresses would seem to be on "Time" and "thief," the epithet intended by the poet. The regularity of the stress pattern is broken by "Stoln," and that break in the rhythm serves to emphasize the deed. Similarly, in the prose passage, the primary stresses of the last phrase would seem to be "highest" and "human" — a link conveying the compliment Milton intends — further reinforced by the repetition of the "h" sound.

Meter

If the rhythmic pattern of a poem is regular, the poem is *metrical*. The arrangement of words into regularly measured, patterned, or rhythmic lines or verses in poetry is called *meter*; a metrical unit in a poetic line is called a *foot*. A foot consists of two or three syllables, one or two of which are stressed. The most common rhythmic foot in English poetry is *iambic*, in which an unstressed syllable is followed by a stressed one, as you see in the sonnet quoted above.

Another two-syllable pattern is the *trochaic*, the reverse of the iambic with a stressed syllable followed by an unstressed — fĭf tў, wóm ĕn. Note the trochaic feet in these lines by Emily Brontë:

> Tell me, tell me, smiling child,
> What the past is like to thee?

As you see in this example, trochaic rhythm tends to have a sing-song effect perfectly suitable for these lines in which an adult questions a child.

Two three-syllable patterns are the *anapestic* (two unstressed syllables followed by a stressed — ĭn tĕr cépt) and the *dactylic* (a stressed followed by two unstressed — beáu tĭ fŭl). Poe uses the anapestic foot in his ballad "Annabel Lee":

> For the moon never beams, without bringing me dreams
>   Of the beautiful Annabel Lee;
> And the stars never rise, but I feel the bright eyes
>   Of the beautiful Annabel Lee:

And Tennyson uses the dactylic in "The Charge of the Light Brigade" as presented in the refrain below:

> Cánnŏn tŏ rîght ŏf thĕm,
> Cánnŏn tŏ lĕft ŏf thĕm,
> Cánnŏn ĭn frónt ŏf thĕm
> Vólleyĕd ănd thúndĕrĕd;

As you can see in these examples, the dactylic and the trochaic feet, called the *falling feet*, are more rapid in movement than the *rising feet*, the iambic and the anapestic.

Two other feet not used for entire lines of poetry but which vary the regularity of other established patterns are the spondaic foot or *spondee* (two stressed syllables) and the *pyrrhic foot* (two unstressed syllables). Notice the last line of the Milton sonnet quoted earlier which combines a pyrrhic foot and a spondee, interrupting the regularity of the iambic feet and emphasizing the theme of the poem, the speaker's lack of fruitful productivity:

> Bŭt mў láte spríng nŏ búd ŏr blóssŏm shów'th.

A line of verse which has one foot is called *monometer*; two, *dimeter*; three, *trimeter*; four, *tetrameter*; five, *pentameter*; six, *hexameter*; seven, *heptameter*. In scansion you would mark a foot by a single vertical line (|):

> And the stars | never rise, | but I feel |the bright eyes

Looking back you will see the Milton poem has iambic pentameter lines, the Brontë trochaic tetrameter, the Poe alternates trimeter and tetrameter anapestic lines and the Tennyson is written in dactylic dimeter.

Some verse contains a pause within the line which causes a slight variation in the rhythmic regularity; this pause, often marked by punctuation, is called a *caesura*. In scansion you would mark the caesura by a double vertical line (||):

> And the stars never rise, || but I feel the bright eyes

The placement of the caesura may be quite regular — for example, always in the middle of the line — or the placement may be varied to create a more free-flowing rhythm. In the example from Milton's sonnet, the caesura quite regularly falls at the end of the second or third foot.

Language

If the thought in a line of poetry runs over one line into the next, this trait is called *enjambment* as in the first two lines of the Milton example. If the thought is contained in the line, the line is called *end-stopped* as in the last two lines of the same example.

As mentioned before, scansion is not an exact science; not all readers will agree on the metrical reading of any given line. What is more important than marking a line exactly as another reader may is noting the effect of the chosen meter on a particular work. How does the rhythm of the line affect the meaning and tone of the poem? Usually, the more stresses per line, the slower and more weighty the line becomes and the more solemn and forceful the thought. Because readers tend to pause at the end of each line of poetry they read, short lines move more slowly than long lines.

Free Verse

Many late nineteenth- and twentieth-century poets have broken away from regular metrical and stanzaic patterns in their poetry, choosing instead to echo the rhythms of speech and let meaning determine form rather than using predetermined patterns. Their poetry, aptly named *free verse* because it does not conform to a fixed pattern, is unified by repetition of grammatical structures, words, sounds, and images. You can easily see the repetition and parallelism in the first stanza of Sylvia Plath's "The Bee Meeting":

> Who are these people at the bridge to meet me? They
>   are the villagers —
> The rector, the midwife, the sexton, the agent for bees.
> In my sleeveless summery dress I have no protection,
> And they are all gloved and covered, why did nobody tell me?
> They are smiling and taking out veils tacked to ancient hats.

Despite its lack of a regular metrical pattern, this is poetry; obviously the way it is lined on the page forces us to treat individual lines as units. But also there is a subtle rhythm in the questions, "Who are . . . ?" and later "Why did . . . ?" echoed by the answer, "They are. . . ."

Writing about Poetic Rhythm

To write about rhythm in a work of literature, you may want to read the work aloud, many times. Emphasize or stress the words as you naturally would. Is a regular pattern established? Copy the work with double or triple spacing and mark or scan the pattern you have detected. Then ask yourself questions such as those below.

1. Is there a perceivable rhythmic pattern?
2. Is the pattern regular or irregular? If irregular, can you detect any reasons for the irregularity?
3. If you cannot detect metrical rhythm in the work, how would you characterize the rhythm?
4. What is the effect of the rhythmic pattern? How does it emphasize the theme and content of the work?

The following draft for a paper on rhythm in poetry shows the work of a student who first scans a poem and then offers preliminary responses to the questions.

Student First Draft for a Paper on Rhythm in Poetry

Loveliest of Trees, the Cherry Now

Loveliest | of trees, || the cherry now | 1

Is hung | with bloom | along | the bough, | 2

And stands | about | the woodland ride | 3

Wearing | white | for Eastertide. | 4

Now, || of my threescore years | and ten, | 5

Twenty | will not | come | again, | 6

And take | from seventy springs | a score, | 7

It only leaves | me fifty more. | 8

And since | to look | at things | in bloom | 9

Fifty | springs | are little room, | 10

$$\underset{\text{About}}{\cup}\ \underset{\text{the}}{/}\ \Big|\ \underset{\text{wood}}{\cup}\ \underset{\text{lands}}{/}\ \Big|\ \underset{\text{I}}{\cup}\ \underset{\text{will}}{/}\ \Big|\ \underset{\text{go}}{\cup}\ \Big/\ \Big|$$

About| the wood lands| I |will go| //

$$\underset{\text{To}}{\cup}\ \underset{\text{see}}{/}\ \Big|\ \underset{\text{the}}{\cup}\ \underset{\text{cher}}{/}\ \Big|\ \underset{\text{ry}}{\cup}\ \underset{\text{hung}}{/}\ \Big|\ \underset{\text{with}}{\cup}\ \underset{\text{snow.}}{/}$$

To see| the cher ry hung|with snow.   /2

A. E. Housman

The dominant rhythmic pattern for this simple little poem is iambic tetrameter. However, the rhythm is varied in five different places at the beginning of lines. The poem begins, not with an iamb, but with a dactyl, "Loveliest" which serves to emphasize the beauty of the tree and makes a definite and rapid beginning, getting the reader quickly into the poem. Lines 2 and 3 are regular lines but the fourth line begins with a trochee, "Wearing." This irregularity recalls the irregularity in line 1, and indeed the two words are linked by meaning also. The cherry tree is lovely because it is wearing white.

The second stanza begins with the definite dactylic opening "Now of my" followed by the emphatic "threescore years" (5). I find the last phrase hard to mark. According to the dictionary "threescore" could be a spondee or an iamb, but since it is followed by "years" which certainly the poet meant to emphasize, I read it with the emphasis on "three," "years," and "ten," that is, with the anapest "of my three" followed by two iambs: "score years" and "and ten." In any case surely what the poet stresses is the Biblical prediction of the normal span of life being seventy years.

Line 6 begins with the trochee "Twenty" and serves to stress the poet's current age, which is just past twenty. This entire line is trochaic rather than iambic until the last word "again." The rest of this stanza is regular iambic tetrameter.

Again in the third stanza, the word which breaks the pattern is another "age" word, the word "Fifty" (10). Linked

with the two words from the second stanza, "Now" and "Twenty"
(6), we almost find an extract for the poem itself: Now I'm
twenty (or just past twenty), but I only have fifty years left,
so I had better concentrate on what is important in life which
is appreciating the beauties of nature.

I find only two caesuras emphasized by punctuation—in
line 1 separating the appositives "Loveliest of trees" and "the
cherry" and in line 5 separating and emphasizing the "Now."

Work Cited

Housman, A. E. "Loveliest of Trees, the Cherry Now."
Literature: The Power of Language. Thomas Mc Laughlin.
San Diego: Harcourt, 1988. 200.

Comment   The previous questions have provided this student with ideas for
a first draft of a prosodic analysis of the Housman poem. The fourth paragraph,
which answers the fourth question, contains a statement which could become
the thesis for a revised draft.

ALLITERATION, ASSONANCE, AND CONSONANCE

Besides rhythmic patterns, you may also find repetition of sounds,
a pleasing effect linking words in close proximity to help unify and
convey meaning, in both poetry and prose. *Alliteration* repeats initial
consonant sounds as in *"Founding Fathers,"* or *"thief"* and *"three."* In
consonance, the final consonant sounds are repeated: "boat, bat, bite"
or "spirit," "acute," "invent" as seen in the Milton prose passage
quoted earlier. In *assonance*, the vowels in stressed syllables are repeated, "moan, groan, phone" or "hasting days" and "late" as seen in
the Milton sonnet.

When sound effects are pleasant, the combination is called *euphonious*; when sound effects are unpleasant, the effect is called *dissonance*
or *cacophony*. A writer may deliberately create cacophony to indicate
the emotions or personality of a character or to describe a scene or
situation. For example, in the following lines, the narrator of Byron's
Don Juan rhymes "matter" and "water":

> I say — the future is a serious matter —
> And so — for God's sake — hock and soda water!

This unpleasant rhyme conveys the satirical mood of the narrator and the cynical tone of the poem.

RHYME

The repetition of identical stressed (and sometimes unstressed) vowel sounds is called *rhyme*. Rhyme is usually appealing; most of you can probably recall, without effort, favorite nursery rhymes or passages from children's books like Dr. Seuss' because of the powerful mnemonic effect of their rhymes:

> Little Miss Muffet
> Sat on a tuffet,
> Eating her curds and whey.
>
> Along came a spider
> And sat down beside her,
> And frightened Miss Muffet away.

Some of your favorite, much more sophisticated poetry may also depend on rhyme; note Wordsworth's "I Wandered Lonely as a Cloud":

I wandered lonely as a cloud	a
That floats on high o'er vales and hills,	b
When all at once I saw a crowd,	a
A host, of golden daffodils;	b
Beside the lake, beneath the trees,	c
Fluttering and dancing in the breeze.	c
Continuous as the stars that shine	d
And twinkle on the milky way,	e
They stretched in never-ending line	d
Along the margin of a bay:	e
Ten thousand saw I at a glance,	f
Tossing their heads in sprightly dance.	f
The waves beside them danced; but they	e
Outdid the sparkling waves in glee;	g
A poet could not but be gay,	e
In such a jocund company;	g
I gazed — and gazed — but little thought	h
What wealth the show to me had brought:	h
For oft, when on my couch I lie	i
In vacant or in pensive mood,	j
They flash upon that inward eye	i

Language

> Which is the bliss of solitude;   j
> And then my heart with pleasure fills,   b
> And dances with the daffodils.   b

The first few lines set up your expectation for a certain pattern of repetition, a rhyme scheme of *a b a b c c*, fulfilled by the remaining stanzas. (Identical rhyming sounds at the ends of lines are marked with the same lower-case alphabet letter beginning with *a* and using a new letter for each new rhyme.) But to be meaningful, rhyme, of course, must be more than simple repetition; it should stress the important words and thus the structure and meaning of the poem. As you can see, "crowd" not only rhymes with "cloud" but is also an antonym for "lonely" ("as a cloud") and reinforces the contrast of the isolated speaker cheered and comforted by the "crowd" of flowers. "Solitude" rhymes with "mood" and is also a synonym for "vacant . . . mood," reinforcing your perception of the speaker's situation. "Fills" as the first verb of the compound verb "fills, / And dances," rhymes with "daffodils," but even more importantly, it shows you that for Wordsworth the heart must first be overflowing, flooded with the remembered beauty, before it can "dance."

The rhymes you have examined so far are *end-rhymes*: they occur in the final position of the line of verse. Some poets enrich the texture of their poems by adding a word in the middle of the line to rhyme with the end word; this rhyming structure is *internal rhyme*. If found in only a few lines of a poem, internal rhyme gives additional emphasis to those lines. Note the internal rhyme pattern of this stanza from Coleridge's "The Rime of the Ancient Mariner" (emphasis added):

> And through the *drifts* the snowy *cliffs*
> Did send a dismal sheen:
> Nor shapes of *men* nor beasts we *ken* —
> The ice was all between.

So far the rhymes you've examined have also been *exact rhymes*. Rhymes which are not identical but only similar are *inexact* or *slant rhymes*; they not only lessen the sing-song effect of too many exact rhymes, but, by creating a slight dissonance, may contribute to a tone of uncertainty. Note the rhyme of the last lines of Dickinson's ". . . Lightly Stepped a Yellow Star":

> All of Evening softly lit
> As an Astral Hall —
> Father, I observed to Heaven,
> You are punctual.

The slant rhyme "Hall" and "punctual" conveys doubt; perhaps Dickinson does not think this punctuality deserves respect.

Rhymes of one syllable (lie, eye) are called *masculine*, rhymes of two syllables (ending, bending) are called *feminine*, and rhymes of three syllables (clerical, spherical) are called *triple rhymes*. Masculine rhyme tends to be final; feminine, fluid; and triple, humorous or satirical.

You should also note that modern poetry often does not rhyme because many modern poets prefer to echo the diction and patterns of ordinary speech. Rather than rhyme, repetition of words and images may unify verses as in this sixth stanza from Margaret Atwood's "Spelling":

> How do you learn to spell?
> Blood, sky & the sun,
> Your own name first,
> your first naming, your first name,
> your first word.

The poem opens with an image of the speaker's daughter playing with colorful plastic letters. The first line of this stanza recalls that opening; "Blood, sky & the sun" repeat the colors red, blue, and yellow mentioned in the first stanza and recall images from the fourth and fifth stanzas. The repetition of "your," "first," and "name" in the last three lines reinforces a theme of the poem: she who controls language is powerful.

STANZAS — PATTERNS OF SOUND AND SENSE

Poems are often divided into units of lines called *stanzas*; these divisions may be based on sound — rhythm or meter and rhyme — or thought and content or both. Let's examine some of the most common traditional English stanzas.

A *couplet* is a stanza of two rhyming lines. When it ends with a strong mark of punctuation and completes a thought, the couplet is a *closed couplet*. A couplet written in iambic pentameter is a *heroic couplet*:

> 'Tis hard to say, if greater want of skill
> Appear in writing or in judging ill;

> (Pope, *An Essay on Criticism*)

A *tercet* is a unit of three lines, sometimes rhymed and sometimes not:

> Whenas in silks my Julia goes,
> Then, then, methinks, how sweetly flows
> That liquefaction of her clothes.

(Herrick, "Upon Julia's Clothes")

A *quatrain* is a unit of four lines, usually rhymed *abab*, *abba* or *abcb*:

> Why should I blame her that she filled my days
> With misery, or that she would of late
> Have taught to ignorant men most violent ways,
> Or hurled the little streets upon the great,

(Yeats, "No Second Troy")

Other stanzaic patterns include the *quintain* (*quintet, cinquain*), a five-line stanza rhyming *ababa* or *ababb*; *rime royal*, a seven-line iambic pentameter stanza rhyming *ababbcc*; *ottava rima*, an eight-line stanza rhyming *abababcc*; and the *Spenserian stanza*, developed by Spenser for *The Faerie Queene*, a nine-line stanza rhyming *ababbcbcc* in which the first eight lines are pentameter and the last line is an *Alexandrine* (iambic hexameter).

Poets may choose to work in one of these traditional forms, some of them incredibly complex, both to exercise their craft and shape their thoughts, or they may choose to let their meaning determine their form. The irregular stanzas of free verse and blank verse, linked by thought rather than a regular number of lines per unit, are called *verse paragraphs*. The stanza from Plath's poem "The Bee Meeting" quoted earlier in this chapter is an example of a verse paragraph.

Writing about Sound Patterns

To generate ideas for writing about the sound patterns of a work, first read the work aloud. Then copy the selection with double or triple spacing. Devise a marking system to link words with similar sounds — boxes, circles, single, double, and triple underlining, or others. Then respond to questions such as the following:

1. Are important words in the work linked by alliteration, consonance, assonance? Why?
2. Do any changes in sound patterns reflect changes in mood or theme?
3. Is there a pattern in the rhyme of the poem?

4. If there is a pattern, is it ever broken? Can you decide why?
5. How do the sound patterns of the work contribute to the meaning?

As in the section on rhythm, your answer to the last question could become the thesis of your essay, supported by frequent illustrations from the work itself.

Closely examine this final draft of an essay on sound in poetry, using the same Housman poem as the earlier student draft on rhythm. The poem is reprinted with sample markings linking sound patterns.

Student Essay on Sound in Poetry

Carpe Diem Emphasized by Sound Patterns

Loveliest of Trees, the Cherry Now

Loveliest of trees, the cherry now   1 *a*

Is hung with bloom along the bough,   2 *a*

And stands about the woodland ride   3 *b*

Wearing white for Eastertide.   4 *b*

Now, of my threescore years and ten,   5 *c*

Twenty will not come again,   6 *c*

And take from seventy springs a score,   7 *d*

It only leaves me fifty more.   8 *d*

And since to look at things in bloom   9 *e*

Fifty springs are little room,   10 *e*

About the woodlands I will go   11 *f*

To see the cherry hung with snow.   12 *f*

Regular meter and rhyme and a repetition of similar vowel sounds link the three stanzas of this lovely poem. The poem is set up almost like an exercise in logic, and the regularity of the sound effects reinforces the certainty of the theme—one must enjoy today.

In the first stanza (lines 1—4), the scene is set, a scene of natural beauty starring the cherry tree, which is clad in garments of symbolic white for Easter. The rhyming words are "now," "bough," "ride," and "tide," three of which emphasize time and its rapid passage while the fourth refers to the object of contemplation, the cherry tree. Lines 2 and 3 are linked by the repetition of the ou sound with the internal rhyme in the third line, "about." Alliteration links "bloom," "bough," and "about" as well as "woodland," "wearing," and "white."

In the second stanza (lines 5—8), the second proposition is advanced. The speaker has already demonstrated the beauty of the tree; now he presents and supports his contention that time is fleeting. Again the rhyming words emphasize this message since they are "ten," "again," "score" and "more." The immediate repetition of the ou sound in "Now" serves to connect this stanza with the preceding one. Alliteration links "ten," "twenty" and "take" as well as "me," "my" and "more," all connections of sense as well as sound. The curt abruptness of the t sound in the numbers "twenty," "seventy," and "fifty" contrasts with the drawn out l sound of "only leaves," upon which the poet dwells to reinforce his meaning. The quick endings also stress the message that time is passing.

The repetition of the l alliteration in line 9, "looks," links the third stanza to the preceding one. In this stanza the speaker builds to his inevitable climax; having proven that the tree is lovely and that he has only fifty years left to live, it remains only to point out that fifty years are not a great deal of time; therefore, he's off to see the tree. The rhyming words are "bloom," "room," "go," and "snow," slow rhymes over which the voice lingers, just as the speaker wants to do when he gets to the woods. Also, the slower pace contrasts with the quicker sounds of the second stanza when the speaker emphasized the swift passage of time. Again a dominant assonance in lines 9 and 10 is repeated internally in line 11, "woodlands." The repetition of "s" links four key words: "since," "springs," "see," and "snow."

So, finally, the reader who takes the time to read this poem aloud will discover that the sound patterns repeat and reinforce the content of the poem.

Work Cited

Housman, A. E. "Loveliest of Trees, The Cherry Now."
Literature: The Power of Language. Thomas Mc Laughlin.
San Diego: Harcourt, 1988. 200.

Comment   This essay analyzes the sounds of language to indicate how the poet reinforces his meaning through skillful word choice.

CHAPTER REVIEW

Writers present their vision of reality through language. A careful study of the language of a work including such elements as diction, denotation, connotation, allusion, imagery, figures of speech, irony, rhythm, meter, and rhyme may help you understand how literature works. Reading a work aloud, marking it, and responding in a journal prepare you for writing about literature. Through a careful selection of language, writers communicate meaning and create style. Recognizing the elements of language and how they work can help you analyze literary works and your response to them.

CHAPTER 8

Theme

When reading a work of literature, you may weave the literary experience into your imagination, making it part of you as you connect the work to your world.

To achieve this assimilation you must discover purpose in the poetry, fiction, drama, or nonfiction prose. We usually think of purpose as the underlying ideas or *themes*. For example, after reading Sophocles' *Oedipus Rex*, you may discover the theme of pride. A classmate, however, may have identified the theme of fate. Another reader may state the theme in a sentence: "The relentless search for truth may lead to destruction."

Clearly, theme in literature is subject to interpretation — your interpretation. Your interpretation of theme will be, of course, a result of your life experiences, your thinking processes, your personality, and your imagination. You construct meaning as you read, so what you bring to the reading is just as important for establishing meaning as what the author intends. Since you are at the center of the interpretive experience, you may want to begin your quest for theme by asking, "What does this work say to me?"

Your interpretation of theme, of course, must be supported by the work itself. As you know, a complex work of literature may have more than one theme, and several themes may be simultaneously validated through the work.

READING FOR THEME

As you read a work, analyze *what* happens — the story, *why* it happens — the plot, and *what* the work means to you — the theme.

When reading for theme consider the parts present in a work such as setting, structure, symbol, language, tone, and character. These elements work together to reveal and enhance meaning. For example, if an author desires to show that we need our illusions about ourselves to survive, he might dramatize what happens to a character who loses her illusions.

In *A Streetcar Named Desire*, Tennessee Williams does not explicitly say, "People need their illusions to survive"; instead, we see the idea dramatized through Blanche's visit to her sister, Stella. As the characters interact during the visit, we see the setting, the dialogue, the symbols, the characters' personalities, and the tone functioning together to reveal this theme.

Look at how the different elements support and reveal theme. At one point in *A Streetcar Named Desire*, Blanche hangs a paper lantern over a light bulb. This simple action is clearly symbolic: Blanche cannot face the light, a traditional symbol for truth and knowledge.

This symbolic interpretation is reinforced near the end of the play. Blanche is arguing with Mitch, whom she has been dating when, having learned from Stanley about her sordid background, he questions why she meets him only in the dark. Angry at her deceptions, he rips the paper lantern from the light bulb. Blanche cries out:

> I don't want realism. I want magic. Yes, yes, magic! I try to give that to people. I misrepresent things to them. I don't tell the truth, I tell what ought to be the truth. And if that is sinful, then let me be damned for it! — Don't turn on the light!

This is only one of many possible examples of how various elements in this play create theme. In literature the elements are skillfully woven together into the web of meaning.

As you know, in many poems very little may actually "happen." Rather, the poet may have recorded a series of images, a descriptive landscape, or an emotion. In William Carlos Williams' poem "The Red Wheelbarrow," you are presented with a series of images: a red wheelbarrow and white chickens. But what do these images mean to you? Because Williams begins the poem "So much depends," you may ask, *what* depends? That "what" has been the subject of numerous thematic interpretations.

Because poetry relies heavily on language devices such as rhythm, rhyme, figurative language, and connotation, meaning may emerge from these intertwining elements. Additionally, verse lines, stanzas, and even punctuation work together to develop theme. In Walt Whitman's "When I Heard the Learn'd Astronomer," for example, the sentence structure, the use of free verse, the length of lines, the connotations, and the musical quality of Whitman's language all work together to create theme. As one student has discovered, "The poem comments on the inadequacies of science to explain the universe. Only a personal and mystical relationship with the heavens can offer satisfactory answers."

To interpret the theme in a work of literature, you might begin by asking some questions:

1. What does this work say to me?
2. How do the parts work together to convey meaning?
3. What is the author's purpose or intent?
4. What vision does the work convey about life?
5. What ideas are being dramatized?
6. Does the author use symbols to develop meaning?
7. What questions or problems does the literature raise?
8. Does any one character or narrator seem to state explicitly a theme?
9. Has my understanding of life been enhanced? How?
10. What truth or insight has been renewed for me?

The theme of a work is usually not a *moral*; that is, a lesson, a rule, or a warning for the conduct of life. These rules or morals often sound like platitudes or sermon topics. For example, "Don't go near fire," "Avoid jealous people," and "Love thy neighbor" are morals. Literature with expressed or implied morals has teaching as its purpose; it is didactic. Since not all literature is didactic, read not for morals, but for themes that help you understand life.

RESPONDING TO THEME

Freewriting is one starting point for discovering theme. The very act of writing about the theme of a work will make you think; initial responses can be refined later. During a freewriting, try to connect the literature to your life; freewriting can be a time of personal exploration. Note how one student discovers theme and something about

herself in Nathaniel Hawthorne's "Young Goodman Brown" by freewriting in her journal:

Journal entry #24: Meaning in "Young Goodman Brown"

    This is a wicked story! It haunts me! Sometimes I feel
like Young Goodman Brown. Why? I, too, have taken walks through
the forest at night. I have been attracted to the forbidden.
And I, too, have left my "Faith" behind to do things—often to
satisfy my curiosity about something—something evil. I think
Hawthorne makes a comment about evil in this tale. Evil is the
theme. But what does he say about evil? I think he says that
when we come to suspect those we trust of evil, then we doubt
those people—we can never really trust them again. Goodman
Brown gradually lost his faith in his ancestors, his church
leaders, members of his village, and eventually his wife. This
knowledge of evil destroyed his life—"No hopeful verse was
carved on his tombstone." If you ask me—better not to have
such knowledge than to live with such terrible doubt. Once
doubt infects your trust of others, you live with suspicion.
Forbidden journeys exact their tolls. We pay dearly for our
curiosity.

Theme

Comment   Note how she begins by weaving the story into her own experience. She is interested in how the story illuminates her life; she feels an
identification with Brown's journey into the forest. After examining the story's
possible meaning in terms of her own experience, she attempts to make a
generalization about the meaning of the story. Ideas developed in this freewriting could later be used as a basis for other types of writing.

    Here is another student's freewriting on Whitman's poem "When
I Heard the Learn'd Astronomer":

    As a science major, I can appreciate the meaning I found
in Whitman's poem. The poem is about knowing the universe. The
speaker identifies two ways to examine the heavens—through

science or through mystical meditation. Of the two ways, the
speaker prefers the latter. The learn'd astronomer, with his
"proofs, books, and figures," bores the speaker. Whitman makes
me feel the boredom when he begins four lines with the word
"When." All the maps, charts, figures, diagrams, proofs,
columns are an endless and boring list of scientific ways of
knowing the universe. When the speaker leaves the classroom
and wanders outside, the sentences are shorter and the
language more poetic. The poem comments on the inadequacies of
science to explain the universe. Only a mystical and personal
relationship with the heavens can offer satisfying answers.

Comment   This journal entry explores how sentence structure and diction
work together to convey a meaning. This entry is a good starting point for an
essay. With some more examples and commentary on line length, the student
could write a formal thematic analysis.

ANALYZING THEME

After exploring your initial reactions to the theme of a work, you
are ready for further, more in-depth analysis depending on a more
detailed study. This study could involve stating a possible theme, proving your idea is based on a consistent interpretation of the facts of the
work, and writing about theme.

Stating Theme

After your first reading of a work, you will probably have a general
idea about meaning. As you examine the evidence during a second,
more intensive reading, you may or may not be able to verify your idea.
Begin your analysis of theme by writing your view of the theme
subject. You might want to do a listing activity if you think the work
embodies several themes. Note this listing of possible theme subjects
in "Young Goodman Brown":

1. guilt
2. loss of innocence

3. evil
4. forbidden knowledge
5. witchcraft
6. suspicion and doubt

Next, expand your theme subject by making a statement about it. For example, the theme subjects "evil" and "suspicion and doubt" could be developed: "Knowledge of evil can make us suspicious of those we once trusted."

Phrase a theme statement so that it applies to the world of the work and also to your world — the real world. A theme statement such as "In Bobbie Ann Mason's short story 'Shiloh,' Leroy's attempts to change his lifestyle to adapt to Norma Jean's settled ways are unsuccessful" is too narrow. This same theme statement could easily be made universal with some rewriting: "In her short story 'Shiloh,' Bobbie Ann Mason reveals that our attempts to change our lifestyles to accommodate other people are often unsuccessful."

Theme

Testing Theme

After writing your theme statement, you are ready to test it by examining the work again. As you obtain the proof to support your theme idea, you may have to refine or discard your idea. As you reread for theme, consider the following questions:

1. Does the title reveal anything about the theme?
2. Does an epigraph suggest possible meaning?
3. Does irony help reveal theme?
4. What major conflicts give rise to theme?
5. Does setting help reveal theme?
6. What imagery enhances meaning?
7. What actions reveal theme?
8. Does the tone contribute to the theme?

Keeping these questions in mind as you read for theme, mark the work: underline key passages and make notes to yourself in the margins.

Writing about Theme

Your essay on theme may take the form of an analytical persuasive paper. Your statement of the theme will be your assertion or thesis, which you will verify with specific examples from the work. Since multiple interpretations are possible, your analysis will have to be convincing. To convince your audience your interpretation is valid you need to find substantial support from the primary source, arrange the support logically, connect the support to the assertion, and synthesize your analysis with an effective conclusion. The student writing the following essay was asked to explain how setting, symbol, plot, and characterization help reveal theme.

Sample Essay on Theme

Theme in Bobbie Ann Mason's "Shiloh"

Bobbie Ann Mason's short story "Shiloh" is about life and its ironies, present and past. The basic irony underlying the story is that when people finally change or adapt to life, it is often too late. Mason carefully weaves her story, using different elements of life such as marriage, death, and personal growth to portray her theme. In addition to using the plot to help her communicate her message, she also employs characterization, setting, and symbols.

The plot begins when Leroy "after fifteen years on the road, is finally settling down with the woman he loves" (527). He realizes that he does not know anything about his wife and very little about his world: "He has begun to realize that in all the years he was on the road he never took time to examine anything" (526). Leroy now awakens and notices "how much the town has changed" (527), "how much time she [Norma Jean's mother] spends with Norma Jean" (528), and "he sees things about Norma Jean that he never realized before" (530). Leroy realizes they need to begin again and get to know each other, but Norma Jean does not seem interested. She adapts to Leroy's permanent return by changing herself. She begins to take body building and then enrolls in a class at the community college. Norma Jean grows in a direction away from her husband and mother.

The setting in the story is also used to convey the theme. Leroy now realizes that their rented house is "small and nondescript. It does not even feel like a home" (526). He has promised Norma Jean a home for years, but now there are subdivisions all over town which would not be compatible with the log cabin he wants to build. Ironically, by the time Leroy realizes his home is inadequate, he is unable to provide another.

Mason also reinforces her theme with the use of symbols. Leroy and Norma Jean's baby is symbolic. The circumstances surrounding the baby's death are similar to those circumstances surrounding their marriage. The baby died unnoticed on the back seat of a car during a double feature at the drive-in, the cause of its death unknown. Leroy, characteristically, can only vaguely remember the baby but can vividly recall the scenes from the movie.

Certainly the location of Shiloh is symbolic of life's ironies. Shiloh is the site of Norma Jean's beginnings, where her parents began their life together. It is also where Leroy finally begins to understand his life with Norma Jean. And here Norma Jean struggles to begin her new life by telling Leroy, "I want to leave you" (535).

Thus, in "Shiloh" Bobbie Ann Mason reveals through characterization, setting, and symbol that our attempts to change our lifestyles to accommodate other people are often unsuccessful.

Work Cited

Bobbie Ann Mason. "Shiloh." The Norton Introduction to Fiction. 3rd ed. Ed. Jerome Beaty. New York: Norton, 1985. 525–36.

Comment   This student discovers change as a theme subject in the story and then comments on this subject by writing a statement of theme: "When people finally change or adapt to life, it is often too late." She supports the theme statement with an analysis of Mason's use of marriage, death, and personal growth and also shows how character, setting, and symbol all contribute to the theme. To persuade readers that her discoveries about theme are valid, the student offers substantial support from the primary source including direct quotations and commentary.

CHAPTER REVIEW

The theme of a work of literature is its meaning — what it says to you. Your interpretation is based on evidence within the work and your experience. The search for theme should begin with an analysis of the elements of literature because theme emerges out of the interplay of elements such as symbol, language, character, setting, and form. In an analytical essay about theme, you should support your carefully worded theme statements with specifics from the text, and logically arrange your examples to persuade the reader of your discoveries.

CHAPTER 9

Character, Setting, and Symbol

CHARACTER

Most of us read fiction for the stories it tells or the people it creates, its *characters*. Responding to characters and to their creation (characterization) expands your knowledge of human behavior, helping you understand the people you encounter daily. Even when characters are fantastic or mythical beings, animals, plants, or even inanimate objects, they generally display human characteristics and abilities. Think for a moment of the heroic and cowardly rabbits in Richard Adams' *Watership Down*. They clearly represent recognizable human "types."

The English novelist E. M. Forster has provided us with valuable categories for characters, dividing them between *flat* or one-dimensional characters who can be "perfectly expressed by one sentence" and *round* or complex characters. Characters can also be designated as *dynamic* (growing, changing, and developing in the work) or *static* (non-changing). The terms flat, round, dynamic, and static are neither positive nor negative; they are merely descriptive. You may find flat characters both interesting and memorable. Because of limited scope, some short stories may introduce flat characters; on the other hand, because of their complexity, novels and dramas may also be populated with some flat characters. You may identify Bartleby in Melville's "Bartleby the Scrivener," the four shipwrecked men in Crane's "The Open Boat," and Paul's mother in Lawrence's "The Rocking Horse Winner" all as flat, but far from uninteresting characters.

Of course, some flat characters are *stereotypes*, standardized representations which fulfill your expectations: for instance, an artist as impractical, a professor as absent-minded, or a factory worker as insensitive to art and beauty. Authors use stereotypes as a form of shorthand to reveal character quickly with minimal development. When a character called a "clown" walks on stage clad in rustic clothing, you can expect some comic relief; the playwright does not have to provide a biography or motives for this character. However, writers may also reverse or modify stereotypes to create round or dynamic characters; the professor can turn out to be a detective whose absent-mindedness is a pose.

You cannot conclusively describe round characters because they resemble the people you associate with daily; they are interesting, complex, and elusive. You cannot easily define Judith in Doris Lessing's "Our Friend Judith." You could argue equally plausibly that she is a stereotypical English spinster, as someone calls her at the beginning of the story, a cold-hearted mistress, or an admirable example of a modern woman.

If the central character of a work is static, then you may find the plot more important than the character, and the conflict in the work will likely be *external*, between two characters, for example, or between a character and a natural force. Montresor in Poe's "The Cask of Amontillado" remains unchanged as he narrates his story fifty years after he lured Fortunato to the wine vaults. On the other hand, you may find that if the main character is dynamic or changing, the plot may revolve around that change, and the conflict may be *internal* or within the character. As you will see in subsequent examples, La Folle in Chopin's "Beyond the Bayou" is forced to grow by a traumatic event, but the event is not nearly so important as the change in her; the climax of the story is not Chérie's gunshot wound but La Folle's crossing the bayou and her collapse.

You may also define characters by their roles in the work. The central character is called the *protagonist*. If this character displays admirable and favorable attributes, then he or she can be called a *hero* or *heroine*. If the central character merely behaves as most of us would in similar circumstances, in a less than desirable but by no means evil fashion, then you may call the character the *antihero*. A wholly evil central character may be referred to as the *villain*. The villain who also opposes the main character is labeled the *antagonist*. However, the antagonist may not be human; it may be non-human or even an aspect of the protagonist's personality.

Characters serving to define or emphasize the central character are called *foils*. (This metaphorical label comes from the thin layer of metal foil placed under a gem to improve its color or sparkle.) When Job's wife tells him to curse God and die, she is his foil, representing a typical human reaction to such horrible catastrophes. Since Job does not act as she suggests, she serves to emphasize his heroic stature.

A character may be revealed *directly* as you see when Mary Freeman in her "Old Woman Magoun" comments on Nelson Barry: ". . . he stood regarding the passing child with a strange, sad face — unutterably sad, because of his incapability of the truest sadness." And characters may be revealed *indirectly* through conversation, dress, physical appearance, thoughts, actions, or even setting; in the Freeman story mentioned above, you know the grandmother has loved the child because she carries the child's rag doll with her long after the child's death. Characters are also revealed by other characters who speak to and about each other and who act with, for, and against each other. However, be cautious when judging a character by what other characters do or say; you must determine how reliable the other characters are and what their motives may be. The townspeople say the grandmother is "a trifle touched" because she carries the doll, but you know better.

Similarly, what the author says about the characters can usually be accepted as true, but what the characters say about themselves and how they act must be carefully evaluated before you can judge them. Sometimes characters respond to a particular circumstance because of their emotional states. You may find a difference between what characters say and do or between what they say and think. You, like a detective or a psychiatrist, must infer motivation from speech and action, whether or not the invitation is as specific as that from the narrator of Poe's "The Tell-Tale Heart." He challenges: "True! — nervous — very, very dreadfully nervous I had been and am; but why *will* you say that I am mad?"

Writing about Character

Again, as suggested earlier, if you are allowed a choice when you write about a character, pick one who appeals to you, perhaps because you can picture that character precisely, or because you know someone exactly like that, or because the character embodies a fascinating quirk you would like to explore in greater depth. In the following sample student essay, the writer is initially puzzled by the unhappy ending of Melville's "Bartleby the Scrivener." She questions why, despite the good intentions of the lawyer-narrator, the story ends with Bartleby's death Although she could have analyzed the title character, Bartleby, she decides she "would prefer" to write about the lawyer.

After you choose a character, reread the work carefully with your notebook or journal at hand, responding to questions such as the following:

1. How does the character you have chosen function in the work? Protagonist? Antagonist? Foil? Villain? Other?
2. Is the character highly individualized or stereotyped? Flat or round?
3. Is the character static or dynamic? If the character changes, how? What causes the change?
4. How is the character revealed? Directly by the author or indirectly through action, speech, thoughts, dress, setting, name, physical appearance, or history?
5. How do other characters treat the character? What do they say and think about him or her?
6. Is the character adequately motivated? Is his or her behavior consistent or inconsistent?

Let's see how the student writing about the lawyer in "Bartleby" might respond to these questions.

```
Journal entry #26: The lawyer in "Bartleby"

1. Well, I'm already stuck on the first question. Is the lawyer
   the protagonist or is Bartleby? After all, the story is
   named after Bartleby. And yet, I feel that I know a lot more
   about the lawyer after I finished the story than I do about
   Bartleby. Maybe it doesn't matter. Neither man is a hero
   although the lawyer has lots of good qualities.

   [Later—we decided today in class that it really doesn't
   matter whether you call Bartleby or the lawyer the
   protagonist. The instructor said you could argue for either
```

one. It seems questions about literature don't just have a
right and a wrong answer.]

2. The lawyer is individualized all right. I'd recognize him,
even today. And he's round (probably even fat!).

3. The character changes. The encounter with Bartleby shakes
his faith in practical Christianity and also the encounter
forces him to recognize things about himself that he'd
rather not have faced.

4. Well, since the lawyer tells his own story, I had to read
between the lines a little. Sometimes when he's
congratulating himself on a decision or an action, I don't
think he's done anything to be too proud of. But he does
give us a little personal history in the beginning and the
books he quotes and mentions tell us more about him. But
mostly it's the way he treats his clerks. So I guess he is
revealed by his actions and his words.

5. What happens in this story happens in part because of the
lawyer's concern for how other people regard him. He wants
to be thought of as a sensible, reasonable, "safe" man by
his Wall Street peers. Certainly his clerks must think him
an easygoing, tolerant boss. The only character he has
trouble with is Bartleby. I don't know how much we can trust
Bartleby's reactions though because he's such an odd
character. Would anybody have been able to save Bartleby? Is
the lawyer a bad person because Bartleby dies in the end? Is
it really his fault?

6. As I read Question 6, it's really asking if the character
is believable or not. And yes, I believe in the lawyer. I

believe there could be a person like him who would act as he
does. Although his behavior is sometimes inconsistent, it
is adequately motivated. (Bartleby is the one I really
couldn't believe in—what planet did he come from anyway? Is
he just a foil so Melville can make the point that Christian
ethics and business don't mix?)

Then the student (and you for your assignment) can jot down or
list all the elements of the character's personality, noting the pages
where the traits are specifically illustrated:

"the easiest way of life is the best" (672)

unambitious—he regards Nippers as the victim of an "evil
    power"—ambition (674)

safe, prudent, methodical—

cares what other people, especially important people, think—
    says this at the beginning of the story (672) and at the
    end, this is what forces him to do something about B.
    despite his having decided that he is predestined to
    keep B.

tolerant of Turkey's and Nipper's odd working habits (673–6)

chooses path of least resistance when dealing with T. and N.—
    and later when dealing with B., at least at first—shows
    consistency. When he first decides to challenge B., he
    backs off. Waffles (678–80).

rationalizes both his behavior and other people's—"Poor
    fellow! thought I, he means no mischief; it is plain he
    intends no insolence; his aspect sufficiently evinces that
    his eccentricities are involuntary" (681).

says it is good for his soul to treat B. kindly—later adds that
    it is prudent and even selfish to act charitably—he does
    offer B. a job, a home, money, visits him in prison and
    provides his food.

at one point decides that he is predestined to have B. as a
   permanent guest (693).

denies B. three times—echo of Peter and Christ? (695–7).

This student then decides that, for her at least, the lawyer's chief traits are his tolerance, his tendency to rationalize his possibly irrational behavior, and his religious beliefs. Another student might prefer to write on the lawyer's sensitivity to other people's opinions or his tendency to choose the easiest way.

When you write on character, you may want to follow a similar pattern of responding informally to the questions, listing character traits, choosing those you regard as most important, arranging them in climactic order (that is, saving the most important trait for the last point of your paper), and grouping the traits around a central assertion. Select those events, conversations, and interactions with other characters supporting your assertion and develop at least a paragraph of support for each trait you discuss. Conclude with a statement about how the traits you have discussed are important to the development of the story as a whole.

Notice in the following student essay that she explains why the lawyer, whom she has characterized as tolerant, rational, and Christian, still is unsuccessful in saving Bartleby. She places the blame on the rigid structure of the Wall Street business community; another writer might have argued equally successfully that the blame for the failure should be placed on Bartleby himself. (This essay was written in a one-hour class period; she could refer to her text and her journal entries.)

Student Essay on Characterization

The Tolerant Lawyer in "Bartleby the Scrivener"

The narrator in "Bartleby the Scrivener" is a mid-nineteenth century New York lawyer who is basically a tolerant man, but the enigmatic Bartleby, who answers his advertisement for a scrivener, stretches his tolerance to the breaking point. Yet the lawyer uses rationalization and Christian spirit in combating the relentless pressure of society to let Bartleby go.

The narrator describes himself as tolerant but reserved
with his employees. His acceptance of the curious tempers
and working habits of Turkey and Nippers shows his enormous
tolerance. He is almost pushed too far when Turkey uses a
ginger cake as a seal, but a simple apology causes all to be
forgiven. At first, when Bartleby disobeys a command, the
lawyer forgives him because he shows no emotion: "[He] . . .
in a wonderful manner, touched and disconcerted me" (679).
The lawyer allows him to stay, even though he "prefers not to"
do some of the work for which he has been hired.

As time passes the lawyer must rationalize to avoid firing
Bartleby. He argues that Bartleby is a steady employee and also
that tolerating him will "purchase a delicious self-approval"
(681). But after a time, the original pity becomes fear. Then
the temporary loss of Bartleby's eyesight rekindles the
lawyer's pity. However, when Bartleby does not return to work
and refuses to be fired, the lawyer rationalizes anew; he
decides that it is his mission in life (Christian duty) to give
Bartleby office space. Eventually, however, peer pressure and
the lawyer's declining reputation cause him to move his
offices, thus removing himself from the problem but avoiding a
real conflict with Bartleby. When he is called back to talk to
Bartleby, he offers Bartleby his home, a very Christian act.
When Bartleby refuses, the lawyer feels he has done all that he
can (697). Both his Christian nature and his rationalizations
fail him in the end, and society scores another triumph.

The lawyer does lose his battle with society but not
without a struggle. Because of his own tolerance, ability to
rationalize, and Christian spirit, the lawyer fights society
by keeping Bartleby for a long time despite repeated
disobedience and eventual uselessness. However, in the end, the
lawyer, and Bartleby as well, lose because those virtues cannot

win on Wall Street. He tries to hide that fact from himself,
but eventually he must give into it.

Work Cited

Melville, Herman. "Bartleby the Scrivener." Literature: The
Power of Language. Ed. Thomas Mc Laughlin. San Diego:
Harcourt, 1988. 671–701.

Comment   Because of the assignment's time limit, this essay is too brief to
develop the character of the lawyer fully, but it is a reasonable beginning
completed in one class period. The one area the student addresses but does not
develop is the Christian spirit of the lawyer. In a fully developed essay, she may
want to show how the lawyer fulfills completely the spirit of the Beatitudes: he
ministers to Bartleby, the strangest of strangers, by offering him his home,
feeding and clothing him through providing a salary, and even visiting him in
prison.

SETTING

The *setting* of a literary work is the physical world of the work —
the place, the time, and the circumstances of the action. Setting,
whether realistic or fantastic, can have symbolic, psychological, and
sociological aspects. For example, Ibsen's settings are realistic but have
symbolic meaning. Over the course of the play, Hedda Gabler retreats
from the large drawing room to a smaller back room, symbolic of her
gradually narrowing choices. O'Neill often specifically describes his
settings as symbolic; for example, he says the two elm trees growing on
either side of the house where *Desire Under the Elms* is set have "a
sinister maternity in their aspect, a crushing, jealous absorption."
    Setting may provide clues to the subject and the conflict as it reveals
character, affects action, and helps communicate theme. In Bambara's
"My Man Bovanne," you see Miss Hazel's flamboyant yet warm and
maternal personality stand out in sharp contrast to the setting of the
Black Power political gathering where an old blind man, invited primarily for local color, is being ignored by the young activists. Miss
Hazel's befriending him in this setting displays integrity. In Lawrence's
"The Rocking Horse Winner," the setting of impoverished gentility
underlies the action, the frantic effort by the young son to win money

for his mother. In Chopin's "Beyond the Bayou," La Folle's transition from fearful isolation to tranquil integration into the life of the plantation is marked by a change in her setting from the narrow sterility of her tiny cabin to the spacious world of Bellissime, the plantation beyond the bayou.

Besides place, you will want to analyze how setting establishes the time of the work, not just its historical period, but also the way time passes in the work. A novel may cover several centuries or several hours. Time may pass quickly for one character and slowly for another. In Bierce's "An Occurrence at Owl Creek Bridge," a clue to the surprise ending is given early in the story when time slows for Peyton Farquar so dramatically that he waits seemingly minutes between each tick of his watch.

As you would expect, setting functions in all genres — poetry, fiction, drama, and even nonfiction. In poetry you may find the setting is not so much described as implied. Browning indirectly tells us a great deal about the Renaissance in "The Bishop Orders His Tomb at Saint Praxed's Church" and about the restricted life and conflicts within a monastery in "Soliloquy of the Spanish Cloister."

On the other hand, in fiction the setting is usually described; you realize that each detail is relevant, each contributes to the work, and that changes in setting or a character's perception of setting are important for understanding plot, theme and character. For example, the garden in Hawthorne's "Rappaccini's Daughter" is a key element in the story. It is a man-made and evil Eden where a fountain, now broken, once gushed pure water. The fountain symbolically suggests Beatrice, an outwardly flawed but inwardly pure woman.

Of course, in drama setting is imparted by the actual sets (or their descriptions if you are reading), as well as the characters' costumes, behavior, and speech. The drawing room environment of Wilde's *The Importance of Being Earnest* is obvious from the first view of the setting (described as a "luxuriously and artistically furnished" morning room in a fashionable location in London where a manservant sets out tea). Lillian Hellman in *The Little Foxes* says almost as much about her characters in this two-line description of their setting as she does in dialogue: "The room is good-looking, the furniture expensive; but it reflects no particular taste. Everything is of the best and that is all." Similarly, Clare Booth Luce satirizes the typical "drawing room" world to establish immediately the difference between her heroine and the rest of *The Women*: "Today, Park Avenue living rooms are decorated with a significant indifference to the fact that ours is still a bisexual society. . . . They reflect the good taste of their mistresses in everything but a consideration of the master's pardonable right to fit into his own home decor. Mary Haines' living room is not like that."

Historical and geographical setting are also significant in nonfiction prose. To appreciate the full impact of Martin Luther King's "Letter from Birmingham Jail — April 16, 1963," you must have knowledge of its setting — the Civil Rights movement of the 1960's, Southern institutions, and the public statement from the Birmingham clergymen which precipitated the letter. Similarly, Virginia Woolf's *Three Guineas* reflects the cultural and social setting of patriarchal Victorian England.

Writing about Setting

To write about setting in a particular work, respond to questions such as the following during and after your reading:

1. In what period in history is the work set?
2. Where does the work take place?
3. What period of time does the work cover?
4. How much time does the writer cover in a typical passage? Does it vary? If so, why?
5. Do all the characters perceive the passage of time similarly? If not, how and why do their perceptions vary?
6. What is the social setting for the work?
7. Is the setting symbolic? How?
8. To what extent does the setting play a role in the work? Is it related to the plot? Does it reveal and develop character? Does it reveal the meaning of the work?

As you did when writing about character, try to answer the questions above in your journal or notebook and then settle on those which seem most relevant to the work you have chosen. Begin with the last question and analyze whether the primary role of the setting is to provide background, precipitate plot, develop character, or convey theme. Develop a thesis explaining this primary effect and then summarize the significant details of the setting. Work through the story, showing how the setting fulfills its role. Your essay will be most effective if you arrange the events in dramatic order from the least to the most significant. However, note from the following student essays that excellent papers do not always follow the same pattern, even when written on the same topic (in this case, the use of setting to reflect psychological changes in a protagonist). A good idea creates its own form.

[Note: Both of the following examples are rough drafts, written in a one-hour class period, using the text of the story only, no pre-written notes.]

Two Student Essays on Setting

Setting in "Beyond the Bayou"

If a Hollywood producer and director were to collaborate on a movie version of Kate Chopin's "Beyond the Bayou," they could approach the production of the setting and transformation of the protagonist using a treatment similar to that in The Wizard of Oz—beginning the story in black and white and ending it in color.

La Folle, a black "mammy" or nurse on the plantation Bellissime, lives in voluntary but complete isolation, having drawn an imaginary circular boundary line around the bayou and into the woods after a traumatic episode in her childhood. Across this boundary she never ventures. Her life within this compound is portrayed in black and white, without color or radiance.

The only color and sunshine to enter her world is Chéri, the son of the plantation owner. When Chéri suffers a gunshot wound, La Folle is confronted head-on by her fear of crossing the bayou. Her love for the boy is strong enough to overcome her irrational fear of leaving her familiar surroundings, and, crossing her physical and psychological boundary, she carries him to the safety of his home.

Afterwards she undergoes a transformation. She awakens the following morning with renewed strength and an altered attitude toward life. She puts on a new dress and walks to the plantation. She no longer hesitates at the edge of the bayou "as she had always done before, but crossed with a long, steady stride as if she had done this all her life" (261). And this is the point in the story where the Hollywood director switches to full technicolor, focusing on the field of cotton, "the thousand blue violets that peeped out from green, luxuriant beds . . . , big waxen bells of the magnolias . . . , the jessamine clumps around her" (261), and innumerable roses. This beauty symbolizes the transformation and renewal of La Folle's life. She realizes this change while sitting on the plantation house veranda watching "for the first time the sun rise upon the new, the beautiful world beyond the bayou" (261).

Work Cited

Chopin, Kate. "Beyond the Bayou." The Norton Introduction to
    Fiction. 3rd ed. Ed. Jerome Beaty. New York: Norton, 1985.
    257–261.

Comment   The clever introduction to this essay implies a thesis; that is, that the color symbolism of the story expresses the meaning of the story — boundaries can prevent the full experience of living. The second paragraph would be stronger with a supporting quotation. The third paragraph makes the important point that psychological boundaries can become physical boundaries as they do in this story. The fourth and final paragraph returns to the opening point, exemplified this time by a quotation.

A Step Forward in Chopin's "Beyond the Bayou"

La Folle in "Beyond the Bayou" by Kate Chopin lives in a world set apart from the other residents of the plantation, Bellissime. She has not left her small patch of land since a traumatic episode in her childhood. Yet because of another accident to a child whom she loves, she must break her habit and cross over to the rest of the world.

In the exposition we find that La Folle ventures no further from her cabin than the space of a "big abandoned

field" (257). There is a bayou beyond the field, and the rest
of the plantation begins on its opposite bank. She refuses to
cross the bayou. She also refuses to venture into the woods
which line its banks.

La Folle lives a solitary life, for the other Negro
workers' quarters are beyond the bayou. She tends her "patch of
cotton and corn and tobacco" (257), awaiting the arrival of the
Maitre's children, especially his son, Chéri. She is not a
slave, for it is a few years after the Civil War, but she is the
stereotypical black "mammy" in her relationship with Chéri.

Suddenly, her routine, habitual life is shattered. Chéri
is injured while hunting in the woods, and she must take him
beyond the bayou for help. She wildly plunges through the
shallow water and the trees as "the pathway spread clear and
smooth enough before her" (260), signifying her transition in
life. The shock of the incident induces in her a semi—catatonic
sleep after Chéri is safe, but she revives the next morning in
sound spirits. She crosses the field and goes through the
"scrub cotton—wood trees." Beyond the opposite bank, she finds
a field of "white, bursting cotton." The dew upon it "gleam[s]
. . . like frosted silver." The perfumes of the blue violets
and roses innundate her. The palms "spread in broad and
graceful curves." She now sees the river "bending like a silver
bow" (261).

La Folle realizes she has nothing to fear beyond the bayou
now. It is probable that she will prefer the beautiful side in
the years to come. Her sure stride and contented demeanor
signal her readiness to participate in "the beautiful world
beyond the bayou" (261).

Work Cited

Chopin, Kate. "Beyond the Bayou." <u>The</u> <u>Norton</u> <u>Introduction</u> <u>to</u>
    <u>Fiction</u>. 3rd ed. Ed. Jerome Beaty. New York: Norton, 1985.
    257—261.

Comment   This essay is more traditional in structure and treatment than the first essay although, like the first essay, the thesis is implied rather than directly stated. Both essays come closest to a direct thesis statement in their last, rather than first, paragraphs, an arrangement typical of first draft writing when you don't know what you're going to say until you've said it. This essay works rather straightforwardly through the story, an obvious time-saver in an in-class writing situation. Although a relevant point, the comment made in the third paragraph about La Folle as a mammy seems irrelevant because it is not smoothly integrated into the paragraph nor is enough information given. The fourth paragraph notes a symbolic aspect of the setting, the smooth pathway. The fifth paragraph contains an acceptable inference about La Folle's future.

SYMBOL

A *symbol* is a person, place, situation, action, color, or object representing more than its physical reality or its literal meaning. Because you can see the symbol as both literally itself and something else, as a flag is both a banner with a colorful design and a representation of a specific country, it concisely creates and enriches the meaning of the work. A symbol is concrete, but the meaning derived from it is abstract. You can look for a clue to its importance in its recurrence in the work and its location at key points in the story, perhaps combined with an element of strangeness or oddity. (Why is a small town, perhaps just like the one where you grew up, having a lottery to pick a sacrificial victim? Why does "A Very Old Man with Enormous Wings" drop into the courtyard of a peasant family?)

For an example of how symbols and symbolism operate in a literary work, let's examine the story of Joseph in the Old Testament book of Genesis, Chapters 37–47. Even on a first reading you can see that Joseph is placed in jeopardy many times in this story and that each episode begins with a dramatic change in his clothing. First you notice Joseph's brothers strip him of his multi-colored robe when they throw him into the pit before selling him into slavery. This exceptionally decorated garment represents or symbolizes Joseph's position as the indulged favorite son of a favorite wife. His brothers, who rather resent this adolescent dreamer and tattle-tale, dip the garment into animal blood and take it to their father Jacob, who assumes Joseph has been killed by wild animals.

You see later, after Joseph the slave has risen to a position of prominence in the household of the Egyptian Potiphar, that he rejects the advances of his master's wife. When she grabs his robe, he is forced

Symbol

to leave it behind as he flees. She then uses the robe to convince her husband that Joseph has attacked her, so Joseph is imprisoned. Even here you may see a pattern emerging. Clothing has been used in the story so far to signal or symbolize changes in Joseph's fortune; he is well-dressed when he is successful and loved, naked when he is in the pit or prison. To check this interpretation of the clothing symbol, try it against another mention of clothing in the text. And you find that later in the story, when Joseph leaves the prison to interpret Pharoah's dream, he washes, shaves, and *changes his clothes* to enter the ruler's presence. After he becomes Pharoah's overseer, he is dressed in "fine linen."

Then you need to ask whether there are other symbolic acts or objects in this story. Journeys also seem to be a recurring motif in the plot. Joseph journeys to Egypt as part of a slave caravan, the brothers journey to Egypt twice to get grain, and at the conclusion, Jacob and all of his sons and their families journey to Egypt to live with Joseph. This may make you wonder whether the journeys are symbolic. They certainly might be; one is never quite the same after a journey as before. Joseph has to suffer as a slave to become a savior. His brothers have to humble themselves before this unrecognized Egyptian overseer, a humility symbolized by their bowing low before him and reinforced by their obedience when he commands them to bring back their younger brother. They are forced to journey home and back again; they feel powerless and fearful when they discover, first, the grain money still in their sacks and, later, Joseph's drinking cup. Joseph is reassured of their change in heart when, instead of allowing Benjamin to return alone to bear Joseph's presumed wrath and become his slave, they journey back as a group and offer themselves instead. You may see their final journey back to Egypt with Jacob and all their flocks and servants and wives and children as a triumphal journey, symbolic of their changed attitudes and signaling their new fortune.

Symbols such as clothing to denote status and a journey to note change are so familiar they are called *archetypes*, that is, patterns, objects, or characters to which most readers respond in approximately similar fashion. (Archetypes are discussed in more detail in Chapter 11.) Some symbols, however, are *private* or particular to the work in which they are found; for example, look again at the elm trees in O'Neill's play *Desire Under the Elms*. Although trees traditionally symbolize shade, rest, refreshment, and stability, these two trees, as we have seen, are described as symbolizing a brooding, possessive, destructive maternalism foreshadowing the infanticide which is the climax of the drama. So even traditional symbols depend on the context of the work for their meaning. Symbols are also elusive; you will find it difficult to pin them down to one specific meaning. Therefore, the most satisfactory papers on symbolism are usually those suggesting a multiplicity of meanings.

Writing about Symbols and Symbolism

To locate possible symbols in a work of literature, read the work looking for those details of setting, characterization, and action emphasized in the work. Pay particular attention to anything odd about the emphasis on a particular object or its location. Examine characters' names for symbolic possibilities. Notice how the writer uses light and dark and whether any colors are mentioned repeatedly. All these might be clues to symbolic meaning.

After you have identified possible symbols in your work, select the element that seems most symbolic or that most interests you and record in your journal answers to questions such as the following:

1. What might these symbols mean?
2. Is there a pattern to the symbols in the story?
3. How does the pattern of symbolism (or a particular symbol) serve the meaning of the work?

To create some ideas for an essay, you might try a freewriting exercise. Let's follow a student who has chosen Hawthorne's "Young Goodman Brown" for an essay on symbolism. She doesn't have any problem finding symbols in this work as she reads through the questions, so she freewrites on several of them to come up with her essay topic.

Student Essay Process on Symbols and Symbolism

```
          Freewriting on "Young Goodman Brown"

     Let's look at the setting first. There are two settings
for the story, the Puritan village (unnamed) and the forest.
Of the two, the forest seems most symbolic, both in the
traditional way of mystery, darkness, hidden depths, nature,
etc., and in Hawthorne's own treatment of it as the earthly
```

Symbol

embodiment of hell: the first thing Goodman Brown says about it
is, "There may be a devilish Indian behind every tree," and
then he thinks that maybe "the devil himself should be at my
very elbow" (347). It's not odd that there is a forest in the
New England wilderness, but it is odd that Goodman Brown should
be going through it, voluntarily, at night, on an unnamed
errand, when his bride doesn't want him to go. It is also some
special night (maybe Halloween?); Faith says, "Pray, tarry with
me this night, dear husband, of all nights in the year!" (347).

Then, the characters. Well, first, their names are almost
too obvious even if it was a Puritan custom to call each other
"Goodman" and "Goodwife." Because the story reveals that they
are anything but good (or at least Brown ends up not thinking
so). Brown can certainly be any man, just like we say "John
Smith" today. And it's significant that he's young. Faith—
faith in everything and nothing, faith which Brown loses after
his night in the forest. One night and he no longer has faith
in his wife or in the village elders he used to respect or in
his religion.

Hawthorne describes darkness very well. The scene of the
Black Mass is particularly well-described but words like
gloom, lurid, black, dusk, etc. are all through the story. The
only light touch is the pink of Faith's ribbon and that's odd.
I didn't think Puritans wore any colors at all except black and
maybe a little white.

The traveler's staff is definitely a symbol that's
mentioned a lot, as is Faith's ribbon.

The primary action of the story is a journey in the night,
a journey of the soul, an initiation into evil for Brown. I
guess it's a journey that is also a quest although we're never
really certain what Brown is after—knowledge? And we don't
really know if he finds what he thinks he does or if it's just
an hallucination.

Comment After freewriting, the student settles on the character Faith, who is both a real flesh-and-blood woman, the wife of Goodman Brown, and the physical embodiment of abstract faith. However, rather than seeing this faith as religious belief only, probably the first meaning which occurs to most readers, she explores the idea of Faith as also symbolic of Brown's faith in his marriage and his fellow man as well. Thus, she finds several levels of meaning in the action of Brown's abandoning Faith for his dreadful journey, meanings which reflect and enhance the ambiguity of the story more completely than a one-dimensional treatment of religious belief could.

Final Essay

Goodman Brown's Faith

Symbolism is well represented in Nathaniel Hawthorne's story "Young Goodman Brown." Hawthorne chooses the name for Goodman Brown's wife carefully. Faith, as he names her, is symbolic of the theme of this story as Brown is confronted with doubts concerning his faith in his marriage, in his fellow man, and in his own religious beliefs.

Faith's name symbolizes the importance of Brown's faith in his marital relationship. In the beginning of the story, Brown is reluctant to leave the wife he refers to as a "blessed angel on earth." He again stresses her importance to him when he says, "My love and my Faith" (347). As a young married man, Goodman Brown trusts his marriage and his wife. Yet overnight, his trust is destroyed. After his journey into the forest Brown passes by his wife without speaking to her and thereafter shrinks "from the bosom of Faith" (357). By doubting his wife's faith, Brown loses his own faith in their marriage.

Before the night in the forest, Goodman Brown also has faith in his fellow man, especially his religious leaders whom he holds in great respect. His minister, the Deacon Gookin, and Goody Cloyse all represent goodness to him, just as his wife does, and he initially hesitates over consorting with the devil for fear of losing his good standing with them. So, he is stunned when he hears Goody Cloyse talking with the devil, and, upon realizing his minister and Deacon Gookin are also in the forest, he feels a "heavy sickness of his heart" (352). Then, he recognizes a "score of the church-members of Salem village, famous for their especial sanctity" (354) at the unholy congregational meeting. When he returns to the village, he shrinks from the minister and snatches away from Goody Cloyse a little girl whom she is catechizing. Brown doubts the goodness of his fellow man the rest of his life and "his dying hour was gloom" (357).

Most importantly, Faith is symbolic of Brown's personal religious faith. While the narrator never states Goodman Brown's reason for going into the forest, Brown does say to his fellow-traveler, "having kept covenant by meeting thee here, it is my purpose now to return whence I came" (348). Clearly it is Brown's appointed time for his faith to be tested. He believes he will withstand the test; however, as the journey progresses Brown begins to doubt the faith of his peers and the faith of his wife and his own faith begins to slip. When he loses faith in his peers, Brown questions rather than states: "Is that any reason why I should quit my dear Faith . . . ?" (351). Then when Brown is alone in the forest and finds the pink ribbon, he doubts his wife and cries out, "My Faith is gone! There is no good on earth . . . " (352). Brown's own personal faith, which seemed so strong in the beginning, cannot stand alone. He needs to believe in the goodness of his wife and of his fellow man. Brown does not go to his grave with his faith; rather, he is "followed by Faith" (357).

Work Cited

Hawthorne, Nathaniel. "Young Goodman Brown." Literature: The
    Power of Language. Ed. Thomas Mc Laughlin. San Diego:
    Harcourt, 1988. 346–357.

Comment   The introduction to this essay is stylistically weak, but the thesis is clearly stated. The essay is tightly structured and well supported. Although most of the points it makes are obvious, it represents a careful attempt to neither overlook nor emphasize the symbolism of the story. The last paragraph, which treats the most important symbolic aspect, is also the strongest and most well-developed paragraph. The last sentence is a particularly apt combination of the student's own conclusion and a concluding phrase quoted from the story.

CHAPTER REVIEW

Characters, the creations who populate literary works; setting, the world of the work, when and where it takes place; and symbols, objects or persons or events in the work meaning more than their physical reality, are three important elements to examine when reading to write. Writing about these elements is easiest when you choose a subject which interests you and when you try not to be dogmatic about your interpretation. The most intriguing characters, symbols, and settings are often the most elusive, resisting a single correct analysis.

Symbol

CHAPTER 10

Point of View
and Tone

POINT OF VIEW

Point of View in Fiction

Many authors adopt a *persona* or a *mask* — they select a *voice* through which they present the work. *Point of view* is the particular voice, angle of vision, or perspective from which the work is told. The point of view affects how the author reports information; narrates action; describes characters, settings, objects and emotions; or even interprets or judges these elements.

In fiction, there are several possible points of view. The *first-person* point of view is presented by a character who narrates the story using "I." This character may be either a major or minor character. For example, in Edgar Allan Poe's "The Cask of Amontillado" Montresor, the main character, is established as the narrator in the first sentence as he confesses to us: "The thousand injuries of Fortunato I had borne as best I could; but when he ventured upon insult, I vowed revenge."

Minor characters may also narrate the action. Although minor characters often appear as spectators or witnesses to the events, they should not be viewed as mere reporters. They are often affected by what they experience; they may even change as a result of what they observe. A seemingly minor character, Nick Carroway, narrates F. Scott Fitzgerald's novel *The Great Gatsby*. As a witness to the action, Nick tells us in the exposition, "I was privy to the secret griefs of wild, unknown men." He then reports the story of Jay Gatsby, the main character. In this novel, Nick portrays himself as a sensible Midwesterner objectively reporting on the extravagant and wasteful lifestyles of Easterners. He thinks only someone like himself could describe the romantic and decadent Gatsby. Although Nick appears to function as a spectator, he is so affected by the extravagance and waste that he decides to leave New York and return to a less complex life in the Midwest.

The narrator in William Faulkner's "A Rose for Emily" is a *first-person collective narrator*, the community who has observed Miss Emily's life. When Miss Emily's father dies, the collective narrator comments on Miss Emily's reluctance to bury her father's body, "We did not say she was crazy then. We believed she had to do that. We remembered all the young men her father had driven away, and we knew that with nothing left, she would cling to that which had robbed her, as people will." By using a collective narrator, Faulkner shows us how the entire village respected her.

You may discover that some first-person narrators are unreliable. *Unreliable narrators* can be mentally deranged, too young to understand what is really happening, or too involved in the action to report the events objectively. Some narrators may even consciously attempt to deceive the reader. Unreliable narrators challenge the reader to make inferences and "read between the lines" to know what is really happening. In Charlotte Perkins Gilman's "The Yellow Wallpaper," the main character, a young woman writing in her journal, tells us she is "sick." Her physician-husband has diagnosed her as having a "temporary depression — a slight hysterical tendency," and he has confined her to her upstairs bedroom. As part of her treatment, she is forbidden to engage in social conversation or to express her negative thoughts. As she slowly goes insane, and hence becomes unreliable as an objective reporter of events, she is convinced a woman is trapped behind the wallpaper on the bedroom walls. Eventually, the narrator rips off the wallpaper to free the trapped woman.

First-person narrators tell their tales from a time perspective as well. Perhaps the narrator is reporting events as they happen or perhaps, as we have seen in Poe's "The Cask of Amontillado," recounting events many years after they have happened.

An author may decide that *third-person* point of view is best suited for telling a story. If the third-person point of view is *omniscient*, the narrator has unlimited knowledge of the events and characters. This narrator may even report what the characters are feeling and thinking. This narrator knows the past and present and perhaps the future. Omniscient narrators may also interrupt the narration to interpret, evaluate, or judge the characters and their actions. The omniscient narrator in Sarah Orne Jewett's "A White Heron" comments on Sylvia's emotions when the hunter decides to leave after she refuses to tell him where he can find the white heron:

> Dear loyalty, that suffered a sharp pang as the guest went away disappointed later in the day, that could have served and followed him and loved him as a dog loves! . . . Were the birds better friends than their hunter might have been, — who can tell? Whatever treasures were lost to her, woodlands, and summertime, remember! Bring your gifts and graces and tell your secrets to this lonely country child.

The *limited omniscient* narrator is usually limited to knowing one character. In Henry James' short story "The Beast in the Jungle," although the narrator tells us what John Marcher is thinking and doing, he reports only what May Bartram does, how she looks, and what she says, but not what she thinks. James himself calls this point of view the "center of consciousness." Unlike the omniscient point of view which lets readers examine the thoughts, feelings, and motives of all the characters, with limited omniscience our responses to all characters are formed through a single perspective.

The *objective* point of view is achieved through reporting factual detail, only that which can be perceived by the senses. Objective narrators never intrude to evaluate, interpret, or judge characters and their actions. In Shirley Jackson's "The Lottery," the narrator reports in a very matter-of-fact manner the events of what at first seems a village celebration. The emotionless narrator reports the events and provides background information. And even when the villagers prepare to stone the main character, Tessie Hutchinson, to death, the narrator remains uninvolved and detached. You, the shocked reader, are left to infer the horror and betrayal Tessie feels. Severely objective narration is called the *dramatic* point of view. The narrator functions much like a "fly on the wall" — a spectator to the events.

Point of View in Poetry

Poetry may also rely on point of view to convey experience and meaning. You might refer to the narrator as the "speaker" in the poem.

Many poets create first-person narrators for their speakers. Robert Browning, in "My Last Duchess," as you have seen has the events conveyed by a duke who has "given orders" concerning his wife. (In this dramatic monologue, you can only speculate what those orders might have been since his wife, the last duchess, is now dead.)

When reading poetry, you need to distinguish between the poet and the speaker. Of course, some poets are the speakers of their own poems; in Gerard Manley Hopkins' "God's Grandeur," you can hear the voice of the Jesuit priest speaking of God's love for mankind in spite of all man's abuses. More often than not, however, poets invent a voice. Emily Dickinson once wrote that the speaker in her poetry is a "supposed person." When reading Dickinson's lines, "Because I could not stop for Death / He kindly stopped for me," do not assume Dickinson herself is the one who could not stop for Death.

Point of View in Drama

Plays, too, can have point of view. As we have seen in Tennessee Williams' *The Glass Menagerie*, the events are told from the memory of Tom Wingfield. As the play opens, Tom enters the stage and reveals, "I am the narrator of the play, and also a character in it. The other characters are my mother, Amanda, my sister, Laura, and a gentleman caller who appears in the final scenes." Tom perceives the actions from the point of view of one who was desperately trapped by an overbearing mother and an all-too-sensitive sister. The play would be quite different had the events been told from the point of view of Amanda, Laura, or the gentleman caller because each of these characters has a different vision of the desperation experienced in the Wingfield household.

Writing about Point of View

If you are going to generate an essay on point of view, slowly reread the work to discover the type of narration. Here are some questions to help you determine and analyze the point of view:

1. Who tells the story, poem, or play?
2. If the point of view is first person, is the narrator a major or minor character?
3. Can you trust the narrator? Is he or she reliable?
4. If the point of view is omniscient, is it limited or unlimited?

5. Why might the author have chosen this angle of vision?
6. Does the narrator tell too much or not enough?
7. Is the narration consistent? If the point of view shifts, can you explain why?
8. What inferences have you made about characters, action, etc. from the narration?
9. How would the work be different if it were told from another point of view?

Creative Project on Point of View

One student decided to do a creative project on the point of view in Faulkner's "A Rose for Emily." To explore the topic, she wrote an objective newspaper account of Miss Emily's death. By doing so, she could see the role the sympathetic narrator played in Faulkner's story.

Mad Woman Slept With Corpse

Miss Emily Grierson, a long-time resident of our city, was found dead this week. But investigators found more than her body. In the upstairs bedroom was found the rotted corpse of a young man. One of her own gray hairs found beside the corpse proves that this deranged woman slept with the corpse.

Those who remember Miss Emily recalled that once before when her father died, she refused to release the body. This town eccentric apparently had a desire to hold on to the dead. Investigators are speculating that she murdered the young man in the upstairs bedroom. The town druggist remembers that years ago she came into his shop looking for rat poison.

Even in a small, peaceful town like ours, necrophilia and murder can lurk beneath the apparently tranquil life of a little old spinster.

Journal Entry

If you are required to write an analytical essay on point of view, a free response in a journal is also a useful way to generate ideas. Note how one student explores the point of view in Fitzgerald's short story "The Rich Boy." By the end of his journal entry, he has discovered an idea he might develop into an essay.

Journal entry #12, February 15

Our next essay in this class is on point of view in a story that we enjoyed. No problem for me. I like F. Scott Fitzgerald's "The Rich Boy." Even though that story was written during the jazz age, it sure has a lot to say about rich people. My roommate is rich—comes from a wealthy family—so I've had a chance to observe him. I'm sorta like the narrator in the story—someone who is not wealthy looking in on the life of someone who is rich. What I've discovered is that I, like Fitzgerald's narrator, am a bit cynical about the way the rich behave.

What's interesting to me about the narrator here is that he is so cynical. Cynical people tell cynical stories. I wonder how Anson would tell his own story? Or what if Dolly told it? Well, I guess she'd be a bit cynical too.

Perhaps an objective narrator should have told the story, a narrator who is not biased and cynical—then we could have discovered Anson's other side. After all, the narrator tells us just what he wants us to know. But by doing so, he's telling us about himself as well! Ah! This very problem may be the topic for my essay!

Comment   As you have seen here and in the chapter on the journal, the very act of writing generates ideas. By the time this student has finished just a few free-response paragraphs in his journal, he has discovered a workable idea for his essay. He obviously feels free to relate the story to his own life as he compares himself to the narrator and his roommate to Anson Hunter. Note the following final essay he wrote in his short fiction course.

Student Essay on Point of View

The Narrator in Fitzgerald's "The Rich Boy"

F. Scott Fitzgerald's short story "The Rich Boy" is about the life of the wealthy Anson Hunter and his inability to love.

The events in Anson's life, however, are not told objectively.
Fitzgerald has chosen a first-person narrator, a minor
character, to convey the story. This unnamed narrator, from a
lower economic class than Anson, is biased against Anson and
slants the reader's perception of this rich boy and his
extravagant life.

First, the narrator reveals that he is one of "us." He is
not rich; rather, he is an observer of the rich and feels that
he knows them well. The narrator states:

> Let me tell you about the very rich. They are
> different from you and me. They possess and enjoy early,
> and it does something to them, makes them soft where we
> are hard, and cynical where we are trustful, in a way
> that, unless you were born rich, it is very difficult to
> understand. (2296)

Although the narrator claims that the rich are cynical, he
seems to express cynicism in his own comments about the rich:
"They think, deep in their hearts, that they are better than we
are because we had to discover the compensations and refuges of
life for ourselves" (2296). After setting himself apart from
the rich and revealing his own cynicism about them, he claims
that he will report Anson's life objectively: "The only way I
can describe young Anson Hunter is to approach him as if he
were a foreigner and cling stubbornly to my point of view"
(2296). His claim that he will approach Anson as if he were a
foreigner is self-delusion. Even assuming that the narrator
could be more objective describing a foreigner than someone he
knows well, his envy of Anson has already surfaced in his
narration.

From time to time, as the narrator describes Anson's life,
he reveals information about himself. Such passing comments
offer valuable proof that the narrator is self-conscious about

his middle–class status. For example, when the narrator describes Anson's house, he also mentions that his own childhood "was much simpler in the series of small and medium–sized houses in which my own youth was spent" (2297). These slight comments offer valuable proof that the narrator is self–conscious about his economic status and that the story is being told from a middle–class perspective.

At one point in the story, the narrator admits that he is unable to report Anson's feelings. After the love of Anson's life dies, the narrator tells us, "For the first time in our friendship he told me not a word of how he felt, nor did I see the slightest sign of emotion" (2312). Instead, the narrator reports Anson's actions, and the reader is left to make inferences. The narrator reports only, "His [Anson's] chief preoccupation was with the fact that he was thirty years old" (2312). Seemingly unaffected by Paula's death, Anson, according to the narrator, is only concerned with himself. From this evidence, the reader infers that Anson is a self–centered rich boy who is incapable of love.

At the end of the story, the narrator and Anson are on vacation. On the ship, the narrator states that Anson is his old self again or "at least the self that I knew, and with which I felt at home" (2313). And that states the problem of narration in this story: the readers know only the Anson that the narrator knows—"the self that I knew." Our estimation of Anson is based on what and how the narrator lets us see. There may very well be another Anson Hunter who has a very different story to tell.

Work Cited

F. Scott Fitzgerald. "The Rich Boy." <u>American</u> <u>Literature</u>: <u>The</u> <u>Makers</u> <u>and</u> <u>the</u> <u>Making</u>. 2 vols. Ed. Cleanth Brooks et al. New York: St. Martin's Press, 1973. 2:2296–2313.

Comment   After discovering an idea during his freewriting, this student develops it with ample use of quotations and analysis. Note the well-developed paragraphs. His analysis of Fitzgerald's narration is valid.

TONE

The *tone* of a work of literature expresses the writer's (or speaker's) attitude toward the subject. Because tone is also an element of voice, it is, as you might assume, closely linked to point of view.

Perhaps someone has said to you, "Don't use that tone of voice with me." You had expressed your thoughts and emotions to that person through your voice — your inflection and pitch — as well as word choice, sentence structure, and content. Perhaps you even added a sarcastic sneer. In literature, printed words convey tone through author's style and diction, especially connotation, figurative language, imagery, and rhythm. Tone, then, is not just attitude, but the *way* the attitude is conveyed.

Some tones you may have encountered in literature are anger, despair, joy, humor, irony, nostalgia, sentimentality, bitterness, vulgarity, or sarcasm.

Reading for tone involves critical thinking just as reading for point of view does. For the most part, you infer tone, and you need valid justifications for your decision about a work's tone.

Questions to Ask about Tone

Here are some questions to help you discover the tone of a work:

1. What are one or two words to describe the tone of the work?
2. What are some synonyms for those words?
3. What evidence in the work supports your description of its tone?
4. Are there any shifts in tone? Are these shifts justified?
5. How does the tone contribute to meaning?

Writing about Tone

An essay on the tone of a work does more than merely describe the tone and support that description with evidence to prove the statement. For an analytical essay, you can also reveal how the tone contributes to meaning you have discovered. Or you can define the tone of a particular work, analyze the effect of the tone on the reader, or even find what creates tone. You may also compare and contrast tones of works on similar subjects and discuss, for example, whether a sentimental tone is more effective than an objective tone in describing the death of a child.

Listing Activity on Tone

As we have seen, one creating activity that works well for many writers is listing. As one student prepared to write about tone in Dr. Martin Luther King's "Letter from Birmingham Jail," she listed as she reread the work:

```
 1. starts off polite, reasonable
 2. logical
 3. organized
 4. effective sentences
 5. uses metaphors and similes
 6. likes figurative devices
 7. essay builds in intensity
 8. King makes allusions to many religious and
    historical figures.
 9. Paragraph 14 is one long sentence.
10. Note King's use of the word "wait."
11. Anger, bitterness
12. Quest for justice
13. sensitivity
14. diction suited to his purpose
15. Who is the reader? Alabama clergymen? A wider
    audience interested in human justice?
16. Vivid images
```

A list can generate a main idea as well as supporting points. Note that in the above list, the student has detected several tones in the essay as well as King's use of stylistic devices. This information was eventually used in the following essay on King's tone. Note how the student has tied her analysis of tone to her discovery of King's style, purpose, and audience.

Student Essay on Tone

Tone in Martin Luther King's "Letter from Birmingham Jail"

In 1963 a group of eight Alabama clergymen sent a public statement to Dr. Martin Luther King admonishing him to be more moderate in the demonstrations he was conducting in Birmingham. This public statement caused him to make a fervent response to state his cause. In his response, "Letter from Birmingham Jail," King chooses tones appropriate for his message and audience. These tones range from patience and reasonableness to controlled anger and sensitivity. His tones are a product of his style, specifically his diction and sentence structure.

King begins his essay with a tone of sensitivity and reasonableness. He chooses these tones in order to win the acceptance of his audience. Rather than burst into an emotional tirade about injustice, he first reveals himself as an organized, thoughtful, and cooperative civil rights leader and spokesperson. King states in his introduction, "But since I feel that you [the Alabama clergymen] are men of genuine good will and that your criticisms are sincerely set forth, I want to try to answer your statement in what I hope will be patient and reasonable terms" (521).

After establishing his "patient and reasonable" tone, he gives examples of how the blacks in Atlanta remained patient, waiting for their civil rights, until they could wait no longer—they had to take reasonable actions in order to gain their equality. King uses balanced sentences to describe his quest for civil rights: "I cannot sit idly by in Atlanta and not be concerned about what happens in Birmingham. Injustice anywhere is a threat to justice everywhere" (522). Furthermore, he uses figurative language to describe injustice. King declares, "We are caught in an inescapable network of mutuality, tied in a single garment of destiny. Whatever affects one directly, affects all indirectly" (522).

King's patient and reasonable tone, though, changes to one of controlled anger midway through the essay. After revealing how black people have waited for justice, he makes an emotional appeal that "justice too long delayed is justice denied" (524). He then launches into a sentence, nearly 300 words long, that gives vivid examples of how long black people have waited for their rights. The tone of this carefully constructed sentence is one of controlled anger as he concludes, "When you are forever fighting a degenerating sense of 'nobodiness'—then you will understand why we find it difficult to wait" (524). The long sentence builds to a climax as the reader is left with the sense that black people have indeed waited too long for equal rights.

King also establishes his angry tone with emotionally charged imagery. King writes of "vicious mobs [that] lynch your mothers and fathers at will and drown your brothers and sisters at whim" (524). He also gives a vivid example of injustice by citing the abuse of having to "sleep night after night in the uncomfortable corners of your automobile because no motel will accept you" (524).

King then regains control and produces a series of examples of how he has tried to cooperate with the system in order to gain justice. The later part of the essay returns to a tone of "reasonableness" as King argues that some forms of extremism are productive. He quotes from Jesus, Paul, Martin Luther, John Bunyan, Abraham Lincoln, and Thomas Jefferson.

King ends his essay with an impassioned plea for justice: "Let us all hope that the dark clouds of racial prejudice will soon pass away and the deep fog of misunderstanding will be lifted from our fear-drenched community, and in some not too distant tomorrow the radiant stars of love and brotherhood

will shine on our great nation with all their scintillating
beauty" (532). This last statement with its figurative
language and imagery creates a tone of sensitivity and hope as
King projects a bright future where justice will exist for all
Americans.

Work Cited

Martin Luther King. "Letter from Birmingham Jail, April 16,
    1963." The Informed Argument. Ed. Robert K. Miller. New
    York: Harcourt, 1986. 521–32.

Comment   During the listing, this student noticed King's use of several different tones for different writing purposes. By analyzing each tone and how it
was created by stylistic devices, the student is able to connect King's tone to
his various purposes in the letter. Support paragraphs contain ample quotations from the primary source.

CHAPTER REVIEW

Discovering point of view and tone in a literary work will help you
understand the voice of an author. Discovering the voice behind the
work can help you comprehend and enjoy the work. Detecting point of
view is a challenge for readers since narrators may be biased and
unreliable. Tone, the author's expressed attitude, is a product of personal style including the choice of sentence structure, diction, and
subject matter. Reading for point of view or tone requires you to exercise your critical reading and thinking skills, particularly your skill at
making inferences.

CHAPTER 11

Other Approaches to Literature

The analysis of literature discussed earlier — analyzing structure; language, imagery, and figurative devices; theme; character, setting, and symbol; and point of view and tone — depends on a close study of the work of literature itself, the structure and style of the text. This intensive study of a work from within has been called the *intrinsic* approach. Although many literary works can be read for and by themselves, applying knowledge acquired in the study of other fields often illuminates or enriches your understanding. For example, if you have studied psychology, you can apply psychological insights to the behavior of characters or analyze your response to the text. Approaches examining extraliterary aspects such as the life and background of the writer or the historical period of the work are called *extrinsic* approaches. Extrinsic criticism requires knowledge in other fields besides literature, but you are already studying many other fields, and extrinsic criticism provides the opportunity to interrelate the study of literature with the study of such varied fields as sociology, politics, fine arts, and even economics.

This chapter introduces a few extrinsic approaches, lists questions you might use to develop a particular response to works, and provides sample paragraphs illustrating the differences among the approaches by applying them to the same work, D. H. Lawrence's short story "The Horse Dealer's Daughter."

HISTORICAL APPROACH

The study of the time of a work, both the time period during which it was written and the time period depicted in the work, uses history to inform literary understanding; literature can also be used to inform historical understanding. War and peace, the great chain of being, the rediscovery of the classics, the development of capitalism, slavery, the emancipation of women, the Industrial Revolution – historical events and movements inform, illuminate, and redefine literature. Many survey courses in literature use the historical approach; many anthologies group authors chronologically in specific historical periods and highlight the main social and intellectual developments of those periods in brief introductory chapters. Some literature – satire, for example – may depend greatly on historical knowledge for a clear interpretation; Swift's "A Modest Proposal" can be misread if one knows nothing of the plight of the Irish at that time.

Further, the historical approach is important not only because history influences writers but also because writers use historical events as sources for their work. Contemporary readers of *The Divine Comedy* would have known that Paolo and Francesca were actual lovers, slain by Francesca's husband after he discovered their affair. That knowledge adds to the pathos of her account of their tragedy. Knowing something about the Spanish Civil War leads to a fuller understanding of Hemingway's *For Whom the Bell Tolls* just as knowledge of World War II will help you appreciate John Hersey's *Hiroshima*.

When this approach emphasizes the study of historical ideas, some critics treat it separately as the *history of ideas*. Certainly the ideas prevalent during a writer's time (referred to as the zeitgeist or spirit of the times) influence his or her work; Chaucer's vivid character portraits in *The Canterbury Tales* are clearly influenced by the medieval theory of the humors. If you know that the medieval church considered suicide a form of murder, you better understand why Dante places suicide victims in Hell.

When literature is read in conjunction with contemporary events, ideas, and traditions, reading becomes more informed.

Questions that Lead to an Historical Approach

1. What are both the author's time period and the time period depicted in the work?
2. From what period of time are most of the allusions in the work drawn?

3. What significant events were taking place at this time? Are they reflected in the work?
4. What ideas or philosophies were most dominant?
5. Does the work reflect or oppose these ideas? How?
6. If you have read other works written during this same time period, how does this work compare in its treatment of subjects, events, or ideas?
7. What literary traditions or movements were especially strong at the time? Does the work reflect these traditions or movements, or is it a reaction against them?

Application of the Historical Approach

Mabel Pervin: Embodiment of Post—War Pessimism

In 1922 when "The Horse Dealer's Daughter" was published, England had just come through World War I. The optimism and the certainties of the Victorian period had been destroyed, and many English felt pessimistic about the future, either their personal futures or the future of their nation. The best behavior in such an uncertain world was simply to endure whatever fate could bring, whether a devastating war or, as in this story, the end of the world Mabel Pervin has known.

With the death of her father and the sale of the family property, Mabel has nothing left. Yet, "nothing . . . could shake the curious, sullen, animal pride that dominated each member of the family. . . . She would not cast about her. She would follow her own way just the same. She would always hold the keys of her own situation" (418). But Mabel isn't completely stoical. The reader learns that she intends to kill herself and sees her actually attempt it because "this was the end, and there was no way out" (419). However, she is stoical in that she asks for no sympathy, no consolation, no savior. In fact, as she tells Dr. Ferguson after he rescues her, "It [the suicide] was the right thing to do. I knew best, then" (423). She is not saved by her choice; in fact, she relinquishes all responsibility for the rest of her life as she accepts Jack's love. Lawrence seems to say that the only cure for the ills of history and individuals—the only antidote to pessimism—is human love,

Work Cited

Lawrence, D. H. "The Horse Dealer's Daughter." The Collected
    Short Stories. London: Heinemann, 1974. 413—427. (All
    subsequent citations to this story are from this volume.)

Comment   Because this particular short story describes domestic rather than national events, the historical approach is used to comment on contemporary attitudes reflected through the protagonist. Also see the discussion below on the sociological approach.

SOCIOLOGICAL AND POLITICAL APPROACH

The sociological approach, while similar in ways to the historical approach, is more specialized because it centers on the social environment of the work — the culture, politics, economics, mores, customs, fashion, manners — to use the French term, the *milieu*. To use this approach you might consider either the ways the forces of society influence a writer or the ways these forces operate in the work. Clearly, literary works reflecting or commenting on social reality (the utopian novel, for example) can validly be approached sociologically, and your understanding of most literary works could be enhanced by this approach because the culture to which writers belong helps determine their understanding of life and even the language they use to express that understanding.

Knowledge of contemporary economic and social theory is important for your understanding of how some works attempt to reflect or even reform their society. For example, to understand the nineteenth-century English novel better, you should understand the plight of dowerless daughters in that society. You wonder why Dante places money-lenders (usurers) in the seventh circle of Hell unless you know the difference between medieval money-lenders and the loan officer at your branch bank. And certainly, your appreciation of Upton Sinclair's *The Jungle* will be increased if you are aware of Theodore Roosevelt's reform movement and of the influence of the muckrakers' attacks on sweatshop labor, unsanitary food processing, and slums.

In fact, the sociological approach is especially helpful for your understanding of such works as Steinbeck's *Grapes of Wrath*, first written as a newspaper series on conditions in migrant worker camps, and Arthur Miller's play about the New Salem witchcraft trials, *The Crucible*, written during the McCarthy "witch hunts."

Questions that Lead to a Sociological Approach

1. What class (or classes) of society is represented in the work?
2. What are the prevailing manners, customs, habits, dress, etc. of that class?
3. Do these manners and mores directly influence the behavior of characters in the work? If so, how?
4. Could the work have been written about any other milieu and still have the same impact?
5. What economic (e.g., Marxist) or social (e.g., women's liberation) movements were taking place either in the time period depicted in the work or in the time period in which the work was written?
6. Is the writer making a statement about social reality? If so, what?
7. If the writer describes a social problem, does he or she seem to offer a solution for that problem?

Application of the Sociological Approach

The Shedding of Gentility in D. H. Lawrence's "The Horse Dealer's Daughter"

The climax of Lawrence's short story "The Horse Dealer's Daughter" comes as an almost comic release from middle-class gentility. Young Dr. Ferguson has just rescued Mabel Pervin from the pond where she has attempted to drown herself. In an attempt to revive her, he removes her "saturated, earthy-smelling" black clothing and wraps her in warm blankets. As she gains full awareness of her surroundings, she realizes she is

naked under the blankets and "with wild eye" asks, "Who
undressed me?" (423). Dr. Ferguson can only reply, "I did . . .
to bring you round" (424). Middle—class mores being what
they were in Edwardian England, to have been viewed naked by a
man can mean only one thing to Mabel. "Do you love me,
then?" (424).

This is almost comic, yet not at all. In Lawrence's hands
the episode has an ache—in—the—throat poignancy, and, with Dr.
Ferguson, the reader's soul seems also "to melt." The reader
can only be glad, then, when Mabel sheds her middle—class sense
of propriety with her clothing and shuffles forward to clasp
him around the knees as, heedless of her "wild, bare, animal
shoulders," (424) she acknowledges and responds to his love.
Dr. Ferguson lets "his heart yield toward her" (425) as he
crosses "over the gulf to her" while "all [bachelorhood,
loneliness, isolation, unhappiness] that he had left behind
had shriveled and become void" (426). Gentility—and with it
stubborn pride and empty life—has been conquered by the
passion of love.

Comment   The sociological approach is used here to show how a writer
such as Lawrence both reveals and opposes contemporary notions of propriety.

MORAL AND RELIGIOUS APPROACHES

Since most literature reflects and comments on life, it is logical that
reading may have an effect on how readers live their lives. The Roman
writer Horace stresses that the purpose of literature is to instruct as
well as to delight. (Works written primarily for instruction are termed
didactic.) To use the moral approach to literature, you might examine
the beliefs and behaviors upheld and opposed by the work or evaluate
the work for its moral content.

If either you or the writer espouse the beliefs of a particular religion, then the approach can be termed a religious one. (Moral and
religious are not synonymous; you need only to remember Shelley to
realize that a profoundly moral writer is not always an orthodoxly
religious one.)

What literature may be validly approached from the religious point of view? Although you might examine any work for its religious content (or lack of it), you can best examine works which form the basis of religious beliefs (the Koran, the Bhagavad-Gita, the Bible, sacred tribal myths), works which express personal religious statements (St. Augustine's *Confessions*, Edwards' sermons, Hopkins' poems), and works with religious content (*Beowulf*, the Greek tragedies, Sartre's *No Exit*).

If you explore either the religious or the moral approach, avoid appreciating and applauding *only* those works with whose religious viewpoint or expressed moral you agree and attacking those works with whose expressed values you disagree.

Questions that Lead to the Moral and Religious Approaches

1. Are any religious or moral beliefs overtly espoused by the work or specifically criticized by it?
2. Is the work written primarily for didactic purposes? Does the work have an explicit or implicit moral? If explicit, is it thoroughly integrated into the work?
3. What religious imagery or symbolism do you find in the work? Is there a pattern of religious imagery?
4. Are there allusions to any sacred texts in the work? What is the effect of these allusions?
5. Is the structure of the work reminiscent of any religious event?

Application of the Religious Approach

Suicide: Self—Determination or Self—Murder?

Using Lawrence's story "The Horse Dealer's Daughter" to determine his attitude toward suicide is difficult because the story seems to support three opposing beliefs. First presented is the belief that suicide is an acceptable means of avoiding disgrace. Mabel Pervin is a proud young woman whose life as the daughter of a prosperous trader has been destroyed by his death and her ensuing poverty. She has "suffered during the period of poverty" because "everything was gone to the dogs, there was nothing but debt and threatening" (418). Therefore, she

rejects the (presumably humiliating) situation with her
married sister which has been planned for her and moves quickly
and single-mindedly "in a sort of ecstasy . . . to her
fulfilment, her own glorification approaching her dead
mother, who was glorified" (419).

Second, the story also supports the belief that our lives
are our own to keep or give up as we will. Mabel is determined
to "hold the keys of her own situation. . . . Why should she
answer anybody?" (418-19). When the doctor spies her tidying
her mother's grave in the churchyard, he is struck by her
independent remoteness; looking at her is "like looking into
another world" (419). Sharing her suicidal intention with no
one, she finishes her chores and walks ". . . slowly and
deliberately towards the centre of the pond" (421).

Finally, though, because her suicide is thwarted, it would
appear from this story that Lawrence ultimately sides with
those who believe suicide, a waste of human potential, is
murder and must be prevented. Further, the act of intervention
may save the rescuer just as it does the victim. At the end of
the story, the doctor and Mabel are planning the beginning of a
life together.

Comment   This analysis presents and illustrates two moral attitudes towards suicide expressed in the story and another inferred from the main action of the story. Although the writer carefully qualifies any generalizations
about Lawrence's beliefs based on this single example, some readers may question the use of fiction to determine a writer's moral or religious philosophy.

BIOGRAPHICAL APPROACH

How important is it for you to know something about the life of a
writer to understand his or her work? Those critics primarily interested in the intrinsic approach may say "not at all"; others may disagree. Studying the author's life can provide valuable insight into a work
of literature. Dante's idealized love for Beatrice, the inspiration for his

greatest work, was based on only two actual meetings; this biographical detail suggests a man imbued in the traditions of courtly love. F. Scott Fitzgerald was turned down by the lovely Southern belle, Zelda Sayre, until his first novel was sold to the movies, thus proving to her that the young man could attain success and riches, and these themes dominate his work. Ralph Ellison's *Invisible Man* is perhaps best understood by relating it to his involvement with left-wing political organizations and his position as a leader of black protest.

Many writers draw on the events of their lives for the subject matter of their literature. Cervantes writes movingly of prisoners and slaves in *Don Quixote*; he was himself a slave for five years before his country ransomed him. Ernest Hemingway was an ambulance driver in Italy before the United States entered World War I; he used his experience in one of his war novels, *A Farewell to Arms*. Tennessee Williams had a shy sister who collected glass animals, no doubt the inspiration for his masterpiece *The Glass Menagerie* in which crippled Laura dotes on her glass unicorn and waits for her gentlemen callers.

Readers are often fascinated by the lives writers have led — their loves, losses, successes, failures, incomes, and various occupations. Your appreciation of the talent lost in the premature deaths of such artists as Keats and Crane, dead of tuberculosis before they were thirty; Sylvia Plath, a suicide; Rupert Brooke, killed in battle; may lead you to reevaluate their works. You may especially want to study the biographies of women writers whose lives and writings are often so inextricably intertwined that to separate them is to risk misreading the texts. Could Virginia Woolf have written *A Room of One's Own* had she not been the daughter of a scholar and the wife of a writer and editor? How did Dorothy Wordsworth's relationship with her brother William and his friend and colleague Coleridge affect her extremely perceptive journal writing? Did Mary Wollstonecraft Shelley's work depend on her unconventional upbringing and her marriage to the poet?

For a further example of how the events of a writer's life may influence his work, examine Eliot's *The Waste Land*. He wrote much of it while on sick leave from his job in a London bank, suffering from a mental breakdown of some kind. His wife was herself mentally unstable. His father had recently died, and Eliot felt guilty at having left America against his father's wishes. Any or all of these factors may have contributed to the fragmented vision he reveals in the poem. However, he was also reading Dante's *Divine Comedy*, and perhaps the recovery of identity found in the last section of the poem is influenced by the experience of Dante's pilgrim.

Other Approaches

In your biographical approach you may want to study what writers themselves have said, written, and felt about their works, during the composition process and afterwards, and how they have reacted to the critical response to their works. Letters to and from writers are considered part of the biographical approach.

If you use the biographical approach, remember, as discussed in Chapter 10, that the persona or speaker of an author's work is not necessarily the author himself or herself. Do not confuse the writer's life with the lives of his or her fictional creations, or necessarily think of the writer as holding the convictions depicted in his or her works. Even when a writer seems to be speaking autobiographically, do not expect details identical with the biographical record.

Second, make certain that you refer to an authoritative biography. Some biographies have been written solely to glamorize their subjects; others, such as Rufus Griswold's study of Poe, to discredit their subjects or their works. One way you can tell if a biography is accurate is whether or not its author had complete access to the records of the life, including published and unpublished letters and manuscripts. A biography authorized by the family or estate of the writer *may* be the most accurate one available. (That is *may* because if families exercise a right of censorship, the biographer may have to present a purified version of a life.) If the subject was living, did the biographer interview or consult him or her? And, finally, as mentioned above, view autobiographies skeptically. Writers are not necessarily the best commentators on their own lives.

As you search for an authoritative biography of your subject, notice that some biographies contain literary criticism while others do not. If you are researching a particular work, then you may prefer reading a biography which includes critical responses.

Questions that Lead to a Biographical Approach

1. Does the writer seem to draw from his or her life in the work? What biographical knowledge seems necessary for a fuller understanding of the work?
2. If any key episodes from the writer's life are reflected in the work, to what extent do the literary events resemble biographical ones?
3. Did any controversies surround the writer in his or her lifetime?

4. How did contemporaries regard the writer and how did that influence the work?
5. Did the writer have any important friendships or other relationships important to a full understanding of the work?

Application of the Biographical Approach

The Working Class in Lawrence: Joe Pervin in "The Horse Dealer's Daughter"

Lawrence in "Nottingham and the Mining Countryside" tells us that his father was a collier and characterizes colliers as men who have neither ambition nor intellect, men who avoid a rational life. Joe Pervin in Lawrence's short story "The Horse Dealer's Daughter" is a perfect embodiment of such working men, displaying the coarseness and vitality that Lawrence's mother taught him to abhor. He is a strong physical specimen, "broad and handsome in a hot, flushed way," but "his bearing" is "stupid." He watches the horses leave on their last exercise with "a certain stupor of downfall" (413). Because he is not intelligent, he will be controlled by others in the same way that the horses are. Lawrence links Joe specifically with the horses in a later passage: "The horses were almost like his own body to him" (414). He is going to be married, but marriage will not provide the companionship that Mabel and Dr. Ferguson will achieve later in the story: Joe "would marry and go into harness. . . . He would be a subject animal now" (414).

Insensitive, helpless despite his strength, Joe Pervin represents the working class for which Lawrence, despite his schoolteacher mother, always felt a kinship.

Comment　　These paragraphs combine biographical and sociological approaches in the comments on the relationships between classes. More than one extrinsic approach may be helpful in understanding a particular work.

PSYCHOLOGICAL APPROACH

Some biographies also provide material for the psychological approach which applies the insights of psychology to literary works. For example, as discussed earlier with the biographical approach, knowing Eliot's psychological condition at the time of his composition of *The Waste Land* adds to your understanding of that poem. The method can also be applied in reverse; a critic may study a writer's works to project his or her psychological state, perhaps illuminating the biography. For example, John Cody's biography of Emily Dickinson, *After Great Pain: The Inner Life of Emily Dickinson*, reconstructs some of the events of her life through the application of psychoanalytic theory and a careful examination of her poetry.

When you relate the behavior of characters in a literary work to relationships of people you know, you are applying an intuitive understanding of psychology (as well as sociology). The psychological approach may also include a more formal application of psychological theory, perhaps beginning with the Freudian aspects of the human mind. Freud's division of the mind into the *id* (the mental image of biological instinct, the primarily unconscious source of desires and aggression), the *ego* (which bridges the gap between mental image and external reality by restraining the desires of the id within social and moral boundaries) and the *superego* (the mental representation of morality, the conscience) has provided many critics with a convenient schema for discussing characters (see, for example, the student research paper, "The Heart Tells the Tale," in Chapter 13), as has his analysis of dreams. Of course, the work of other psychologists can also be used; for example, Elizabeth Kubler-Ross's stages of grief could provide a structure for examining Hamlet's action (and inaction).

You do not need to know whether a writer was aware of a particular psychological theory before you can examine it in connection with the writer's works. Psychologists have not invented the behavior they observe; they record, analyze, and, in some cases, name the reactions and responses they observe. The behavior Freud metaphorically termed the "Oedipus complex," the strong attraction a child feels to the parent of the opposite sex, appears in Sophocles' *Oedipus Rex* (but in a rather different form) long before Freud described it.

However, many modern authors are well aware of psychological theory and consciously employ its terms, symbols, and patterns in their work, as, for example, Joyce does in the pure stream-of-consciousness monologues of his characters, or O'Neill does with the brooding embodiments of subconscious desires he characterizes in many of his plays. The psychological approach is particularly appropriate applied to such authors and their works.

You may apply psychological theories to writers, works, or readers. The figments of a writer's imagination can be analyzed as "real" people, motivated by the same desires and conflicts as the readers themselves. You may examine a character as a case study of a particular form of behavior — Lear in Shakespeare's play as senility or Iago in *Othello* as jealousy.

You may also use psychological criticism to consider the effect of the work on the reader and how that effect might depend on unconscious feelings. If you have participated in class discussion with a heterogeneous mix of students — perhaps eighteen to fifty in age, male and female, grandmother and son, professional and student — you have probably observed that reactions to a work vary widely; some vociferously declare a work such as Alice Munro's "Boys and Girls" the best they've read all semester while others find it too depressing to finish. Is that because of the work itself or its readers? You must say both as you analyze the students' reasons for appreciation and dislike. Perhaps one student says that she loved the story because she has a sister just like the heroine and now she understands why her sister sometimes acts as she does. Another dislikes it because she sees aspects of her own personality in the heroine, aspects she abhors yet feels helpless to change. Powerful literature arouses powerful emotions; the psychological approach can illuminate those emotions.

Use caution when making judgments about an author's psychological profile because your viewpoint is certainly less complete and rigorous than a trained analyst's. Don't assume, for example, that O'Neill's treatment of infanticide indicates a desire on his part to do away with his own flesh-and-blood children. Similarly, avoid applying psychological criticism too broadly; not every father–son quarrel in literature means the son really wants to murder the father to establish his own identity. However, used wisely, the psychological approach can give you the chance to apply what you know about human behavior to the literature you read.

Questions that Lead to a Psychological Approach

1. What is your immediate response to the work? What single word best describes that emotional response?
2. What is the emotional condition of each of the characters?
3. Would you like to know any of the people in the work? Why or why not?

4. Do any characters display perceivable psychological problems?
5. Do any psychological theories seem particularly applicable to the work?
6. How do these theories illuminate the work?

Application of the Psychological Approach

Love in Lawrence's "The Horse Dealer's Daughter":

A Painful Necessity

Lawrence's presentation of love in "The Horse Dealer's Daughter" is complex and psychologically precise, particularly in its portrayal of the pain involved as the self is changed in the union of the couple. Yet, as he makes clear through his description of Mabel Pervin and Dr. Ferguson before Mabel's attempted suicide, this painful alteration of the individual is necessary if either is to become a full human being. Mabel and Jack are lonely, incomplete, and unfulfilled. She is described as "alone" because she does not "share the same life as her brothers" (413). Her solitude is so profound that she looks forward to joining her mother in death as a "fulfilment, her own glorification" (419). The doctor too will be lonely with Fred's leaving; "the only company he cared for in the alien, ugly little town he was losing." Besides his friendship with Fred he has only the vicarious life he leads through his patients; "the contact with the rough, strongly-feeling people was a stimulant applied direct to his nerves" (420).

When Jack rescues Mabel and she naively assumes that means he loves her, he resists at first: "He had no intention of loving her: his whole will was against his yielding. It was horrible" (424). Rationally and logically, he is not ready to commit himself to her. But under the driving power of his feelings, his unwillingness to hurt her, he loses control of

his actions and crosses "over the gulf to her, and all that he
had left behind" shrivels and becomes "void" (426). Even though
Lawrence believes, as Freud did, that the ability to love
another person is the hallmark of the mature adult, still, the
powerful force of the emotion of love is terrifying. Mabel is
almost as frightened by the "terrible intonation" of Jack's
voice when he says that he wants her as she was by the thought
that he might not want her (427). Love is complex, painful, and
frightening, but Lawrence demonstrates in this story that only
through loving as men and women can we be fully human.

Comment   The important psychological theory in this essay is that the ability to love is the hallmark of true maturity. Certainly, Lawrence presents both Mabel and Jack as incomplete and unfulfilled human beings.

ARCHETYPAL APPROACH

The archetypal or mythological approach is an approach combining insights from both psychology and anthropology. Carl Jung, once a student and colleague of Freud's, broke with him over what Jung considered Freud's too narrow approach to psychoanalysis. Jung believed that beyond the personal unconscious, all humans share a deep level of unconsciousness, the "collective unconscious." This collective unconscious contains patterns of memory and thought called *archetypes* predisposing people to respond similarly in certain situations. (That people of different cultures do respond similarly has been recorded by anthropologists, notably Sir James Frazer in *The Golden Bough*, a twelve-volume treatment of the similarity of primitive rituals among different cultures.)

Literature of lasting appeal such as *Hamlet, Moby Dick,* or "The Rime of the Ancient Mariner" achieves that appeal in part through its embodiment of archetypal figures and situations, universal symbols, to which readers unconsciously respond. Thus in *Hamlet* readers respond to the corruption of the kingdom by the unnatural murder of the king by his brother, a corruption which can only be purged by Hamlet's avenging his father. In *Moby Dick* readers respond to Ishmael, the innocent witness swept along on an unholy quest into the nature of evil. Like the wedding guest in "The Rime of the Ancient Mariner," readers are enthralled by tales of universal human suffering, of mistakes made, and consequences suffered.

Dreams, art, and myths are the means by which these unconscious, universal patterns or archetypes become articulate and accessible to consciousness. A collection of myths, or cultural mythology, is comprised of the stories, beliefs, and traditions common to a certain people, representing their attempts to explain natural events, to develop and pass on their history, and, in general, to give meaning to life. Literary myths include such works as the *Iliad, Beowulf,* and the Icelandic sagas, the *Elder* and *Younger Edda.* "The American Dream," a folk myth unique to this country, presumes that America is a present Eden, populated by innocent and morally stalwart Adams and Eves. The inevitable fall of these Adams and Eves and the destruction of Eden is also a motif throughout American literature.

Archetypal literary criticism identifies archetypal images, patterns, and characters. For example, water might symbolize redemption, fertility, growth, and creation. T. S. Eliot uses this archetype most specifically in *The Waste Land*, contrasting it with another archetypal image, the desert, representing sterility and hopelessness. Circles can symbolize perfection; thus, Dante presents the Trinity as three concentric circles in *The Divine Comedy.*

Archetypal patterns include the quest, the journey, the initiation, the battle, and the sacrifice. In these patterned activities, an archetypal hero is transformed. King Arthur, for example, "quests" for the Holy Grail to save his kingdom, Camelot. Both Huck Finn and Don Quixote set off on journeys that will change them before they reach their destinations. Sophocles' Oedipus offers to sacrifice himself so the city of Thebes will no longer be plagued by drought. During their ordeal in a lifeboat, the four men in Stephen Crane's "The Open Boat" are initiated into a sense of community, and Billy Budd in Melville's novel is initiated into the knowledge of human evil.

Characters also can be archetypes. The *clown* is an archetype as old as Roman comedy. The *hero* can be Odysseus or Aeneas, the Archbishop of Canterbury or Natty Bumppo, Mary Rowlandson or Barbara Frietchie. The hero as *warrior* archetype includes characters like Beowulf, Hector, Achilles, Gideon, David, and the Red Cross Knight. The *earth mother* is Mrs. Piggoty in *David Copperfield*, Aunt Sally in *Huck Finn*, or the nurse in *Romeo and Juliet*.

Using the archetypal approach will help you detect recurring images and patterns, analyze your responses to literature, and become aware of how authors both use and reverse archetypes in the works you read. Melville uses the archetypal quest in *Moby Dick* as does the author of *Sir Gawain and the Green Knight*, but for far different purposes. Ahab maniacally searches for the white whale, archetypal symbol of the unknown, that had torn away his leg; Sir Gawain rides in search of a green knight, an archetype of spring and vegetation, to fulfill an honorable promise.

Clearly the archetypal approach is also related to the sociological approach in its study of a particular culture; to the religious, moral, and historical approaches in its study of the ideas which influence or dominate a particular society; and to the psychological approach when it analyzes unconscious responses.

In noting the elements a particular work has in common with universal archetypes, don't lose sight of the individual work itself, even though concentrating on how a specific text uses archetypes may help you understand why and how that work has achieved such a universal and lasting appeal.

Questions that Lead to an Archetypal Approach

1. Do any symbols, situations, motifs, or characters in the work seem familiar? Why?
2. How are these archetypes used in the work?
3. Does the use of archetypes explain some of the work's appeal? Why or why not?
4. Does the writer reverse any expectations you may have? Does thinking about archetypes explain those expectations?

Application of the Archetypal Approach

Water as Rebirth: The Pond in Lawrence's

"The Horse Dealer's Daughter"

Mabel Pervin's immersion in the pond in "The Horse Dealer's Daughter" is a deliberate use by Lawrence of the archetypal significance of water as baptism, a rite involving

the destruction of the old life and the birth of a new one.
Mabel has chosen the pond as her means of committing suicide so
that she can join her mother in death. Lawrence has already
shown the reader enough of her current life for one to realize
that it is a living death; isolated and destitute, Mabel has
no plans and no hope. She marches steadily toward her goal of
glorification by death; the doctor observes her walking
"slowly and deliberately" (421) into the water and thence to
the deep center of the pond. She has gone under by the time
he reaches the bank, so he slowly and reluctantly wades out
to find her. However, he cannot reach her until he too is
submerged "horribly, suffocating in the foul earthy water,
struggling madly" (421-2). This "baptism" of total immersion
enables him to be reborn; after what seems an "eternity" he
"rises" and "gasps" and knows he is "in the world." The newly-
born man can be a savior; he grasps Mabel who "rises" near
him and, after carrying her to shore, he is able to restore
her to life (421). Having been reborn to an awareness of their
humanity, it is only natural then, that in the next scene, they
accept their love for each other.

Comment   The paragraph points out the significance of both characters'
having to be totally immersed before rebirth is possible. The paragraph could
easily be rewritten to reflect the religious approach.

FEMINIST APPROACH

Having its roots in the women's movement of the 1960s, the feminist approach to literature is relatively new. Feminist criticism includes several different strands: examining works for bias in their
portrayal of women; rescuing from oblivion the works of some women
writers; analyzing works written by women for specifically "feminine"
language and images; developing new standards of evaluation for literature to include more works by women; and looking at literature

from social and political standpoints. You can see from even this tentative list that feminist criticism can and does overlap many of the approaches already considered: feminist criticism is historical when relating women's suffrage to contemporary literature, sociological and political when discussing the position of women in society, and archetypal when examining universal images of women.

Certainly, having been born male or female has an impact on an individual's life, but you will have to determine if gender is the deciding factor in literature for the writer, the work, or the reader. Can a reader tell the difference between a work written by a man and one written by a woman? Having first established your deciding hallmarks — subject, plot, style, setting, or theme — your class may want to circulate unsigned poems, paragraphs, or short stories and try to decide authorial gender. However, do not be surprised if you cannot decisively determine the sex of writers.

If you cannot find any significant differences between works written by women and works written by men, you may want to consider another feminist issue: have women writers betrayed their gender to achieve recognition in an art predominantly written by men, taught by men, and criticized by men?

Finally, you may want to consider, as part of your stylistic analysis, the possibility that there are distinctly feminine and masculine styles of writing but that these styles cannot be sex-determined; that is, some women write in a masculine style and some men write in a feminine style. You may find that feminine writing is characterized by such themes as gender-specific experiences, subjugation and deprivation, madness and entrapment, escape and flight, themes perhaps reflecting sociological and psychological conditions. You may agree with French feminists that feminine language (which they call "writing the body") is more metaphorical, more intuitive, and more abstract than masculine language which is more authoritative, rational, and concrete. You may also discover that feminine writing is more fluid, formally more open, showing less concern for the conventions of language such as punctuation and paragraphing, and that it is more reckless and daring in tone, more mocking, ironic, and playful.

Another intent of the feminist approach is to examine all literature, men's and women's, for portrayals of women. For example, consider whether a work accepts or defends, implicitly or explicitly, a social structure which elevates men and devalues women. If it devalues women, examine the strategies used. Ask how a particular work treats self-expression and self-realization.

Does gender also affect you as a reader? Some feminist critics have called into question the traditional literary canon and literary evaluation, saying that reading is also a gender-oriented activity controlled too long by male readers. Thus the canon ignores, or designates as "secondary" or "minor," that literature which women have produced and to which women readers have traditionally and instinctively responded such as diaries, journals, letters, and sentimental or romantic novels. Critical standards need to be evaluated in light of the importance of these nontraditional texts to women as writers and readers. The feminist approach asks questions such as: Have women-authored literary works been treated fairly by critics? Why were critics so long in realizing the acute perception of nature and vivid description in Dorothy Wordsworth's journals? Why wasn't it until the 1950s that critics discovered Kate Chopin's 1899 novel, *The Awakening*? Can a male critic really understand Emily Dickinson?

Just as the feminist approach may lead you to criticize other critics for ignoring women's contributions to literature or their distorted image in literature, so too proponents of the gay and lesbian approaches have criticized feminist critics for ignoring homosexuality in literature and life. Perhaps, as Carolyn Heilbrun in *Toward a Recognition of Androgyny* (New York: Knopf, 1973) has theorized, the best literature and criticism would be culturally androgynous, humanizing both men and women, with neither dependent for identity on the other, with both sexes able to express the self fully, with both self-actualized in reality and in literature.

Questions that Lead to a Feminist Approach

1. How are women portrayed in the work? (Consider such roles as virgin, temptress, witch, monster, mother, nurse, wife, servant.)
2. What are their relationships with men? with each other? with their children? with themselves?
3. Do you detect any specifically female images or symbols such as nets, wombs, traps, vases, the earth, the moon? How are these images used?
4. Is the writer male or female? If female, has she used a male pseudonym? Why?
5. Is the subject "typically" feminine? How?

6. Do female characters accept their "places" in the family (society, marriage) or are they struggling for self-definition?
7. How does the author's own biography relate to the characterization of women (and men) in the work?

Application of the Feminist Approach

Daughter or Wife: A Woman's Role

Lawrence's short story "The Horse Dealer's Daughter," whether intentionally or not, presents in vivid microcosm the limited choices allowed a woman of that time. At the beginning of the story, Mabel Pervin, "a rather short, sullen-looking woman of twenty-seven" (413), has lost her societal role as the horse dealer's daughter because the horse dealer is dead and his business has "gone to the dogs" (418). Her brothers see only one option for her: living with a married sister (as unpaid spinster help, one assumes). Mabel, however, plans another destiny since "it was enough that this was the end, and there was no way out" (419). She will commit suicide and thus join her dead mother in "glorification." At least in this plan Mabel demonstrates the "curious, sullen, animal pride that dominated each member of the family" (418).

However, her independent action is forestalled by the young doctor who sees her walk "slowly and deliberately towards the centre of the pond" (421) and rushes to rescue her. When she revives, she abdicates responsibility for her life and actions, "'It was the right thing to do. I knew best, then'" (423; final emphasis added), turning them over to her savior. When, after an inner struggle, he accepts that responsibility, the reader realizes that Mabel Pervin has merely exchanged one role for another: horse dealer's daughter for doctor's wife. How sad that she could not be permitted to make a life for herself as an independent woman.

Comment   This brief essay exemplifies one of the strands of feminist criticism: how works portray the position of women in their society. It criticizes the society for not offering Mabel more choices and even uses the title as supporting evidence.

OTHER APPROACHES

This chapter has provided only an introduction to some possible approaches to literature; there are many other extrinsic approaches not covered. What are you studying in your other classes? Economics? Research in that field might help you appreciate Virginia Woolf's theme in her essay *A Room of One's Own*: all one needs to be a writer is five hundred pounds a year and a private room. How much in current dollars is five hundred pounds? How generous a stipend does Woolf think necessary for the artist? How does that relate to incomes today?

Perhaps you are a fine arts major. There have been some good critical studies of the parallels between painting and literature in such areas as impressionism and the use of chiaroscuro. You need look no further than William Blake, poet, painter, engraver, and publisher, to see that a fine arts approach to his work would contribute to your understanding. Are you a musician? Can you draw a parallel between musical repetition and patterns in a specific literary work?

To illuminate literature, bring to its study what you know as well as who you are.

CHOOSING AN APPROACH

Now that you have sampled some of the extrinsic approaches to literature, which one should you use for an essay topic? In part the answer depends on you — your interests and your knowledge. As the application of several different approaches to Lawrence's "The Horse Dealer's Daughter" shows, complex works can support a variety of approaches. However, some approaches will not be suitable for some texts because of the subject, the length, the intended audience, or your purpose for writing. Use the questions provided for the approaches to help you decide. If a set of questions does not fit your work, choose another work or another approach.

However, since one object of literary criticism is to account for your response to the work, the best approach may be (some critics would say must be) a pluralistic reading. Certainly, approaching all works of literature with a single approach, whether religious, historical, or feminist, is too restrictive. Since writers may be simultaneously young, female, Jewish New Yorkers or middle-aged, black, southern clergymen and politicians, how can there be a single "right" reading of works written from such pluralistic backgrounds? The richer the text, the more possible interpretations.

CHAPTER REVIEW

The specialized approaches examined in this chapter — historical, sociological and political, moral and religious, psychological, biographical, archetypal and feminist — indicate how you can use your knowledge gained in other fields, as well as your own background, to illuminate literature. Many literary works are complex enough to be approached plurally; the approach you choose to apply to a specific text depends on your knowledge and interest as well as the potential of the text.

Other Approaches

PART IV
WRITING PAPERS
FROM SOURCES

CHAPTER 12

Researching
a Literary Topic

WHEN IS RESEARCH NECESSARY?

*W*hen taking a literature class, you may research literary topics to investigate issues or make connections to enhance your enjoyment or increase your understanding of the works you read. Reading a *primary source* (the work itself) often leads to questions needing to be researched in *secondary sources* (including criticism and interpretation of the work, commentaries on the work, histories, biographies, reviews, interviews, films, recordings, and specialized encyclopedias) before the work can be fully appreciated and understood. The research may be as simple as dating the work or learning biographical details about the author, or you may want to explore other works in the same genre, other works by the same author, major political events of the period, or comments on the work by other readers. Research in a literature class may result in writing a formal research paper, answering questions generated by reading, or preparing for class discussion or oral reports. Other assignments may require you to compile a bibliography on an author or work or even to *annotate* the bibliography (find, read, and evaluate secondary material). This chapter outlines the process of research itself; the following chapter explains the process of writing a formal research paper.

CHOOSING AND NARROWING A TOPIC

If your instructor has assigned a specific topic or if you are researching for your own satisfaction, you do not have to worry about choosing a topic. However, if you are assigned a research paper on a twentieth-century American author, you may not know where to begin. Try some of the creating techniques discussed in Chapters 2 and 3. What interests you most in the material you are studying? What issues have you discovered? What subjects would you like to explore further? Also review Chapter 11 on other approaches to literature. Can you relate your interests in fields such as psychology, history, religion, sociology, or feminism to a literary topic?

If you are researching for a class project, carefully list all requirements on an index card to carry with you as you work. If aspects of the assignment are obscure, now is the time to clarify them. If the requirements state the project should be typed, and you compose with a word processor and a dot matrix printer, make sure that form is acceptable. Ask whether you can use articles as well as books or whether you are supposed to avoid general encyclopedias.

Be certain to note the audience and purpose for the assignment. If not specified, assume an audience of classmates who, having read the text, are equally puzzled by the issue intriguing you.

Note one student's "carry card" for an American literature research project:

Class: American Literature I
Topic: a short story by Poe
Due date: Dec. 7
Requirements: 6-8 typed pages,
    8-10 sources, formal outline,
    1988 MLA documentation.

If possible, narrow your subject now. The length of the assignment, the resources of local libraries, your resources of time and energy, your audience and purpose for writing can all help you narrow your subject to a specific topic.

Let's follow this student as she works through some of these decisions for her paper on Poe. First, she must choose the Poe short story she may wish to write about. Since she will have to work with her choice for many weeks, she wants to select a story she enjoys, so she rereads several. She also decides to work with a story her class has already discussed because the discussions provided her with different perspectives on the works. She finally chooses "The Tell-Tale Heart" because she is also studying psychology and finds the portrait of the madman fascinating. The story is also brief enough for her to keep all its details in mind; indeed, after several careful rereadings, she feels she almost has it memorized.

Having decided on a psychological approach to the story, she asks herself questions about the story to determine her specific interest. After considering the questions for the psychological approach found in Chapter 11, she thinks about other issues that occurred to her during her reading, questions she has marked in her text or jotted in her journal:

Could someone who was really mad plan a murder so carefully?

Why does the murderer move so slowly during the actual murder?

Why is it necessary for the murder to be committed at night?

Why does the eye of the old man disturb the murderer so profoundly?

Why does the murderer end up revealing his deed to the police?

As this student has done, ask yourself questions about the work you have chosen. (Remember that Chapters 6–11 all contain lists of possible questions.) Choose the question you find most intriguing as your *working* or *preliminary thesis* to guide your initial research. Add this question to the "carry card" listing the audience, purpose, and requirements for the project — length, minimum number of sources and citations, due date, format, and other data:

Class: American Literature I
Topic: a short story by Poe
Due date: Dec. 7
Requirements: 6-8 typed pages, 8-10 sources,
*   formal outline, 1988 MLA documentation*
Narrow topic: Poe's "The Tell-Tale Heart"
Working thesis: Why does the narrator plan
*   the murder of the old man so carefully,*
*   then reveal the deed to the police?*

(You may also narrow your topic by background reading in encyclopedias and by scanning secondary sources. See the sections "Encyclopedias" and "Using Indexes and Bibliographies" in this chapter.)

THE PRIMARY SOURCE

Now that you have a topic, before you head for the library to investigate it with secondary sources, set aside some time to reread the primary work with your topic in mind. Review Chapter 1 on critical reading and take notes as you reread. Jot down significant quotations or record the page numbers on which such material can be found. You may even want to use a dictionary and an annotated text to look up words and allusions you don't understand. Then use your journal to record how these terms seem to function in the work. A literature handbook such as this one can help with literary terminology.

Also check with your instructor to see if the text you are using is the standard and complete text of the work you are researching. If you are reading a work in translation, choose the translation the instructor prefers because different versions of a work may even emphasize different themes.

Many instructors also prefer one edition of a standard work to others. Always check. While some inexpensive reprints are excellent, others may contain errors, and your hard work deserves an authoritative text. For example, some editions of Crane's *The Red Badge of Cour-*

age include a short story featuring the protagonist, Henry Fleming, back home after the war. Students reading this edition may consider this story an epilogue and thus form a false impression of the tone of the novel.

USING THE LIBRARY

After carefully rereading the primary work, you will want to refer to secondary sources, which usually means using a library. Most college libraries offer orientation tours or brochures; your first step should be to become familiar with your library. Find out the library hours, the loan system, whether there is an inter-library loan system, where the card catalog or computerized catalog is, whether you can access databases, and where reference works are shelved.

Get to know the librarians by asking questions showing you have begun to think about a topic. Most reference or information librarians are well trained and willing to help student researchers, but recognize there are limits to what they can do. Do not expect them to choose or narrow a topic, to know the primary work, or to evaluate sources for you.

ENCYCLOPEDIAS

Before you start locating books and articles, you may want to do some background reading in an encyclopedia. The following specialized encyclopedias are helpful for narrowing literature topics:

> Benét, William Rose, ed. *The Reader's Encyclopedia.* 2nd ed. New York: Crowell, 1965. One-volume presentation of alphabetically listed information on literary characters, terms, authors, and books.
>
> Browning, D. C., ed. *Everyman's Dictionary of Literary Biography: English and American.* Rev. ed. London: Dent, 1958. London: Pan, 1972. One volume of minibiographies.
>
> *Cambridge History of American Literature.* Ed. William P. Trent et al. 3 vols. New York: Putnam, 1917–1922. An authoritative and informative general history of American literature in chapter form. Indexed.

Cambridge History of English Literature. Ed. A. W. Ward and A. R. Waller. 15 vols. Cambridge: Cambridge UP, 1907–32. An authoritative general history of English literature from the earliest times to the end of the nineteenth century. Chapter form. Indexed

Drabble, Margaret, ed. *The Oxford Companion to English Literature.* 5th ed. New York: Oxford UP, 1985. A one-volume, alphabetically arranged compendium of brief entries on authors, works, genres, movements, characters, literary societies, and periodicals.

Hart, James D. *The Oxford Companion to American Literature.* 5th ed. New York: Oxford UP, 1983. Coverage and format as in the *Oxford Companion to English Literature.*

Hoffman, Daniel, ed. *Harvard Guide to Contemporary American Writing.* Cambridge: Belknap, 1979. Essays providing a critical survey of American writers from 1945 through 1979.

Howatson, Margaret C., ed. *The Oxford Companion to Classical Literature.* Oxford: Oxford UP, 1989. One volume, alphabetically arranged. Covers classical literature, authors, genres, and works as well as historical, social, political, and religious backgrounds.

Spiller, Robert E., et al., eds. *Literary History of the United States.* 2 vols. 4th ed. rev. New York: Macmillan, 1974. Volume I is a literary history arranged in chapter format covering American literature from Colonial times to the present. Especially good in relating writers to their historical periods.

USING A CARD CATALOG OR COMPUTERIZED CARD FILE

If you want just to scan the available books on your topic, you will want to use the card catalog. All libraries list their book holdings three ways: by author, by title, and by subject. The quickest way to find critical or interpretative books is to look under subject headings for the author (obviously, alphabetized by last name followed by first name), and then look for the subject heading, "Criticism and Interpretation" and/or the title of the work being criticized following the author's name. (Sometimes you can start your search for criticism by checking your textbook for a bibliography on your author. Many anthologies have basic bibliographies on individual authors, and some casebooks even include reprints of articles.)

Make a list of all books that might be relevant. Be certain to copy all necessary information, especially the call number and location of the book. (Can it be found at the library you are using? In what room or on what floor? Will it need to be loaned by another library?)

INDEXES AND BIBLIOGRAPHIES

You may also want to check articles because they may be more current (it takes time to collect material for a published book); they are shorter, so you can obtain several viewpoints in the same time you could read a single book; or your topic may be so specific you won't find a whole book on it. To find articles you will want to use indexes. An *index* is a book or a set of books containing lists of articles. Some indexes such as *Reader's Guide to Periodical Literature* are general while others such as the *Literary Criticism Index* are more specialized. The following specialized indexes are particularly helpful for researching literary topics:

> *Arts & Humanities Citation Index*. Philadelphia: Institute for Scientific Information, 1978 to date. Annual cumulation. Indexes many journals in the arts and humanities including fiction, drama, and poetry.

> *Essay and General Literature Index*. New York: Wilson, 1934 to date. Semiannual. Five-year cumulations. As well as articles, this index lists chapters and parts of books, thus leading to information not easily found in the card catalog. For example, the 1980–84 volume lists under Poe and "The Fall of the House of Usher," a book entitled *Ruined Eden of the Present* (G. R. Thompson, ed.) with four articles on this short story.

> *Humanities Index*. New York: Wilson, 1974 to date. Quarterly. Annual cumulations. From 1916 to 1974 published as *Social Sciences and Humanities Index*. Indexes newspapers and magazines.

Literary Criticism Index. Comp. Alan R. Weiner and Spencer Means. Metuchen: Scarecrow, 1984. Master index to 86 multiple-author bibliographies including criticism of individual works.

Magill, Frank N. *Magill's Bibliography of Literary Criticism: Selected Sources for the Study of More Than 2,500 Outstanding Works of Western Literature*. 4 vols. Englewood Cliffs: Salem, 1979. Arranged alphabetically by author and then work. Thorough.

MLA International Bibliography of Books and Articles on the Modern Languages and Literatures. Chicago: MLA, 1921 to date. Annual. Classified listing of critical books and articles on modern languages, literature, folklore, and linguistics, arranged by forms, national literatures, periods, and authors.

Moulton, Charles Wells, ed. *Library of Literary Criticism of English and American Authors*. 8 vols. Buffalo: Moulton, 1901–1905. Comments and criticism by and about major English and American authors. Especially helpful for finding what one author wrote about another.

The New Cambridge Bibliography of English Literature. Ed. George Watson. 5 vols. Cambridge: Cambridge UP, 1969– 1977. A selective bibliography covering major authors, movements, and historical periods.

Nyren, Dorothy. *A Library of Literary Criticism: Modern American Literature*. New York: Ungar, 1964. One volume extension of the *Library of Literary Criticism of English and American Authors* into twentieth-century American authors.

Spiller, Robert E. et al., eds. *The Literary History of the United States*. 2 vols. 4th ed. rev. New York: Macmillan, 1974. Volume II is a bibliography including major American authors.

There are also many other specialized indexes and bibliographies organized by genres, periods, national literatures, or authors: for example, *The Mexican American: A Critical Guide to Research Aids* (Barbara J. Robinson and J. Cordell Robinson, Greenwich: JAW, 1980) and *Poetry Explication: A Checklist of Interpretation since 1925 of British and American Poems, Past and Present* (Joseph Marshall Kunitz and Nancy C. Martinez, 3rd ed., Boston: Hall, 1980).

USING INDEXES AND BIBLIOGRAPHIES

Indexes and bibliographies will usually be found in the reference section or room of your library; they cannot be checked out. Although most indexes and bibliographies are arranged alphabetically by author, check the front of each volume for specific instructions on use. After you find an intriguing entry on your topic, copy the information you need to find the article as well as the name, volume, and page of the index you are using (you may need to recheck your information later). Also look up any abbreviations used in the index to be certain you interpret them correctly. (You will usually find a list of abbreviations and their meanings at the beginning or end of the index.)

Once you have found a useful index, you also have an aid to narrowing your topic. How does the index subdivide information about your author or work? What are the topics of some of the articles?

Next, check with the reference librarian for information about the periodicals your library orders, the number of back issues it shelves, where they are to be found, and whether you can order copies of periodical articles your library does not have.

DATABASES

You may also be able to investigate indexes by computer. Unlike most library services which are free, you will be charged for computer searches. However, they may save you hours of library work, may include searching indexes your library does not have, and may uncover material found only in databases (for example, unpublished papers presented at conventions or conferences). Computerized databases usually correspond to printed journal indexes in format and may be searched by author, title, or subject. They may also search for other information such as specific time periods or even specific words.

You may get an immediate printout of a bibliography if the search is done *online*, or later if it is done *offline*. (Offline is cheaper.) Or you may choose to have the citations loaded directly onto your own disk from which you can later edit a bibliography.

Some databases can also provide abstracts or summaries of the cited articles (which adds to the cost but eliminates searching for and locating useless articles). Other databases will even print out entire articles. Your library may have a quick search service for you to use yourself, or you may have to make an appointment with a searcher who will discuss the topic, suggest the database(s) to use, and perform the search, a more costly procedure. Check with your librarian for available services.

When is a computerized search worth the cost? When time is limited, when the search involves two or three subject headings (for example, combining an author and subject such as "Poe" and "cryptography"), when you would like to specify a time period for resources (only criticism written since 1970, for example), when the topic is so current you must have access to unpublished material or to material too recent to be listed in printed indexes (material is listed in databases much more quickly than in printed indexes), or when the topic is too specific to be listed as a subject heading in printed indexes. (Databases include many more subject headings than printed indexes, and, as mentioned, it is also possible to program a search for specific words in titles). To research a single subject heading with no restrictions on date of publication of resource materials, you will probably still want to do a manual search.

OTHER RESEARCH RESOURCES

Remember you can also research a topic outside the library. Your instructor is a valuable resource who may be able to suggest additional readings or recommend someone for you to interview about your topic. Class discussion is another resource to consider. Quality video cassettes, films, filmstrips, or cassette lectures may add to your understanding of the subject. Most libraries or Instructional Materials Centers catalog relevant media.

PRELIMINARY OR WORKING BIBLIOGRAPHY

As you copy information on sources when you locate them in card catalogs or indexes, you are compiling a *preliminary* or *working bibliography*. You will find this bibliography easiest to work with if you list each source on a separate card and separate your cards into books and articles. As suggested, on each card you should list pertinent information such as where the book is to be found (your library or another library) and whether you will manually search for an article or if you need to order a copy. Your working bibliography will grow as your research progresses. As you scan the books and articles related to your topic, check their bibliographies and add relevant references to your bibliography.

PRELIMINARY OR WORKING OUTLINE

Now that you have an idea of the material available on your topic, try to form a rough outline of the divisions of the topic you will possibly explore. You may have found so much material you will need to narrow the topic again, or perhaps you have found very little and need to broaden your topic. Maybe you have decided to approach the topic from a slightly different perspective. In any case, sketch the outline on a card just as you did the working thesis (perhaps the same card), and begin to locate your sources. Again, expect this working outline to expand and change as your investigation continues. Note the following working outline and revised preliminary thesis:

Working thesis: In "The Tell-Tale Heart," Poe's narrator carefully plans the murder of the old man with the "evil eye" because the old man represents his evil side.

    I. Careful planning of the murder

        A. Preplanning

        B. Seven days

        C. Slow-motion action

    II. The evil eye

        A. Represents the ego

        B. Inevitable destruction

    III. The burial

        A. Actual

        B. Psychological

    IV. The arousal of guilt

        A. Old man resurrects?

        B. Necessary confession

LOCATING, READING, AND EVALUATING SOURCES

Start by examining either the books or the articles. Many instructors recommend reading for an overview by first scanning a book by a reputable critic. How do you determine if a critic is reputable? You might examine his or her credentials, often mentioned on the book jacket, or you might read a review of the book. (Two useful reference books are *Book Review Digest* [New York: Wilson, 1905 to date] and *Book Review Index* [Detroit: Gale, 1965 to date]. The first contains summaries of selected reviews both favorable and negative and is published monthly with annual cumulations. Look in the volumes for the year of publication of the book and the year after. The *Index* includes more references but does not summarize reviews.) You will also want to check the book's publication date because critical studies often begin with a review of past criticism, so a recent book may be most helpful.

To scan a book effectively, find the thesis of the work in the preface or foreword and use the table of contents and the index to check what material is included in the book. Skim the work to examine the development of the argument and type of evidence before taking notes.

NOTE-TAKING

First, make a bibliography card for each source you locate (or add to the card you have already written for the preliminary bibliography) — even if it does not immediately seem useful. (You may need to backtrack later; the information will save your having to relocate your sources.) On the card, note the possible usefulness, the call number, and where the source may be obtained, as well as necessary information for your final bibliography or works cited page (author and/or editor, title, edition or volume, place of publication, publisher, date, and page numbers if an article). Note the following sample bibliography card:

Hoffman, Daniel.   813.39

Poe Poe Poe Poe Poe Poe Poe   HOF

N.Y.: Random, 1972.

Great book! Pages 221-227 very helpful for my topic because he brings in other Poe stories, talks about symbols, and about the conscience of the narrator.

When you have located, read, and evaluated the reliability and usefulness of the sources for your topic, you will want to start taking notes. Actual note-taking falls into three general categories: quoting directly, paraphrasing, and summarizing. In each case, the note card should be labeled with a brief description of the contents of the card ("Definition of Romanticism," "Initial Public Response to Wordsworth's *The Prelude*"), the last name of the author, an abbreviation of the title of the work if you will use more than one work by the same author, and the page number(s) of the information.

You will first want to record on note cards direct quotations from the primary work that support or illustrate the assertions you wish to make. You may also wish to use direct quotations from secondary sources when you find you cannot possibly do justice to material by paraphrasing or summarizing. However, be sparing with your use of these quotations. Remember, this is your paper; instructors will not be happy with a series of direct quotations loosely strung together by your brief comments.

USE QUOTATION MARKS ON YOUR CARD AND TRANSCRIBE THE MATERIAL EXACTLY AS IT IS WRITTEN. If lines of poetry have unusual spacing or spatial arrangements, copy them as exactly as possible. If a direct quotation covers more than one page, be certain to indicate with a slash (/) exactly where the page break occurs. When you have finished the transcription, double-check it against the original and place a check mark at the end of the quotation to verify you have done so. You may even want to circle the quotation marks so you won't overlook them later and end up plagiarizing the source. Examine the following sample note card:

> Hoffman 223-4   "the evil eye"
>
>   In the story it is always just
> one eye: " Come to think of it, it is
> always referred / to in the singular,
> as though he had but one. An old
> man with one all-seeing eye, an Evil
> Eye — " ✓

If you wish to omit material from the original source (and your instructor allows this practice — some do not), be fair to the original author. (Despite the common practice in advertisements that quote reviews, it is patently unfair to distort a criticism to make it appear to support your point.) You may omit words, phrases, sentences, or paragraphs by using *ellipsis points* (spaced periods) to indicate the omitted material. (See the next chapter for examples of ellipsis.)

Paraphrase the original when you want to use most of the material, but you want to make it yours by restating it. (Of course you still give the original author credit for the ideas in the final paper. Carefully examine the next section on plagiarism.)

Summarize original material when you want general ideas from a large amount of material (perhaps chapters in a book). Summary note cards may have more general page references (for example, 96–110), especially if your summary rearranges the original material considerably.

Plagiarism

In 1987 Delaware Senator Joe Biden did irreparable harm to his presidential campaign but a great service to many college students by making the issue of plagiarism as clear as possible in definition and consequence. As you recall, some of the most stirring elements from his campaign rhetoric were revealed to be exact quotations from other politicians. This would have been acceptable had he given the original speakers credit, but he did not. *Plagiarism* — using another person's ideas or words without acknowledgement — is stealing. It may be intellectual robbery, but it is robbery all the same.

Although student plagiarism may often be unintentional, it is not taken lightly by instructors. Expulsion, failing a class, or, at the very least, failing a paper may be the consequence of even inadvertent "borrowing." Prevent plagiarism when quoting directly by quoting exactly and giving full credit to the original author. Changing a word or a phrase in material and calling this "paraphrasing" is still plagiarism because you are virtually quoting.

Suppose, for example, you are writing a research paper on Cooper's novel *The Deerslayer*, and you have discovered Samuel Clemen's delightful essay "Fenimore Cooper's Literary Offenses." Here is a passage from the essay, quoted exactly, using the MLA system of parenthetical documentation (explained in the next chapter). Because the quotation is longer than four lines, it is indented and set off from the text, so it needs no quotation marks.

> Cooper was certainly not a master in the
> construction of dialogue. Inaccurate
> observation defeated him here as it defeated
> him in so many other enterprises of his. He even
> failed to notice that the man who talks corrupt
> English six days in the week must and will talk
> it on the seventh, and can't help himself. In
> the <u>Deerslayer</u> story he lets Deerslayer talk the
> showiest kind of book-talk sometimes, and at
> other times the basest of base dialects.
> (Clemens 75)

Here is another quotation from the same essay:

> Cooper's word sense was singularly dull.
> When a person has a poor ear for music he will
> flat and sharp right along without knowing it.
> He keeps near the tune, but it is <u>not</u> the tune.
> When a person has a poor ear for words, the
> result is a literary flatting and sharping;
> you perceive that he doesn't <u>say</u> it. This is
> Cooper. He was not a word-musician. His ear
> was satisfied with the <u>approximate</u> word.
> (Clemens 76)

The following transcriptions would be plagiarism even though the writer acknowledges Clemens as the author because they are really quotations with slight rearrangement rather than paraphrases:

Cooper was certainly not a master in the construction of dialogue and his word sense was singularly dull (Clemens 75-6).

Cooper was not a master of dialogue (Clemens 75).

Researching a Topic

Cooper was not a word—musician (Clemens 76).

Sometimes Deerslayer talks the showiest kind of book—talk and sometimes the basest of dialects (Clemens 75).

To make such transcriptions acceptable, quote directly:

Clemens has pointed out that "Cooper was certainly not a master in the construction of dialogue" (75).

Clemens says that Cooper "lets Deerslayer talk the showiest kind of book—talk sometimes, and at other times the basest of . . . dialects" (75).

Or restate in your own words and acknowledge the original author:

Clemens has previously pointed out that Cooper has no sense for the sound of words (76).

Or combine paraphrase and direct quotation:

Cooper does not have an ear for words and is often "satisfied with the approximate word" (Clemens 76).

One way of preventing plagiarism of paraphrased material is to read carefully the material you are going to paraphrase and then close the work and put it aside. While the content, but not the exact wording, is still fresh in mind, write your note card. After paraphrasing the original, recheck to make certain you have not inadvertently quoted exactly and to verify you have been faithful to the intent of the author.

When you write a summary note card, be certain to give credit to the author; even though you have made the material your own, the author must be given credit for the original ideas. Even if all you borrow from an author is an outline or division of a subject or a suggested approach to the topic, you must give credit.

Finally, minimize your use of the photocopy machine. When time is short, it is tempting to copy whole articles and passages rather than reading, digesting, and then summarizing or paraphrasing the material onto note cards. You may tell yourself that you will complete the process later, but when time continues to be short, you end up cutting and pasting the photocopies into a semblance of a paper. Even if you manage to give full credit for these sources in the finished paper and so avoid plagiarism, such a paper will not be successful because it will not be your work. (Note: Some instructors may require that you turn in photocopies of all of your source material so that they can check your use. This is an entirely different matter.)

COMPLETING THE RESEARCH PROCESS

Your project may end here if researching a literary topic was its sole aim. Some instructors may require only an annotated bibliography on a specific subject, and you now have the material to write one. Other instructors may want an oral presentation of your research. (But it is still a good idea to have made detailed note cards because you may be called upon to verify statements or to write up a brief synopsis after delivering your report.) If, however, like the student we have been following, you have been assigned a formal research paper, read the next chapter on writing a literary research paper.

CHAPTER REVIEW

Investigating issues and making connections in literary works can increase your enjoyment of those works. Steps in the research process include choosing and narrowing a topic; reading and rereading the primary work; using library resources including the card catalog, indexes, bibliographies, and databases; using other media resources; compiling a working bibliography; writing a preliminary outline; locating, reading, and evaluating secondary sources; and taking notes.

CHAPTER 13

Writing and Documenting a Research Paper on Literature

*A*s noted at the end of the previous chapter, sometimes you need only research a topic as a project in a literature class, but the student we have been following has been assigned a formal research paper for her American literature class. This chapter will examine her progress as, having finished her library research, she organizes her note cards into a probable order for a rough draft and revises her preliminary outline and working thesis. Then she writes a rough draft, submits it to her instructor for suggested revisions, prepares a "Works Cited" page, and revises and submits a final draft. As you recall from the previous chapter, she is investigating why the narrator of Poe's "The Tell-Tale Heart," who has carefully planned a murder, reveals himself to the police.

ORGANIZING NOTE CARDS AND REVISING THE OUTLINE

She begins by sorting through her note cards to see whether she has found information on all the topics her preliminary outline covers and whether she has located additional information which now needs to be incorporated into the outline. Remember, a preliminary outline is just that — preliminary and tentative. She revises her outline to reflect a chunk of new material on the psychological symbolism of the two characters and even decides to begin her rough draft with this section. Similarly, you will want to include new material and findings in your outline and delete items for which you have insufficient evidence. After sorting note cards by topic, arrange them in the most effective order, grouping similar topics, perhaps saving your strongest assertions for last. Notice how the student's preliminary outline has grown and changed.

Preliminary outline

    I. Careful planning of the murder

       A. Preplanning

       B. Seven days

       C. Slow-motion action

   II. The evil eye

       A. Represents the ego

       B. Inevitable destruction

  III. The burial

       A. Actual

       B. Psychological

   IV. The arousal of guilt

       A. Old man resurrects?

       B. Necessary confession

Revised outline

    I. Symbolism of the characters

       A. Narrator-id

       B. Old man

          1. Eye-ego

          2. Heart-superego

   II. Planning the murder

       A. Preplanning

       B. Spontaneous

  III. Ingenious burial

       A. Concealing the corpse

       B. No evidence

Writing a Research Paper

```
IV. Haunting of the heart
    A. Narrator's fear
    B. Noise of the heart
    C. Confession
```

REVISING THE THESIS

Once you have organized your note cards and revised your outline, write the strongest assertion you can make about your assembled evidence. Although your preliminary thesis may have been a question, you have now answered the question by your research, so the revised thesis can be a statement rather than a question. The student's preliminary thesis read as follows:

```
Why does the narrator plan the murder of the old man so
carefully, then reveal the deed to the police?
```

She revised this preliminary thesis once:

```
In "The Tell-Tale Heart," Poe's narrator carefully plans the
murder of the old man with the "evil eye" because the old man
represents his evil side.
```

But she still didn't feel that she had stated her assertion clearly, so she revised again:

```
In "The Tell-Tale Heart," Poe's narrator carefully plans the
murder of the old man with the "evil eye," attempting to bury
his conscience, which eventually overpowers the irrational
side of his brain with guilt.
```

WRITING THE ROUGH DRAFT TITLE

Selecting a title helps keep you on track as you write your rough draft. The title should relate to your thesis, stimulate interest in your topic, be relatively short (but more than a single word), and reflect the tone of your paper. Since our student knows that her audience — her instructor and her classmates — also appreciates originality and creativity, she changes the simple "The Tell-Tale Heart" she has been using as a working title to "The Heart Tells All."

WRITING THE ROUGH DRAFT INTRODUCTION

The introduction to a research paper prepares the audience for the material to follow by engaging their attention and interest, stating the point or thesis of the paper, and establishing a tone. It could include one or more of the following:

1. a brief summary of the work being analyzed or even a copy of the work if it is short
2. the reason a particular topic is being investigated (for example, no one you've read seems to have noticed what to you is an interesting point, or perhaps you disagree with a common interpretation)
3. a statement of the limits of the study (just one short story or an author's earliest works only)

Because she knows her audience is quite familiar with the short story she has chosen (it had been required class reading), she introduces her rough draft with a dramatic quotation from the story to engage the reader's attention. (Note: This order implies that introductions are written first, but as you know, writing does not always progress in a linear fashion. Many students write introductions last. If you are having problems with "first things first," begin by writing the section of your paper you feel most comfortable with. Perhaps you will even choose to write your conclusion first so you know where your paper is heading.)

WRITING THE ROUGH DRAFT BODY

Once you have organized your cards, written an outline, formed a good thesis, and (possibly) sketched out the introduction, plunge into the body of the paper. Using a word processor makes drafting much easier because you can shift material around, add, and delete as you go. If you have not yet joined the computer age, leave lots of room in the margins of each page, double-space or skip lines, and write on only one side of the paper to make revision easier. (You may eventually cut your pages apart and reorder them.)

Writing a Research Paper

Work with one group of note cards at a time, following your outline if possible. For each generalization, try to provide at least one concrete example — facts, details, summaries, paraphrases, or quotations from both primary and secondary sources. If you cannot support a point, either omit it or do some additional research. Keep your thesis in mind as you write. Try to maintain a consistent tone, neither overly formal nor excessively chatty. Remember, you are sharing information with an informed and interested audience.

One difficulty of drafting from note cards is a tendency to present chunks of material without adequate connections. As you move from one aspect of your topic to another, provide transitions to guide your audience. Show them how the second point is related to the third point and how both lead to the fourth and final point.

Introduce all borrowed material — quotations, summaries, and paraphrases. Simply to state that "Hoffman says" is not sufficiently helpful. It's usually better to write that "Hoffman agrees with this point when he says that. . . ." Depending on the audience and topic, you may even need to give the credentials of your sources, "noted critic of American literature X," or "respected French critic Y" or "Z, leading proponent of the psychoanalytical interpretation." Similarly, if you quote the primary work, don't just insert the quotation; explain what the quotation illustrates or proves. Do not string together long series of quotations or paraphrases with brief intervening comments. Use borrowed material for support and illustration, not padding.

Incorporating Quotations

The previous chapter contains a brief discussion of quoting source material exactly. Now let's examine in more detail incorporating quotations, omitting material from quotations, commenting on quotations, and interpolating comments or emphasis into quotations, using as an example the following paragraph from "The Tell-Tale Heart":

```
It is impossible to say how first the idea
entered my brain; but once conceived, it haunted me
day and night. Object there was none. Passion there
was none. I loved the old man. He had never wronged
me. He had never given me insult. For his gold I had
no desire. I think it was his eye! yes, it was this!
One of his eyes resembled that of a vulture—a pale
```

```
blue eye, with a film over it. Whenever it fell upon

me, my blood ran cold; and so by degrees—very

gradually—I made up my mind to take the life of the

old man, and thus rid myself of the eye for

ever. (Poe 1598)
```

Because the quotation is longer than four typed lines, it is indented ten spaces from the left margin and double-spaced exactly as the rest of the paper. Since the indention indicates an exact quotation, using quotation marks is unnecessary. Close the quotation with the final punctuation mark, skip two spaces, and then cite the documentation. (The MLA system of documentation, discussed in the next section, uses parenthetical references to the work being cited rather than footnotes. "Poe" is the author of the quotation and "1598" refers to the page on which the quotation will be found.)

Using part of this quotation to illustrate a point, you could write:

```
The mad narrator finally decides to kill the old man because he

cannot bear the "evil eye": "One of his eyes resembled that of

a vulture—a pale blue eye, with a film over it" (Poe 1598).
```

Quotations can go at the beginning, end, or middle of your own sentences or be divided by your words:

```
Poe's narrator tells us that the old man's eye makes his

"blood" run "cold," so he finally decides to get rid "of the

eye for ever" (1598).
```

(Since it is clear in this example that Poe is the author of the quoted material, it is unnecessary to repeat his name in the parenthetical documentation.)

To quote this paragraph and omit part of a sentence, use three spaced dots (ellipsis):

```
The narrator is obsessed by the idea of murdering the old man:

"It is impossible to say how first the idea entered my brain;

but . . . it haunted me day and night" (Poe 1598).
```

To quote while omitting more than a sentence of intervening material, use a period and three spaced dots:

The narrator does not explain his motivation: "It is impossible

to say how first the idea entered my brain, but. . . . I made

up my mind to take the life of the old man, and thus rid myself

of the eye for ever" (Poe 1598).

In the short quotation examples above, punctuation marks follow the parenthetical documentation. However, if a quotation ends with a question mark or an exclamation point, include the mark as part of the quotation and then close the documentation with a period as usual:

The old man's eye powerfully affects the narrator: "I think it

was his eye! yes, it was this!" (Poe 1598).

To indicate that a mistake in the text is original and not your error, use the term *sic* (thus or so) in brackets immediately after the error:

One of the first literary descriptions of the warfare between

settlers and Indians is A Narrative of the Captivity and

Restauration [sic] of Mrs. Mary Rowlandson.

To interject a comment into a quotation or to emphasize a word or phrase not emphasized in the original, indicate you have done so, either in *parentheses after* the quotation or in *brackets within* the quotation:

The old man's eye powerfully affects the narrator: "I think it

was his eye!" (Poe 1598; emphasis added).

or

The old man's eye powerfully affects the narrator: "I think it

was his eye! [italics mine] yes, it was this!" (Poe 1598).

To quote a brief passage which includes a direct quotation, set off the quotation within the quotation with single quotation marks:

Fortunato refers to the Masonic order in Poe's "The Cask

of Amontillado" in the following passage: "He laughed and

```
threw the bottle upwards with a gesticulation I did not
understand. . . . 'You do not comprehend?' he said. . . .
'Then you are not of the brotherhood . . . of the masons'"
(1621).
```

To quote more than three lines of poetry, indent as you would for a prose quotation of more than four lines, imitating the original spatial arrangement as closely as possible. Poetry is usually documented by line numbers.

```
The third stanza from Poe's "To Helen" contains a powerful
image:

        Lo! in yon brilliant window-niche
            How statue-like I see thee stand,
            Thy agate lamp within thy hand!
        Ah, Psyche, from the regions which
            Are Holy-Land. (11-15)
```

To omit one or more lines from an indented poetry quotation, use a line of spaced dots that equals the length of the poetic line:

```
The speaker of Poe's "To Helen" compares Helen to Psyche:

        Lo! in yon brilliant window-niche
            . . . . . . . . . . . . . . . .
        Ah, Psyche, from the regions which
            Are Holy-Land. (11, 14-15)
```

Incorporate fewer than three lines of verse in your text by enclosing in quotation marks; use a slash (/) with a space before and after to indicate the divisions between lines; retain the original punctuation and capitalization:

```
If "Psyche" in Poe's "To Helen" is an allusion to Helen, then
she is from sacred Greece, "the regions which / Are Holy-Land"
(14-5).
```

Writing a Research Paper

We have dealt at length on incorporating quotations because quoting the primary work selectively illustrates your points, while quoting secondary sources provides support for your opinions. However, you should use all quotations judiciously and integrate them smoothly into your paper. The bulk of the paper will not be quotations but rather a thoughtful presentation of the opinions you have formed as a result of your research.

Writing the Rough Draft Body — In-Text Citation

In 1984 the Modern Language Association simplified the documentation of source materials in student research papers and scholarly works by replacing footnotes or endnotes (except explanatory ones) with brief parenthetical citations within the text referring the reader to an alphabetical bibliography or "Works Cited" page at the end of the paper. This system is usually called "in-text citation" or "parenthetical documentation." (For a full treatment of this method, see the *MLA Handbook for Writers of Research Papers* [Eds. Joseph Gibaldi and Walter S. Achert. 2nd ed., New York: MLA, 1984; 3rd ed. New York: MLA, 1988.] The following comments are based on this invaluable handbook.)

As we have seen, in-text citation refers the reader to a bibliography, most often by parenthetically listing the author's last name and the page number on which the material will be found. Place the parenthetical reference as close as possible to the material it documents but also where a pause would naturally occur (often at the end of the sentence). As noted earlier, a parenthetical reference follows the final quotation mark but precedes the final mark of punctuation unless the material documented is set off from the text — then it follows the concluding mark of punctuation by two spaces.

If the bibliography lists more than one work by the same author, you will have to include an abbreviation of the title of the work being cited to distinguish among the works:

(Poe, "Tell-Tale" 1598)

If a work has no author, use the first important word in the title (the word by which it will be alphabetized in the bibliography) and the page number:

("Review" 63)

If you are using more than one volume of a work, include the volume number after the author's name, followed by a colon and the page number in the parenthetical documentation:

```
(Daiches 2:36)
```

To quote a classic verse play or poem, omit the page number and instead cite the division (or act) followed by a period and the line numbers:

```
(Sir Gawain 2.552)
```

To quote a classic prose work available in many editions, it is helpful to add, to the page number of the edition used, additional information that would help the reader locate the passage in another edition:

```
(Twain, Huck Finn 189; ch. 8)
```

Finally, as mentioned earlier, documentation information included in the text itself is not repeated in the parenthetical reference:

```
Authors Rubin and McNeil define anxiety as "a fear that seems
unjustified by any objective threat or danger" (336).
```

Writing the Rough Draft — Using Content Notes

Even when using in-text citations, you may wish to use footnotes or endnotes for explanatory material that cannot be accommodated in your text or to document bibliographic references too bulky or too complicated to be included in parentheses in the text. Chronological superscript Arabic numerals refer readers to footnotes or to endnotes. Do not overdo this option.

WRITING THE ROUGH DRAFT CONCLUSION

An effective conclusion restates or reaffirms, without repeating, your thesis. You may want to summarize your key points or present a logical conclusion drawn from the key points, or you may conclude with a dramatic quotation from either the primary source or a secondary source. The conclusion is not the place to present new or contradictory information. Do not repeat the introduction or the thesis verbatim, and maintain a tone consistent with the tone of the rest of your paper

REVISING THE ROUGH DRAFT

After you have written the rough draft, set it aside for a few days (or at least overnight) and distance yourself from it. Then reread it, silently or aloud, have a classmate read it, or submit it to your instructor for evaluation. When planning your revision, think large — content, organization, and tone — and think small — sentence structure, diction, and mechanics. Check at least the following areas:

1. Outline — Does the outline accurately reflect the divisions of the paper? If it is a topic outline, are all the topics nouns or noun phrases? If it is a sentence outline, are all the sentences complete?
2. Thesis — Is it narrow and specific or too broad or general?
3. Development — Is there appropriate development to support each point you make?
4. Tone — Is it effective, appropriate, and consistent?
5. Organization — Is the strategy of the paper (the arrangement of your points) effective and logical?
6. Coherence — Are there adequate transitions to move the audience smoothly from point to point?
7. Diction — Are all words, especially literary terminology, used correctly?
8. Sentence structure — Are there any ungrammatical constructions? Is the sentence structure monotonous? Is the paper too wordy?
9. Documentation — Are all borrowed ideas documented? Has correct in–text citation been used? Are all citations accurate?

Here is the rough draft of the student paper we have been following with her instructor's suggestions for revision. Notice that she has revised her title once again, and rewritten her topic outline as a sentence outline because her instructor requires a sentence outline with the final paper.

The Conscience Tells All

Thesis: In the "Tell-Tale Heart," Poe's

narrator carefully plans the murder of the

check use of semicolon

old man with the "evil Eye"; attempting

ref.?   *Do you mean "Conscience" or "conscious"?*

to bury his conscious, <u>which</u> eventually

overpowers the irrational side of the brain   *Thesis is*

a bit awkward and

with guilt.   *wordy — revise.*

I.   The Characters are symbolic of the three

no cap

     parts of the brain.

    A. The Narrator symbolizes the id.

       1. The narrator acts irrational and

          insane.

wordy - reduce

       2. He fears the evil eye because the

          heart fills him with guilt when he

          hears the heart's pounding.

both

    B. The old man symbolizes the ego and

      the superego.

       1. The eye (ego) mediates between the

          narrator and the heart.

          a. The eye reflects the soul.

Writing a Research Paper

b. The "Evil _Eye_" is a pun on *cap here is a stylistic choice*

the "Evil I"

2. The heart (superego) represents

the conscious. *check meaning*

a. The conscious releases guilt

when the id attacks.

b. The Tell-Tale heart forces the *no cap— use quotation marks to set it off*

narrator to tell society the

truth.

II. The narrator carefully plans the

psychological murder.

A. He takes seven days until he murders

the old man. *use the infinitive*

1. He slows down time in order to

perform perfectly.

2. The(description of)preplanning is ○

explicitly described.

Transition ⋀ B. The actual murder is spontaneous.

1. He carries no murder weapon.

The 2. ⋀Murder occurs at midnight.

Blanca, develop this part. Explore and research possible symbols here—see Weber and Hoffman

III. The (N)arrator ingeniously prepares the

burial.

    A. The corpse is concealed beneath the

       floor.

       1. The narrator dismembers the body

          to make sure that it will not

          resurrect.

       2. The burial temporarily stops the

          sound of the pounding heart.

    B. No visible evidence remains. *(vague)*

       1. The narrator believes society will

          never know the truth.

       2. The invisible heart is the only

          remaining evidence.

IV. The old man's heart haunts the narrator.

    (A.) The old man does not resurrect.

no "A" without a "B"

       1. The narrator hears the pounding

          heart as it sounds louder and

          louder.

       2. The narrator fears the heart,

          because the eye (ego) does not

mediate between the himself (id)

and the heart (superego).

3. The heart (conscious) haunts the

    irrational side and conquers it

    with guilt, forcing the narrator

    (Poe) to admit his evil to

    society.

"True!—nervous—very dreadfully nervous

I had been and am; but why will you say that

I am mad?" (Poe 1598) Madness! Watch out!

Engaging introduction!

We know that we will be placed in a strange,

foreign place—a madman's brain. In the *check title*

"Tell-Tale Heart," Poe's narrator carefully

plans the murder of the old man with the

"evil Eye," attempting to bury his own

conscious, which eventually overpowers the

irrational side of the brain with guilt.

I believe the story represents Poe's inner

struggle with his Oedipus complex. Since he

cannot control his impulse, he tries to

suppress his conscious in order to relieve

himself of anxiety.

Reword to clear up confusion on use of words "conscious/conscience" and omit personal pronouns. Audience assumes this is your belief unless you give another source for the idea.

use [ ] for your inserts rather than ( )

Fagin states, "He (Poe) was in nearly

everything he wrote his own protagonist: he

describes himself, reveals acuteness, his

aristocratic and aesthetic sensibilities, his

ideal steadfastness and actual vulnerability,

No need to repeat authors name if used in text.

and his pale feverish dreams" (Fagin, 191).

Poe unconsciously wrote about the id, ego,

Introduce your sources to your audience — "noted critic N.B. Fagin."

are you sure this is exact wording?

and superego before they were defined by

Sigmund Freud. He ingeniously placed these

three elements in a narrative to describe,

not only his troubles, but everyone's

lifelong struggles. Hoffman agrees:

". . . the terrible war of superego upon the

id, the endless battle between conscience and

impulse, the unsleeping enmity of the self

and his Imp of the Perverse—these struggles

are enacted and reenacted in Poe's work, but

yes!

and good support but try to paraphrase

always in disguise ∧ (221).

close quotation before documentation

dgl mod (In order to comprehend this story,)

Sigmund Freud's psychoanalytic theory should

be explained. Rubin and McNeil stated:

Use present tense

Freud believed that instinctual

biological urges, primarily sexual

and aggressive forces motivate every

aspect of a person's behavior.

People are merely creatures who are

perpetually at war with themselves.

A major emphasis was placed on early

childhood which determined the adult

behavior. Freud divided the human

personality into three interrelated

parts. The id remains an unchanging,

powerful, active force throughout

life, but its insistent demands are

tempered by the ego. The actions of

the id usually remain unconscious and

out of our awareness.

The ego moderates and restrains

the id by requiring it to seek

gratification of impulses within

realistic and socially acceptable

bounds. . . . Unlike the id,

You have combined paraphrasing and direct quotation here—indicate which is which and break up this too-long citation by summarizing and condensing the material.

most of the ego's actions are

conscious. . . .

The superego is the force within

the ideals of parents and society.

The superego is the moral part of the

personality—similar to what most

people call "conscience.". . .

Further, the superego limits the

sexual and aggressive impulses of the

id. . . . In this three-part

structure, the ego mediates between

the impulses of the id and the

controls of the superego. (286)

In "The Tell—Tale Heart" the narrator *Freud these*

represents the id. The insane represents an *called parts of the*

entire side of the brain which holds the most *personality rather than*

power. The old man represents the other side *the brain*

of the brain which is divided in two. Its

two elements work coherently against the id.

The eye (ego) mediates between the id and

superego. The heart (superego) releases guilt

when the ego transmits a message of the id's

wrongdoing. Weber believes this to be an

inner struggle of Oedipal feelings (93),

Maybe, the irrational sensation is the

Oedipal feeling for his dead mother which

he can not control. He wants to kill the *Who? narrator or Poe?*

"Evil Eye" because it watches over him. *Integrate*

". . . His Eye becomes the all-seeing *quotation*

surveillance of the child by the father" *with your thoughts*

(Hoffman 223). The irrational man does not

want the "eye" to tell his "heart" that he *yes!*

has these Oedipal temptations. He fears the

pounding of the heart because it fills him

with guilt. Guilt will force him to tell

society the truth. Therefore, he attempts to

conceal his troubles and tries to convince

himself that he is a *sp.* genious. Yet, we know

that he is mad.

The narrator stresses his madness. He *Explain this apparent contradiction— sentence combining might make the point clear*

repeatedly states his sagacity. Yet, he

states that he had a disease that sharpened

[handwritten margin note: stay in present tense for summary]

[handwritten margin note: not ‖]

his senses. He _heard_ all things in the heaven

and earth˅ and (things ⁰in) hell. "How, then,

am I mad?" (Poe 1598). Hoffman states:

[handwritten margin note: Indent quotations over 4 lines long]

[handwritten margin note, left side: Avoid stringing together two quotations without commentary]

"When a narrator commences in this vein,

we know him to be mad already. But we also

know his author to be sane. For with such

precision to portray the methodicalness of a

madman is the work not of a madman, but of

a man who truly understands what it is to

be mad. Artistic control is the warrant of

auctorial sanity" (222).

The mad narrator finally decides to kill

the old man. He _could_ not bear the "evil   *t*

Eye." "One of his eyes resembled that of a

vulture—a pale blue eye, with a film over it"

[handwritten margin note, left side: Good observation]

(Poe 1598). It is said that the eye is the

reflection of the soul. Could it be that the

narrator _did_ not want to see the reflection of   *t*

his evil soul? "Whenever it fell upon me,

my blood ran cold; and so by degrees—very

gradually—I made up my mind to take the life

Writing a Research Paper

of the old man, and thus rid myself of the

eye forever" (Poe 1598).

The narrator carefully planned the ⨏

murder of the old man. "It took me an hour

to place my whole head within the opening so

far that I could see him as he lay upon his

bed" (1599). He repeated this for seven 𝓉

nights at midnight. Finally, "upon the *why midnight?*

eighth night . . . a single dim ray fell *Could be a*

upon the vulture eye" (1599). It was time to *powerful symbol?*

attack. Suddenly he heard the old man's heart *Can you develop?*

which increased his fury. Davidson calls the

narrator a "god-player," who makes "the

mistake of thinking it was an eye which was

so vexatious; all the while it was a sound,

the beating of the old man's heart" (190).

The eye was merely the messenger of

information, transmitting everything it saw.

Weber claims, ". . . the murderer hears the

tick-tock of the 'tell-tale heart,' which at

length becomes the 'hellish tattoo' ('louder—

louder') and eventuates in cries which, as

usual, can be recognized as the chimes of the

clock'' (qtd. in Regan 93). He became very *List the Weber essay separately.*

nervous as the pounding increased. In a

matter of minutes, the murder had been *Why is the murder weapon a bed*

committed. He jumped and killed him with *(or mattress)? This*

the (bed) *may be another symbol that could add to your interpretation*

     "And now a new anxiety seized me—the

sound would be heard by a neighbor!" (Poe *If this is a direct quote, use quotation marks*

1600). Rubin and McNeil define anxiety as a

fear that seems unjustified by any objective

threat or danger (290). In order to relieve

this anxiety," the ego must use a maneuver *a* *Blanca, your paraphrase is too close to the original quotation. make this a direct quotation to avoid plagiarism.*

called defense mechanisms. Repression is the *a*

mechanism that excludes unacceptable

unconscious impulses from the conscious" *ww*

(290). In this case, the narrator had been

battling within himself. Since he could not

bury his temptations, he had to hide it from *ref?*

his conscious. "I placed my hand upon the

heart and held it there many minutes. There

sp.

was no puslation. He was stone dead. His eye

would trouble me no more" (Poe 1600).

Blanca, react to this statement. analyze and interpret what has happened here. Explain the effect of the murder on the murderer.

The narrator continues to stress his

sanity as he describes the precautions taken

for the concealment of the body. "The night

waned, and I worked on hastily, but in

silence" (Poe 1600). Notice, he does not

hear the beating of the heart. The corpse had

been "dismembered" and placed under "three

planks."

what do you think might be the significance of the three planks?

The clock struck four—"still dark as

midnight," when a knocking was heard at the

door. The narrator began feeling the

conscious arising as he opened the door with

a "light heart"—"For what had I now to

fear?" (1600). He attempts to convince

himself that his conscious is buried deeply

beneath him. No guilt will be seen by the

three police officers (society). He feels

incarcerated by society because he cannot

tell them the truth. They will not understand

his Oedipus complex; therefore, guilt must

not show through. "I was singularly at ease"

(1600). He had no traces of consciousness *}* awkward—
reword

and finally thought that he had triumphed.

trans.
needed Soon, he grew pale and uncomfortable—

the noise grew "louder and louder." (As he

reword
became frightened with guilt,) he grew

nervous, fearing that the truth might slip

out. "It was a low, dull, quick sound—much a

sound as a watch makes when enveloped in

cotton" (1601). The familiar sound of the

clock? No! It was the sound of the "tell-

tale heart." It is being constrained but
diction
wants (to burst the secret out.) The heart will

succeed! "It grew louder, louder—louder!"

or
the (1601). The guilty conscience is haunting him
murder?
with the guilt of his Oedipus complex. His

heart finally forces him to admit the deed.

"'Villains!' I shrieked, 'dissemble no more!

Writing a Research Paper

I admit the deed—tear up the planks!—here,

here!—it is the beating of the hideous

heart!'" (1601). He finally gave up and told

society the truth. He felt that he must

"scream or die"! Typical of Poe—always

escaping reality.

In fact, Poe was an outcast from

society. Freud believed that "failure to   *Work on this ¶—*

resolve the Oedipus conflict means growing up.   *incoherent—*

with an intense fear that a powerful and   *points are unrelated*

jealous father might punish the boy for his

feelings toward his mother" (Rubin and

McNeil 289). Marie Bonaparte believes that

"Poe was a potential sado-necrophilist

and all of his work shows it" (qtd. in

Symons 118).

In the "Tell-Tale Heart", Poe pieces

the puzzle together. He feels society with

its
their "hypocritical smiles" know of his   *agr*

Oedipal complex. Yet, they pretend (of not   *agr*

reword
knowing.) Poe tries to hide this evil, but his

> w w
> <u>conscious</u> forces him to tell the truth. His
>
> w w
> <u>conscious</u> finally conquers the id with guilt.
>
> The secret is out. The "Tell-tale Heart"
> ✗ <u>said</u> it all!

I like the way you used your reading in psychology to help you analyze this story. You may have overlooked some symbols—I've marked a few places where a little more exploration may help you develop your interpretation. You may think of others. I look forward to reading your final paper.

Note: Ordinarily a rough draft would also include a bibliography, but since preparing the bibliography is not discussed until the next section, the rough draft bibliography has been omitted. You will find one at the end of the final draft.

PREPARING THE BIBLIOGRAPHY

After you have revised the rough draft and are certain of the works referred to, you should prepare the bibliography or list of works cited. (Title this section "Works Cited" if you list only those works you actually cite in the paper; title it "Bibliography" or "Works Consulted" if you also include those works you have read in preparation for the paper but have not actually cited in your paper.) Start by alphabetizing your note cards; then follow a guide for proper format. The examples below follow the 1988 *MLA Handbook* and provide a brief reference for the most commonly used research sources. Note the following general conventions:

1. Page numbers are not indicated with "p." or "pp."
2. Line numbers are not indicated with "l." or "ll."
3. The publisher's name is shortened to the first important word.
4. There is no comma after a journal title.

Writing a Research Paper

Books

One Author

Davidson, Edward H. Poe: A Critical Study. Cambridge: Belknap,
    1976.

Two or Three Authors

Rubin, Zick, and Elton B. McNeil. Psychology: Being Human. New
    York: Harper, 1985.

More Than Three Authors

Guerin, Wilfred L., et al. A Handbook of Critical Approaches to
    Literature. 2nd ed. New York: Harper, 1979.

Anonymous

Beowulf and The Fight at Fennsburg. Ed. Fr. Klaeber. 3rd ed.
    Boston: Heath, 1950.

[List and alphabetize by title.]

More Than One Volume

Fairchild, Hoxie Neale. Religious Trends in English Poetry. 6
    vols. New York: Columbia UP, 1939–1968.

Editor

Watson, George, ed. The New Cambridge Bibliography of English
    Literature. 5 vols. Cambridge: Cambridge UP, 1969–1977.

[Use this form to refer to the work of the editor. Use the form of the
Beowulf example to refer to the work itself.]

Translation

Alighieri, Dante. The Inferno. Trans. John Ciardi. New York:
    New American, 1954.

[Use this form to refer to either the poet or his work.]

Ciardi, John, trans. The Inferno. By Dante Alighieri. New York:
New American, 1954.

[Use this form to refer to the translator's work.]

Encyclopedia or Other Reference Work

"Emerson, Ralph Waldo." Encyclopedia Americana. 1978 ed.

Anthology

Perrine, Laurence, with Thomas R. Arp. Literature: Structure,
Sound, and Sense. 4th ed. San Diego: Harcourt, 1983.

Work Included in an Anthology

Poe, Edgar Allan. "The Tell-Tale Heart." The Harper American
Literature. Ed. Donald McQuade, et al. 2 vols. New York:
Harper, 1987. 1: 1598–1601.

Article Reprinted in a Collection

Wilbur, Richard. "The House of Poe." From Anniversary Lectures
1959. 1966. Rpt. in Poe: A Collection of Critical
Essays. Ed. Robert Regan. Englewood Cliffs: Prentice,
1967. 98–120.

Cross-references

In the example above, if you use two or more articles from Regan's
Poe: A Collection of Critical Essays, you may list it separately in the
bibliography and cite the individual articles by cross-reference.

Regan, Robert, ed. Poe: A Collection of Critical Essays.
Englewood Cliffs: Prentice, 1967.

Wilbur, Richard. "The House of Poe." From Anniversary Lectures
1959. 1966. Rpt. in Regan 98–120.

Treat pamphlets exactly as books:

Ross, Marilyn, ed. National Survey of Newspaper Op-Ed Pages.
    Saguache: Communication Creativity, 1986.

Articles in Periodicals

Monthly Journal Paginated Continuously Through the Year

Kraft, Quentin G. "On Character in the Novel: William Beatty
    Warner Versus Samuel Richardson and the Humanists."
    College English 50 (1988): 32-47.

Weekly Magazine

Roelofsma, Derk Kinnane. "Easing Access to Daunting Talmud."
    Insight 16 May 1988: 56-7.

Monthly Magazine Not Paginated Continuously

Schell, Orville. "China's Andrei Sakharov." The Atlantic May
    1988: 35-61.

Newspaper

Mehren, Elizabeth. "After 24 Years, Novelists Leave California
    Home." Houston Chronicle 12 May 1988, sec. 6:1+.

Nonprint Sources

Film

Last Tango in Paris. Dir. Frederico Fellini. United Artists,
    1972.

Mack, Maynard. Lessons in Hamlet. Encyclopedia Britannica
    Educational Films, 1955.

[Use this form to discuss Mack's interpretation of the play. Notice that a title such as *Hamlet* is not underlined when it forms part of another underlined title.]

Filmstrips, Slides, and Videotapes

Faulkner, William. <u>Barn Burning</u>. Videocassette. Dir. Ray

  Wilson. American Playhouse, 1980.

Interview

Terhune, Robert. Personal interview. 2 Feb. 1988.

Recording

Chaucer, Geoffrey. <u>Prologue to</u> The Canterbury Tales. Narrated

  in Middle English by Robert Ross. Caedmon, TC 1008,

  1971.

Television

<u>Hal Holbrook's Mark Twain Tonight</u>. NBC. KNBC, Los Angeles, 21

  May 1984.

Computer or Information Service

Cole, SuzAnne. "Using Required Departmental Grading Profiles."

  Nov. 1987. ERIC ED 289 179.

PREPARING THE FINAL DRAFT

When you have revised the rough draft and prepared the "Works Cited" page, you are ready to type the final draft. Look over Chapter 15, "Reviewing Manuscript Mechanics," block out a few hours of undisturbed time, change your typewriter ribbon or check the disk on your word processor, and begin. As you read the following final draft, notice the revisions the student has made from her rough draft.

i

Blanca Esthela Silva

Professor Smith

English 101

12 December 1988

The Heart Tells the Tale

Thesis: In "The Tell-Tale Heart," Edgar Allan Poe's
narrator attempts to bury his conscience, an act which
eventually overpowers the irrational side of his brain
with guilt.

   I. The characters are symbolic of the three parts of
      the personality.

     A. The narrator symbolizes the id.

       1. The narrator acts irrational and insane.

       2. He fears the evil eye because the pounding
          of the heart fills him with guilt.

     B. The old man symbolizes both the ego and
       superego.

       1. His eye (ego) mediates between the narrator
          and the heart.

         a. The eye reflects the soul.

         b. The "evil eye" is a pun on the "evil I."

       2. The heart (superego) represents the
          conscience.

         a. The conscience releases guilt when the
           id attacks.

         b. The "tell-tale" heart forces the
           narrator to tell society the truth.

ii

II. The narrator carefully plans the psychological murder.

   A. He takes seven days to murder the old man.

      1. He slows down time in order to perform perfectly.

      2. The preplanning is explicitly described.

   B. Yet the actual murder is spontaneous.

      1. He carries no murder weapon.

      2. The narrator kills with the bed.

      3. The murder occurs at midnight, a time of mass confusion.

III. The narrator ingeniously prepares the burial.

   A. The corpse is concealed beneath the floor.

      1. The narrator dismembers the body to make certain it will not resurrect.

      2. The burial temporarily stops the sound of the pounding heart.

   B. No visible evidence of the murder remains.

      1. The narrator believes society will never know the truth.

      2. The invisible heart is the only remaining evidence.

IV. The old man's heart haunts the narrator.

   A. The old man does not resurrect.

   B. The narrator fears the pounding heart because the eye (ego) cannot mediate between himself (id) and the heart (superego).

Writing a Research Paper

iii

C. The heart (conscience) haunts the irrational
   side and conquers it with guilt, forcing the
   narrator to admit his evil to society.

Blanca Esthela Silva

Professor Smith

English 101

12 December 1988

The Heart Tells the Tale

"True!—nervous—very dreadfully nervous I had been
and am; but why will you say that I am mad?" (Poe 1598).
Madness! Watch out! We know immediately from this
exposition that we will be placed in a strange, foreign
place in Poe's story—a madman's brain. In "The Tell-
Tale Heart," Poe's narrator carefully plans the murder
of the old man with the "evil eye," and then he attempts
to bury his conscience as well as his victim, an act
which eventually overpowers the irrational side of his
brain with guilt. Someone who cannot control his
impulses may try to suppress his conscience in order to
relieve himself of anxiety. Thus, it is possible that
the story represents Poe's inner struggle with his
Oedipus complex (Weber 93).

Many critics agree that Poe's works are filled with
self-revelation; for example, critic N. Fagin states
that Poe "was in nearly everything he wrote his own
protagonist," using his works to display his "mental
and emotional acuteness, his aristocratic and aesthetic
sensibilities, his ideal steadfastness and actual
vulnerability" as well as "his pale feverish dreams
and fancies" (191). Interestingly enough, Poe

Writing a Research Paper

unconsciously wrote about the id, ego, and superego
before they were defined by Sigmund Freud. Noted
scholar of American literature Daniel Hoffman agrees
that Poe's works portray ". . . the terrible war of
superego upon the id, the endless battle between
conscience and impulse, [and] the unsleeping enmity of
the self and its Imp of the Perverse . . . ," but he
also states that "these struggles" are "always in
disguise" (221). "The Tell-Tale Heart" describes both
the "pale feverish dreams" (Fagin 191) of its author
and the lifelong struggles of almost everyone.

In order to comprehend this story, one should
examine Freud's psychoanalytic theory in more detail.
According to Freud, every person's mental processes are
largely unconscious, most behavior is motivated by
sexuality, and many memories and desires are repressed
because of social taboos on sexual impulses. Mental
processes can be divided into the id, the ego, and the
superego. The id is totally unconscious, irrational,
and amoral, motivated only by an instinctive desire for
pleasure. (In many respects the id is similar to the
Devil.) The ego restrains the id, protecting both the
individual and society and moderating between the
unconscious and the world. It is rational. The superego
is what most people call conscience and consists of the
values of the society in which one lives, usually
taught by parents and schools (Rubin and McNeil 284-6).

Silva 3

(It is also responsible for what is called the "guilt
complex.")

In "The Tell-Tale Heart," the narrator represents
the id. This insane man represents the side of the
personality which holds the most power. The old man
represents the other side which is divided into two
elements working together against the id. His eye
represents the ego and mediates between the id and
superego, represented in the story by his heart. The
heart releases guilt when the ego transmits a message
of the id's wrongdoing. As Hoffman observes, the eye
". . . becomes the all-seeing surveillance of the child
by the father" (223). Perhaps, then, the irrational
element created in the story is a result of Poe's
Oedipal feeling for his dead mother which he cannot
control. Poe, like the narrator, wants to kill the
"evil eye" because it watches over him.

The irrational man does not want the "eye" to tell
his "heart" that he has these Oedipal temptations. He
fears the pounding of the heart because it fills him
with guilt. Guilt will force him to tell society the
truth. Therefore, he attempts to conceal his troubles
and tries to convince himself that he is a genius. Yet
we know that he is mad.

Although the narrator denies his madness ("How
then, am I mad?" [Poe 1598]), and repeatedly states his
sagacity, he also claims that he has a disease that

Writing a Research Paper

sharpens his senses. In fact, he hears all things in
heaven and earth and hell. This, as Hoffman points out,
is proof of his madness: "When a narrator commences in
this vein, we know him to be mad already" (222). But,
as Hoffman also observes, the portrayal of an insane
narrator does not mean that the author is also mad:
"For with such precision to portray the methodicalness
of a madman is the work not of a madman but of a man
who truly understands what it is to be mad. Artistic
control is the warrant of auctorial sanity" (222).

The mad narrator finally decides to kill the old
man because he cannot bear the "evil eye": "One of his
eyes resembled that of a vulture—a pale blue eye, with
a film over it" (Poe 1598). Since the eye is often
regarded as the reflection of the soul, could it be
that the narrator does not want to see the reflection
of his evil soul? As he himself admits, "Whenever it
[the eye] fell upon me, my blood ran cold . . ." (Poe
1598). Therefore, the only "sane" course of action is
to eliminate the eye: ". . . and so by degrees—very
gradually—I made up my mind to take the life of the old
man, and thus rid myself of the eye forever" (Poe
1598).

The narrator carefully plans the murder of the old
man. "It took me an hour to place my whole head within
the opening so far that I could see him as he lay upon
his bed" (Poe 1599). He repeats this for seven nights

Silva 5

at midnight, a significant time. Midnight is the
deepest, most unconscious, part of the night and
therefore the time when the id, the darkest part of the
personality, may be assumed to be the strongest. So it
is also the time when a struggle between the id and the
superego is sure to occur. Massive confusion!

Finally, "upon the eighth night . . . a single dim
ray . . . fell upon the vulture eye" (1599). With the
illumination of the hated ego—eye, it is time to
attack. Suddenly he hears the old man's heart
(superego) which increases his fury. Davidson says, in
fact, that the narrator, a "god—player," makes "the
mistake of thinking it was an eye which was so
vexatious; all the while it was a sound, the beating of
the old man's heart" (190). The eye is merely the
messenger of information, transmitting everything it
sees. Weber also emphasizes the sound of the heart as
the precipitating event: ". . . the murderer hears the
tick—tock of the 'tell—tale heart,' which at length
becomes the 'hellish tattoo' ('louder—<u>louder</u>') and
eventuates in cries which, as usual, can be recognized
as the chimes of the clock" (93). The narrator does
become very nervous as the pounding increases, and, in
a matter of minutes, the murder has been committed. He
leaps and kills the old man with the mattress from the
bed. An odd weapon, but Weber hints that it may be
symbolic of Poe's attempt to kill his Oedipal complex (93).

Writing a Research Paper

Silva 6

But soon a new fear replaced the murderer's fear
of the eye: "And now a new anxiety seized me—the sound
would be heard by a neighbor!" (Poe 1600). Rubin and
McNeil define anxiety as "a fear that seems unjustified
by any objective threat or danger" (290). In order to
relieve this anxiety, "the ego must use maneuvers
called defense mechanisms. . . . Repression . . . is
the exclusion of unacceptable unconscious impulses from
the conscience" (290). In this case, the narrator has
been battling within himself. Since he cannot bury his
temptations, he has tried to hide his Oedipal feelings
from his conscience by killing it, and he thinks he has
succeeded. "I placed my hand upon the heart and held it
there many minutes. There was no pulsation. He was
stone dead. His eye would trouble me no more" (Poe
1600). Now that his conscience has died, society (the
eye) will no longer be able to recognize his evil. He
can live with his temptation without fearing an
explosion of guilt which would cause him to reveal his
problems to the world. Since society must not know his
secret, he must bury the body ingeniously and secretly.
Guilt must not escape!

The narrator continues to stress his sanity as he
describes the precautions taken for the concealment of
the body. "The night waned, and I worked on hastily, but
in silence" (Poe 1600). (Notice he does not hear the
beating of the heart.) The corpse is dismembered and

placed under "three planks." The three planks symbolize
the entire personality while the ego and superego are
buried underneath them. The only survivor: the id—the
madman!

The clock strikes four—"still dark as midnight,"
when a knocking is heard at the door. The narrator
opens the door with a "light heart" since ". . . what
had I now to fear?" (Poe 1600). He attempts to convince
himself that his conscience is buried deeply beneath
him. The three (again, that number!) police officers
(society) will see no guilt. He cannot tell them the
truth because they will not understand his Oedipus
complex. Therefore, guilt must not show through. And,
at first, he shows no trace of a guilty conscience and
thinks he has triumphed: "I was singularly at ease"
(Poe 1600).

Yet, soon he becomes pale and uncomfortable; he
hears a faint noise, ". . . a low, dull, quick sound—
much a sound as a watch makes when enveloped in cotton"
(Poe 1601). The familiar sound of the clock? No. It is
the sound of the "tell-tale heart" which gradually
sounds louder and louder. As guilt overcomes him, he
feels nervous, fearing the truth will slip out. It has
been constrained but wants to tell the secret. The
heart will succeed! "It grew louder, louder—louder."
His heart (conscience) finally forces him to admit his
Oedipal murder. "'Villains!' I shrieked, 'dissemble no

Silva 8

more! I admit the deed!—tear up the planks!—here,
here!—it is the beating of the hideous heart!'" (Poe
1601). Because he feels that he must "scream or die,"
he finally gives in and tells society the truth.

Can we relate this story to Poe's life? Poe was an
outcast from society, the orphan son of vagabond
actors. Freud believed that "failure to resolve the
Oedipus conflict means growing up with an intense fear
that a powerful and jealous father might punish the
boy for his feelings toward his mother" (Rubin and
McNeil 289).

In "The Tell-Tale Heart," Poe pieces the puzzle
of his life together. He feels society with its
"hypocritical smiles" knows of his Oedipal complex. Yet
it pretends not to know. Poe tries to hide his evil,
but his conscience forces him to tell the truth. His
conscience finally conquers the id with guilt. The
secret is out. "The Tell-Tale Heart" tells the tale.

Silva 9

Works Cited

Davidson, Edward H. Poe: A Critical Study. Cambridge:

Belknap, 1976.

Fagin, N. Bryllion. The Histrionic Mr. Poe. Baltimore:

Johns Hopkins P, 1942.

Hoffman, Daniel. Poe, Poe, Poe, Poe, Poe, Poe, Poe.

1972. New York: Vintage, 1985.

Poe, Edgar Allan. "The Tell-Tale Heart." The Harper

American Literature. Ed. Donald McQuade, et al. 2

vols. New York: Harper, 1987. 1: 1598-1601.

Regan, Robert, ed. Poe: A Collection of Critical

Essays. Englewood Cliffs: Prentice, 1967.

Rubin, Zick, and Elton B. McNeil. Psychology: Being

Human: Brief/Update. 4th ed. New York: Harper,

1987.

Weber, Jean-Paul. "Edgar Poe or The Theme of the

Clock." La Nouvelle Revue Francaise, 68 and 69

(Aug., Sept., 1958), 301-11, 498-508. Trans.

Claude Richard and Robert Regan. Rpt. in Regan 79-

97.

Wilbur, Richard. "The House of Poe." From Anniversary

Lectures 1959. 1966. Rpt. in Regan 98-120.

Writing a Research Paper

Proofreading and Editing

After you have typed or printed your final draft, read it meticulously. Sometimes it helps to read backwards, sentence by sentence, from the end to the beginning. (This technique will help you spot omissions. When you read in the usual order, your marvelously adaptable brain will fill in the missing spots — you know what you meant to say and your brain will read that. Reading backwards distorts your expectation; you are more apt to spot mistakes and omissions.) Neatly correct all errors. (See Chapter 15, "Reviewing Manuscript Mechanics," for suggestions.)

Submitting the Final Project

Since many instructors are interested in the process of your research as well as your final paper, be prepared to submit all your working material. You may need to assemble a final package with note cards and bibliography cards neatly rubber-banded, rough drafts paper-clipped separately and clearly marked "Draft #1," "Draft #2," etc., as well as the final draft with title page, outline, and "Works Cited" page. Enclose your project in a large manila envelope clearly marked with your name and course number. If you are asked to turn in the final paper only, your instructor will probably specify the method. Generally, avoid stiff binders which are awkward to handle.

CHAPTER REVIEW

Continuing a research project past the initial investigation to the writing of a formal research paper allows you to practice many skills: organization, drafting, revision, proofreading, and editing. Creating a rough draft from stacks of note cards, discovering a title, integrating quotations and other borrowed material with your ideas, mastering parenthetical documentation, and preparing a bibliography are scholarly accomplishments. When you have finished your research paper, you have added your insight, analysis, and interpretation to the collected body of knowledge on your research topic. Be proud of yourself for its successful completion.

PART V

FINAL CONSIDERATIONS

CHAPTER 14

Improving Study Skills and Taking Literature Exams

Success in a literature class requires continuous practice and refinement of those study skills used in other classes — preparing for class; listening to and participating in class discussion; taking notes on reading, discussion and lectures; and preparing for and taking different types of exams. This chapter reviews those essential skills.

PREPARING FOR CLASS — SETTING A STUDY SCHEDULE

To get the greatest benefit from your literature class, prepare for each class meeting. You probably know you should allow two or three hours outside of class to prepare for each hour spent in class. You may actually want to set up a study schedule at the beginning of each semester, taking into account personal considerations such as:

1. Goals — What do you want to accomplish? Set goals such as "This semester I want to improve my research skills." "I want to learn more about short stories." "This year I want to find out about Renaissance literature."
2. Priorities — Be clear on the difference between what you *must* do and what you *want* to do. If you want to skip ahead and read all the short fiction in your book, do so, but also

Improving Study Skills

read the poetry for class tomorrow. And though you want to work on your research project due at the end of the term, first complete the essay due at the end of the week.

3. Balance — Don't set impossible tasks for yourself such as a marathon research session in the library on party night if you're a party person. Be realistic about your needs for relaxation, pleasure, exercise, and companionship. If you have an outside job, be reasonable about your work hours.

After you've thought about goals, priorities, and a balanced life as a student, set up your study schedule allowing ample time for reading, writing, and researching, and stick to it.

PREPARING FOR CLASS — THE RIGHT ENVIRONMENT

Try to have a quiet corner of your own for studying, an area where studying is the only activity. It should have a comfortable (but not too comfortable!) chair, a good light, a desk or table large enough to spread out study materials, and it should be equipped with pens, pencils, paper, and reference books such as a dictionary, a thesaurus, and an English handbook. Every time you sit in this area remember you are there to study. Try to get the cooperation of your family or roommates not to bother you at certain study times; if possible, ask them even to take phone messages for you during these times.

The right environment is psychological as well as physical. Try to clear your mind of all distractions and problems before you sit down to study. Promise yourself to concentrate only on studies for one or two hours and then reward yourself with a short walk or a phone call or fifteen minutes of your favorite TV program.

PREPARING FOR CLASS — READING AND TAKING NOTES

When you begin your assigned reading, follow the advice given in Chapter 1 on marking the text, reading, and rereading. Read a poem or a short section of prose and then ask, "What is happening or what has happened in this work?" Stop frequently during the reading to anticipate what may happen next. Use your journal (see Chapter 2) to jot down these predictions and to summarize the content after you have finished reading. If your instructor has given you study questions, answer the questions. Decide how the work compares with other works you have read earlier. Do you see a pattern in the works? Are there common themes running through works from the same historical period? After having read several works in the same genre, can you now define the genre for yourself? Can you recognize when an author breaks the pattern of a genre and why? Take notes on these and other ideas and formulate your own questions to ask in class.

When you have finished the assigned reading, take a few minutes to review what you have read. What do you recall first? If you cannot recall some works, reread them.

CLASSROOM DISCUSSION

The opportunities for class discussion will vary according to the size and responsiveness of the class and the style of the individual instructor. Obviously, if the class is held in a large and crowded lecture hall, discussion will be limited. Some instructors may not wish to deviate from a planned lecture to include class response, or a detailed lecture may be the only satisfactory method to cover all the material. Since the value of class discussion depends on student preparation, however, don't be surprised if you are graded on participation.

If your class does have at least some discussion, you can benefit from it by being prepared for a variety of possible discussion situations. Your instructor may ask questions to develop lectures, asking a class, for example, about the characteristics of Romantic literature before lecturing on the Romantic influence on a certain writer. This type of questioning prompts critical thinking. Or the instructor may give out study questions or assign particular topics for reader-response journal entries; anticipate discussion based on these questions.

During class discussion, listen carefully to your classmates' responses and jot down comments that seem valid or novel. If you have a contribution, voice it. Remember, literature is complex, and a variety of readings is always possible. Your prior knowledge and experience may illuminate a passage or question.

As discussed earlier, part of the pleasure of reading is discovering how others respond differently to a work. Some of your classmates may attempt to fit every work into their personal world visions and reject those interpretations they cannot easily assimilate. Others may automatically resist all works by a certain author because they have disliked

Improving Study Skills

a previously read selection. Try to be open and fair in your discussion and active listening — appreciating different points of view is an essential part of becoming educated in a culturally diverse world.

TAKING LECTURE NOTES

When your instructor presents a formal lecture, you will probably want to take notes. Prepare for a lecture as you would for discussion by reading the assigned material; then, listen carefully, date and title each day's notes, and keep the notes for each course you study in a separate folder or binder. Concentrate on the lecture and try not to allow yourself to be distracted.

Outline the lecture as you take notes. Often instructors will write key terms or major divisions of the lecture on a board. Listen for verbal clues indicating the important topics and subtopics: "The three most important aspects of Romanticism are . . . ," "Having examined the characteristics of realism in fiction, let's look at the work of two leading proponents. . . ." Record unfamiliar terminology at the top of a page and define later. If you get temporarily lost or confused, simply skip a few lines and resume taking notes as soon as something begins to sound familiar again. You may want to jot down question marks by material you do not understand; there may be time at the end of class for questions. Also, instructors will often review main points at the end of the lecture. Use these summaries to check your notes. Have you recorded the major points? Use numbers, letters, or arrows to keep your notes organized or highlight notes by drawing boxes or circles around important headings.

As soon as possible after class, review and even rewrite or revise your notes. Flesh out the bare bones of the notes with examples from your reading. As suggested above, highlight or mark the notes to make them useful for you. You may want to summarize each day's notes.

PREPARING FOR SUBJECTIVE EXAMINATIONS

Subjective examinations include short-answer, short- or long-essay, open-book, and even take-home formats. (Although some students consider the last two the easiest of all exams, both require a

thorough familiarity with all the works studied.) The following suggestions will be helpful for all types of subjective exams:

1. Study in several short sessions and avoid cramming. (This advice goes for objective exams as well.)
2. Begin your preparation by rereading the assigned material (even reading key passages and works aloud) and then reviewing class notes.
3. Rewrite class notes using a different method of organization — for example, grouping notes around certain themes or specific subgenres.
4. Anticipate possible questions. Look for patterns in the works; compare and contrast authors, styles, themes, and works. Try to define the genres you've studied; classify works into subgenres. Think of examples of different themes, styles, points of view, and literary techniques.

TAKING SUBJECTIVE EXAMINATIONS

1. Preview the test. Notice how much each question is worth and how much time each will take to answer; considering that information and the time allowed for the exam, set a personal time schedule.
2. Read each question carefully to make certain what you are asked to do. (See the sample questions below.)
3. Take the time for a brief organizing activity. List the points you want to make for each answer in the margin. After you make this list, number the items in order from most to least significant. (Since there is seldom time to rewrite or revise an essay answer, a marginal list helps keep your answer focused. Additionally, if you do not have time to complete the essay, the instructor still may give you some points for the list.)
4. Begin your answer with a thesis or assertion which answers the test question. If the question asks, for example, "What is the Puritan doctrine of predestination and the elect?" your answer could begin with the assertion, "The Puritan doctrine of predestination states that only an indeterminate but limited number of souls will be saved."

5. Be concise with your answers, but give all relevant information. Support your assertions with examples from the works you've studied (and quotations if this is an open-book test).
6. Do not apologize for an answer.
7. If you cannot answer a question, but you have time remaining, write to trigger your memory. Begin by restating the question and list everything you can remember about the topic. Examine your list for possible ideas to expand. Do not "pad" your answer with irrelevant information (you will lose your credibility), but do attempt to generate an appropriate response even as a partial answer.
8. Do not make flippant remarks. Remember your audience. You want to maintain your credibility with your instructor.
9. Proofread. Many good essays have been weakened by the simple omission of a key word such as "not" or the misspelling of an author's name. Proofread quickly but thoroughly and neatly make any necessary corrections.

THE MOST COMMON SUBJECTIVE EXAMINATION TASKS

A subjective examination may require you to fulfill one or more of the following tasks. Each task is illustrated with a sample question and *short* response; you may be expected to write longer answers.

1. Define. To *define* is to place something into a general classification and then exclude it from other members of the same class. For example, "Marxism is the economic and political philosophy [general category] developed by Karl Marx, who believed that history is a class struggle motivated by economic forces and that the ideal society is a classless one in which goods are distributed according to need" [difference between Marxism and other economic and political philosophies]. To prepare for definition questions, carefully study definitions in your text and those given in lecture.

Question: Define the nonfiction novel, especially in its relation to journalism.

Response: The nonfiction novel is a genre which resembles nonfiction and journalism because it presents real events and real people, yet it differs from straight reporting in three respects. The writer is present in the work, even sometimes as a character as Norman Mailer is in *The Armies of the Night*. Dialogue and characters are invented, or a character may be a composite of several real-life characters. Finally, chronology is not strictly historical; the writer may move back and forth in time to dramatize events.

2. Compare/contrast. Of course, to *compare* is to find similarities while to *contrast* is to find differences. Usually, the point of comparison/contrast questions is to have you note similarities between those works, elements of literature, or authors that at first glance appear to be quite different, or to note significant differences between works, elements of literature, or authors who appear to be similar. Prepare for such questions by comparing and contrasting each new work and author with those previously studied.

Question: Compare/contrast the resolutions of Milton's "When I Consider How My Light Is Spent" and Hopkins' "Thou Art Indeed Just, Lord."

Response: Although these poems are similar in autobiographical content (both poets plead for justice from God during periods of nonproductivity), they express quite different resolutions. Milton, after an admittedly foolish complaint, accepts the advice of Patience, who tells him that he will serve God best by standing and waiting. His poem ends with this stoic resolution. However, Hopkins ends his sonnet on the same note of pleading as it began: "Mine, O thou Lord of life, send my roots rain."

3. Analyze. To *analyze* is to break something into its parts; for example, to analyze a work of fiction, you could comment on plot, theme, characterization, symbols, language, setting, tone, or point of view. To prepare to write an analysis, group class notes by elements such as these and note these elements in each work as you read. (For a review of the elements and their functions in specific genres, see Part III, "Discovering and Responding to Elements of Literature.")

Taking Literature Exams

Question: Analyze the title of Blake's "Infant Sorrow," relating it to a theme of the poem.

Response: The title is ambiguous: if "infant" modifies "sorrow," then the poem is a sentimental piece about an infant mourning a trifle; more likely, however, after one reads the poem carefully, is the realization that the sorrow is not suffered by the infant but caused by it. The theme supported by this reading of the title is that the birth of a child is not always a joyous occasion.

4. Illustrate. To *illustrate* is to cite examples to support and develop your points. For example, if asked to illustrate the theme of the hunt in Hemingway's fiction, you might refer to "The Short Happy Life of Francis Macomber" or "The Snows of Kilimanjaro." Note that although many questions may not specifically ask you to "illustrate" your answer, you will still be expected to provide examples to prove your points. To prepare for illustration questions specifically, be familiar with the main details of all of the works read.

Question: Illustrate the relationship between the setting and the psychological situation of the protagonist in "Beyond the Bayou" with a specific quotation.

Response: Before her routine life is shattered by an accident to the child she loves, La Folle isolates herself from the plantation and the other workers. After she has to go "beyond the bayou" to seek help, her attitude toward that world is transformed; a transformation symbolized by her crossing the bayou "with a long steady stride as if she had done this all her life" and by the beauty that greets her: "the thousand blue violets that peeped out from green, luxuriant beds . . . , big waxen bells of the magnolias . . . , the jessamine clumps around her," and the roses (261).

5. Summarize. Of course, to *summarize* is to restate briefly and in your own words, and in the present tense, the content of a work. Prepare for summary questions by summarizing assigned readings in your journal and reviewing those summaries before the examination. (To review how to summarize, see Chapter 2.)

Question: Summarize the plot of Shirley Jackson's story "The Lottery" in one sentence.

Response: In Shirley Jackson's "The Lottery," Tessie Hutchinson is stoned to death by her townspeople (including her own family), who blindly act out a ritual sacrifice.

6. Paraphrase. As we have seen, to *paraphrase* is to explain in your own words the content of a work. You may be asked to paraphrase a short selection to demonstrate your understanding. Be certain you have defined any unfamiliar words in the works you've read. Prepare for paraphrasing questions by experimenting with paraphrases in your journal. (To review paraphrasing, see Chapter 2.)

Question: Paraphrase William Butler Yeats's "The Coming of Wisdom with Time."

Response: A person's life has many shapes and forms, including youth and old age. In youth, one celebrates life gaily and joyously but deceitfully; in old age, life is shriveled but truthful.

7. Enumerate (list). To *enumerate* means to list briefly. Check with your instructor to see if the items on your list should be complete sentences or if phrases and single words are acceptable. To prepare for listing questions, arrange your class notes into lists: "five soldier poets of World War II," "four characteristics of free verse," "six symbols in 'The Lottery,'" (See Chapter 3, "Responding through Creative Activities," for a discussion of listing as a creative activity.)

Question: List the chief characteristics of the picaresque novel.

Response:
1. a tale of adventure and wandering
2. realistic portrayal of society
3. point of view of a rogue who is usually the protagonist
4. often an element of moralizing

8. Classify. To *classify* is to group items into categories by recording a series of random observations, discovering logical principles which unite some of the observations, organizing the observations into logical categories based on the

principles, and labeling the categories. To prepare for classification questions, rearrange the works you've studied, your journal entries, or class notes according to different categories; for example, realism, naturalism, and romanticism, or comedies and tragedies

Question: Classify the following examples of nonfiction novels: *Witness, The Autobiography of Malcolm X, The Electric Kool-Aid Acid Test, The Woman Warrior, Hiroshima, In Cold Blood, The Armies of the Night.*

Response: *Witness, The Autobiography of Malcolm X,* and *The Woman Warrior* are autobiographies. *The Electric Kool-Aid Acid Test* and *In Cold Blood* are studies (and indictments) of contemporary society. *Hiroshima* and *The Armies of the Night* are reported (and recorded) but also fictionalized histories. (*The Armies of the Night* also has elements of autobiography.)

9. Trace. To *trace* is to follow something — a theme, subject, or style — through several authors, works, or a single long work or time period, usually chronologically. Prepare for a tracing question as you would for a classification question, but make the categories more specific and pay particular attention to chronological order.

Question: Briefly trace the loss of Goodman Brown's faith in Hawthorne's "Young Goodman Brown."

Response: At the beginning of the story, Goodman Brown has faith in his young wife and his recent marriage, his neighbors and his religious leaders, and in his own religious beliefs. However, in his trip into the forest, he loses all of his faith. First, he spies his religious leaders in apparent league with the devil. When he thinks his wife Faith has also been carried to the Black Mass, he rejects his religion and rushes to join the others in the devil's ceremony. Although he refuses the communion at the last minute and cannot even be certain in the morning that he really experienced that terrible night, it has been enough to turn him into a misanthrope. He carries this loss of faith to the end of his gloomy life; he goes to the grave not *with* faith, but "followed by Faith."

SAMPLE RESPONSES TO AN ESSAY QUESTION

The following essays were written in class in response to the question: "Discuss the theme of education in *King Lear* with reference to one character only." Students could use their texts; they had approximately thirty minutes to write their essays.

Response #1

In <u>Lear</u> many of the characters learn something about themselves and human nature. Lear learns that to be king in name only is not to be king at all. Gloucester learns that he should not be superstitious and should investigate things before leaping to conclusions. Edgar has to learn how to defend himself and how not to be so gullible. Cordelia learns that it wouldn't have hurt to have placated her old man a little bit. I guess Reagan and Goneril learn not to fall in love with the same man. And I learned that I really don't like reading Shakespeare (just kidding, teach!).

Comment   Although this student gives a fairly accurate summary of the lessons learned in the play, this is a poor essay because it tries to cover too many characters. The attempt at wit at the end will probably not endear the student to the instructor.

Response #2

One of the characters who learns a lot in the play <u>King Lear</u> is the main character, Lear himself. At the beginning of the play, he divides his kingdom into three parts, intending to give the biggest part to his favorite daughter because he expects her to praise him the most. When she doesn't, he gets mad and doesn't give her anything. Then he expects his other two daughters to gladly support him and his whole group of knights; he wants the privileges of kingship, despite having given up the powers and responsibilities. When Reagan and Goneril realize that he is powerless, they throw him out into the storm with no help and no support. Then he realizes how foolish he has been and that Cordelia really does love him. At the end of the play he is given a chance to ask Cordelia to forgive him, but she is murdered, and he dies of a broken heart. A little knowledge is a dangerous thing!

Comment   This is a better essay than the first because the author limits the discussion to only one character. However, the greatest part of the essay is straight summary. There is never a clear assertion of what Lear learns in the play, and the essay is weakened by an unexplained cliché as a final sentence.

Response #3

One of the central themes of King Lear is education or the acquisition of wisdom, shown in this play as a painful and even tragic process. Lear himself learns several lessons in the course of the drama: that love is not measured by fancy speeches but by deeds; that real friends tell the truth about each other's actions; and that being a king means being aware of the situation of all the people in the kingdom. In the beginning of the play, Lear disowns Cordelia because of an unwise decision to play his daughters against one another. But when Kent tries to intervene and prevent such a mistake, Lear ignorantly banishes him from the kingdom.

The Fool tries to make Lear see his foolishness with his banter and poems. (It is ironic that the person who is wise enough to foresee the results of Lear's mistakes is considered a fool.) When Lear asks the Fool if he is accusing Lear of foolishness, the Fool replies, "All thy other titles thou hast given away; that thou wast born with" (1.4.132).

Lear acquires his social awareness during a storm in the
wilderness when he is stripped of all his glory, his retine
reduced to the Fool and a supposed madman. Forced to look
inside himself, Lear realizes that he has been ignorant of the
condition of many in his kingdom: "O, I have ta'en / Too little
care of this" (3.4.33–4). Later, reunited with Cordelia, Lear
is sick, tired, and aware of his mistakes. He acknowledges his
past ignorance and asks her forgiveness, "You must bear with
me: / Pray you now, forget and forgive. I am old and foolish"
(4.7.84–5).

Comment   This is an excellent essay with a clear thesis, each point of which
is developed with examples and brief quotations from the work. If an examination is open-book, the instructor usually expects the student to use quotations to support assertions.

PREPARING FOR OBJECTIVE EXAMINATIONS

Objective examinations in a literature class may be true-false, multiple-choice, fill-in-the-blank, or matching (usually author-to-work or quotation-to-author, -work, or -speaker). To prepare for objective tests, concentrate on specific details such as the correct spelling of titles and names, and review facts such as which characters appear in which works and which poems are sonnets. If your course has been taught chronologically, review the progression of authors and works and know who wrote what approximately when. Be aware of patterns in works and periods and be able to trace them. If your instructor has read selections from works aloud, by all means mark those selections in your text and reread them carefully before the examination.

TAKING OBJECTIVE EXAMINATIONS

Be confident as you begin the test. If you have studied and prepared, this exam is your opportunity to demonstrate your knowledge.

   1. Preview the test. Note the types of questions, the number,
   how much time you have, and the general level of difficulty.

Taking Literature Exams

Distinguish questions requiring analysis — "In 'Self-Reliance,' the author believes that the self-reliant person is likely to suffer in the world because. . . ." — from those involving only recall: "Who wrote the poem 'Concord Hymn'?"

2. Set a time schedule for answering the questions. Divide the time you have to take the test by the number of questions and stick to that schedule, saving until last those questions whose answers do not come immediately to mind.

3. Proofread your answers before you turn in your paper. If the answer sheet will be mechanically graded, make certain your marks are dark and in the correct lines. Completely erase any stray marks. Make certain you have not inadvertently omitted any words or answers.

TIPS FOR ANSWERING DIFFERENT TYPES OF OBJECTIVE QUESTIONS

True-False

1. For a statement to be true, all parts must be true. If any part, no matter how small, is false, the statement is false.

2. Look carefully for absolutes such as "never," "always," "every." Such questions are usually false.

3. Check for more than one negative in a statement. Two negatives make the statement positive.

Multiple-Choice

1. Read the first part of the question carefully; look for negative words which can affect your choice; for example, "In *Walden*, the author demonstrates his self-sufficiency in all of the following ways *except*. . . ."

2. Also, just as with true-false, look for absolutes. Choices with absolutes in them will usually not be correct.

3. Read all of the answers before choosing the correct one. Remember, the last choice may be "all of the above." Also, some questions may ask you to choose the "best" of several correct answers.

4. Mark out the obviously incorrect choices first; then choose the correct answer from those remaining.

Fill-in-the-Blank

1. Look for clues in the statement. For example, "a" before a blank is a clue that the answer begins with a consonant; "an" means that the answer begins with a vowel.
2. Sometimes the length of the blank or the number of blanks determines the length of the answer or the number of words in the answer.

Matching

1. Read through both lists quickly before beginning.
2. If the instructions state that items cannot be used more than once, cross out each answer as you use it.
3. If you are stuck, try matching verb to verb, noun to noun, etc.

CHAPTER REVIEW

Skills which help you in a literature class include developing a study schedule, taking notes on reading and lectures, and preparing for and participating in class discussion. Knowing the different types of information different questions ask for and being prepared for both subjective and objective examinations can make them an opportunity and a challenge.

Taking Literature Exams

CHAPTER 15

Reviewing Manuscript Mechanics

FORM

A good paper can be ruined by a poor presentation. Think of your audience, and follow the conventions to give your ideas the best possible form.

1. Typing your paper or using a word processor is preferable and may be required. If you are an average typist, type on erasable bond paper, and turn in a photocopy. If you print your paper on a word processor or computer, tear apart the sheets and remove the punched hole edges. For typed or word-processed papers, observe the following conventions:
   a. Double-space.
   b. Use a reasonably fresh ribbon.
   c. Leave a one-inch margin on all four sides.
   d. Indent five spaces from the left margin to begin a new paragraph.
   e. Leave two spaces after the period that ends a sentence and one space after commas and semicolons.
   If handwritten papers are permitted, skip lines on narrow-lined paper, write on only one side of the paper, use blue or black ink, and avoid using paper ripped from a wire spiral.

2. If a title page is not required, put your full name, professor, class, and date in the top left-hand corner of the first page, skip one line, and center your title. Capitalize all important words in the title, but don't underline it or put it in quotation marks. However, if your title includes the title of a literary work or works, follow the conventions for punctuating the title of the work: underline long poems, plays, and novels and put short stories and short poems in quotation marks, as in the examples below:

Skepticism and Faith in Jay Parini's

"The Missionary Visits Our Church in Scranton"

The Role of the Narrator in Ralph Ellison's

<u>Invisible Man</u>

Witness for the Defense: The Lawyer

in "Bartleby the Scrivener"

3. Number each page, including the title page, with a small Arabic numeral in the top right-hand corner. Also, it is a good idea to repeat your last name in the same spot in case your pages get separated.
4. Connect your pages with a paper clip rather than a staple. Although your pride in your work may motivate you to enclose it in a crisp, colorful folder or binder, subdue the impulse. Most instructors prefer just the paper itself.

CORRECTIONS

If you have more than two or three errors per page, retype or rewrite the paper. However, a few minor errors can be corrected on the final copy as shown below.

1. To add a word or mark of punctuation, use a caret (∧).
2. A vertical line (|) indicates a separation of one space.
3. A closure (⌣) indicates no separation was intended.
4. The symbol (⁋) indicates a new paragraph; (No⁋) means no paragraph was intended.

5. Cross through words to be omitted with a single line:

```
That should not ~~be~~ be a mistake.
```

6. Letters or words transposed may be corrected in this way:

```
That should be not a mistake.
```

CONVENTIONS FOR WRITING ABOUT LITERATURE

1. When referring to the author and the title of a work for the first time, use the full name of each. (If the work has a subtitle, include it too, separating it from the title with a colon and a space.)

```
Maxine Hong Kingston's The Woman Warrior: Memoirs of a
Girlhood Among Ghosts is both an autobiography and a
nonfiction novel.
```

After the initial full reference, you may shorten lengthy titles, omit subtitles, and refer to authors by last name only (no first names only or Mr. or Miss).

```
     Kingston's The Woman Warrior, as previously
mentioned, is also a nonfiction novel.
```

2. Spell authors' names correctly and use the name they prefer: Edgar Allan Poe, not Edgar Allen Poe; Imamu Amiri Baraka, not LeRoi Jones.

3. Use the present tense when writing about literature, even when referring to a long-dead author: Poe *is* a poet who *describes* the pathos of lovers separated by death. However, use the past tense to state an obviously historical fact: Poe *was* born in 1809, not Poe *is* born in 1809.

QUOTATIONS AND QUOTATION MARKS

(For more detailed discussion of using quotations and examples of the following points, see the section "Incorporating Quotations" in Chapter 13.)

1. Do not overuse quotations.
2. Introduce quotations, either with the reason the quotation is relevant or by identifying the speaker or writer of the quotation, or both. When referring to the narrator or speaker in a work, it is preferable to use those terms rather than "writer" or "poet."

Imprecise:

```
The poet Raymond Carver describes an inexplicable
feeling of fear in "The River."
```

Clear:

```
The speaker in Raymond Carver's poem "The River"
describes an inexplicable feeling of fear.
```

3. Avoid using two or more quotations in a row without explanatory commentary.

Unclear:

```
The narrator of James Baldwin's "The Rockpile"
implicitly criticizes the values of the parents: "below
them, men and women and boys and girls, sinners all,
loitered. . . ." ". . . They did not believe this story
ever, but, adopting toward her their father's attitude,
assumed that she had just left some sinful place which
she dared not name, as, for example, a movie palace"
(555-56).
```

Clear:

```
The narrator of James Baldwin's "The Rockpile"
implicitly criticizes the values of the parents: first,
when the boys describe the people they see below them
as "sinners all," which is hyperbole, and second, when
they are said to have adopted "their father's attitude"
```

Reviewing Mechanics

and believe their aunt has come from "a sinful place
which she dared not name, as, for example, a movie
palace" (555–56).

1. Try to work short quotations into your own sentence structure, but notice that they must fit grammatically.

Ungrammatical:

In Baldwin's "The Rockpile," the narrator describes the
young boy John as "seemed to her astonished vision just
below him [the father], beneath his fist, his heavy
shoe" (560).

Grammatical:

In Baldwin's "The Rockpile," the narrator describes the
young boy John, who "seemed to her astonished vision
just below him [the father], beneath his fist, his
heavy shoe" (560).

You may alter the punctuation and capitalization of the original to fit your sentence structure as long as you do not change the meaning of the original.

5. Long quotations (more than three lines of poetry or four lines of prose) should be introduced with a colon, set off from the text by a double-space, and then indented ten spaces from the left margin. Quotation marks are not used. Lines of poetry are arranged as in the original.

To justify the children's lack of freedom in "The
Rockpile," the narrator describes the drowning of
another child:

>   Once a boy, whose name was Richard, drowned
>   in the river. His mother had not known
>   where he was; she had even come to their

```
house, to ask if he was there. Then, in the
evening, . . . they had heard from the street
a woman screaming and wailing. . . .
        Down the street came the woman,
Richard's mother, screaming. . . . Behind
. . . walked a man, Richard's father, with
Richard's body in his arms. (556)
```

```
In the poem "Homage to Elvis, Homage to the Fathers,"
Bruce Weigl describes the effect of a visit by Elvis
Presley on a group of steel town boys:
```

```
He changed us somehow; we cleaned up.
We spun his 45's in the basement,
Danced on the cool concrete and plastered
Our hair back like his and twisted
Our forbidden hips. (25-29)
```

6. Short quotations (a sentence or less) are incorporated into your text with quotation marks and introduced with a comma. Indicate the end of a line of poetry with a slash and capitalize the beginning of each line as in the original.

7. Mark any alterations or additions *within* a quotation in brackets.

8. To omit material from a quotation, use an ellipsis (three spaced dots) to indicate the omission. If a quotation is the beginning or the end of a sentence, you do not have to use an ellipsis to indicate that the quotation is part of a longer section, nor do you have to use an ellipsis when you are obviously quoting only a word or a short phrase. Otherwise, however, use ellipses to indicate omissions. If the material you have omitted is longer than a sentence, you will also use a period with the ellipsis.

9. Periods and commas are placed inside quotation marks; colons and semicolons are placed outside quotation marks. However, when using parenthetical documentation with a short quotation (one that is not indented), the closing mark of punctuation follows the parenthetical documentation,

after the quotation mark. In parenthetical documentation of a long quotation (one that is indented), the quotation is closed before the parenthetical documentation.

10. Single quotation marks are used to indicate quoted material within a quotation.

CHECKLIST FOR MANUSCRIPT MECHANICS

Before you turn in a literature paper, you may want to reread it one last time, reviewing the following areas:

1. Is the paper in the most attractive form possible, clearly and neatly typed or written on acceptable paper?
2. Is the title properly punctuated and capitalized?
3. Is the paper correctly paginated?
4. If there are any errors, have they been neatly corrected?
5. Have the conventions of the literary essay been followed?
6. Are quotations used correctly? Are they introduced? If short, are they incorporated smoothly and grammatically into the text? If long, are they set off from the text?
7. Are quotations properly punctuated, including the use of brackets and ellipsis?

CHAPTER REVIEW

Present your ideas for literature papers in the best possible form by following manuscript conventions in typing the paper, writing the title, making corrections, and using quotations. Also observe the conventions for writing about literature: refer to authors correctly and use the present tense.

Glossary of Literary Terms

This glossary, while not exhaustive, is a comprehensive dictionary of those terms and genres you are likely to encounter in an introductory survey course in literature. When responding to literature, you need to use the appropriate terminology. In some cases the terms have been defined and discussed more fully in the previous chapters but are repeated here in condensed form for ease of reference. Many definitions are illustrated with quotations. Cross-references refer you to more comprehensive discussions; for example, all terms specific to plot are grouped under the listing **plot.**

accent   stress or emphasis. *Word accent* means the syllable receiving the most emphasis in pronunciation is accented, as *sin* in sinner. *Metrical stress* is a pattern of emphasis in poetry (see **meter**).

act   a major division of the action of a play. Dramas usually have from one to five acts, with three being typical of twentieth-century drama, but there is no set number. The end of an act is often signalled by a dropped curtain or a black-out. Acts are often composed of shorter segments (see **scene**).

Alexandrine   an iambic hexameter (see **meter**) line, used and criticized by Pope in his *Essay on Criticism:* "A needless Alexandrine ends the Song, / That like a wounded Snake, drags its slow length along."

allegory   a literary work in which objects, characters, and events have a surface meaning and another correlated meaning; they continually refer to another simultaneous structure. Allegories can be religious, moral, philosophical, scientific, political, historical, or national, sometimes simultaneously. For example, in Spenser's *Faerie Queene*, the Red Cross Knight is a knight, and simultaneously represents the virtue of holiness, the Christian hero, and also St. George, the patron saint of England.

alliteration   the repetition of initial consonant sounds in two or more words in close proximity: ". . . when you have seen hate-filled policemen *c*urse, *k*ick, and even *k*ill your black brothers and sisters . . ." (Martin Luther King, "Letter from Birmingham Jail — April 16, 1963").

allusion   a reference to something — event, person, time — outside the immediate world of the work. Yeats' poem "Second Coming" contains an allusion to the birth of Christ in the lines: "That twenty centuries of stony sleep / Were vexed to nightmare by a rocking cradle."

ambiguity   multiple meanings; language can have several different meanings simultaneously. While ambiguity may be considered a flaw in informational writing, in literature it may puzzle readers, but it also concentrates their attention and enriches their reading. When Anne Sexton in the last lines of her poem "Housewife" writes: "A woman *is* her mother. / That's the main thing," what can she mean? "Mother" in what sense? How can the paradox be explained? What is "the main thing"? All these questions engage our active attention.

anachronism   an event, person, or object out of its proper place in time, sometimes caused by a writer's slip, but also used deliberately for humorous or dramatic effect. Thornton Wilder's play, *The Skin of Our Teeth*, which supposedly takes place in the present, includes events such as the ice age and the invention of the alphabet; this use of anachronism supports a theme that humankind, because it always has, can adapt to catastrophe.

anapest   see **meter**.

anecdote   a brief, single episode, usually used for illustration in a longer work. An example would be the story of Mr. Lovelady in Faulkner's "That Evening Sun."

annotation   a note or commentary to explain a passage. T. S. Eliot, for example, provides numerous annotations to explain the references in his poem *The Waste Land*.

antagonist   see **character**.

antecedent action   significant action that has taken place before the events portrayed in the work. Antecedent action in Shakespeare's *Hamlet*, for example, includes the murder of Hamlet's father and the marriage of his mother.

anticlimax   the deliberate ordering of events from the impressive to the trivial or the linking of the serious and the not-serious, providing a humorous effect. An example would be, "Three things another's modest wishes bound, / My friendship, and a prologue, and ten pound" from Pope's "Epistle to Dr. Arbuthnot."

antihero   see **character**.

aphorism   a short, pointed statement of a truth. Frost's "Home is the place where, when you have to go there, / They have to take you in" from "The Death of the Hired Man" has become an aphorism. (Also *axiom* or *maxim*)

apocalyptic literature   a work such as Yeats' "The Second Coming" describing or predicting the end of the world.

apostrophe   addressing a person or quality not currently present as though it were present and could answer: "Milton! thou shouldst be living at this hour" (Wordsworth, "London, 1802").

approximate (slant) rhyme   see **rhyme**.

archetype   characters, symbols, events, patterns, and images which recur in similar fashion in so many types of literature, myths, and dreams that they are regarded as universal. The English epic poem *Beowulf* exemplifies several archetypes: Beowulf, the warrior, is an archetypal hero; he journeys to Hrothgar's land to fight the dreaded monster, Grendel; their battle is an archetypal struggle between good and evil, fought under water which often symbolizes death; his victory is rewarded with gold, regarded by many cultures as the most perfect of metals.

aside   an actor's speech, supposedly heard only by the audience and not the other actors. In Shakespeare's *Lear*, after Cordelia hears her father decide to give the daughter who praises him most highly the biggest share of his kingdom, she says in an aside, "What shall Cordelia speak? Love, and be silent."

assonance   the repetition of stressed vowel sounds in close proximity, as in "So many steps, head from the heart to sever / If but a neck, soon should we be together" (Anne Bradstreet, "A Letter to Her Husband").

atmosphere   the general effect of a work of art created by details of setting, character and plot. Such short stories as Poe's "The Cask of Amontillado" and "The Fall of the House of Usher" often convey moods of decay, antiquity, and horror.

ballad   a narrative poem with short, simple words and sentences, usually with a refrain. Examples include Keats' "La Belle Dame sans Merci" and Langston Hughes' "Mama and Daughter."

blank verse   poetry written in unrhymed iambic pentameter (see **meter**) lines such as Shakespeare's dramas and Milton's *Paradise Lost*. This verse form is close to the natural rhythm of English speech.

cacophony   discordant, harsh, and jarring sounds; a perjorative term for dissonance. Sylvia Plath uses cacophony in her description of "The Colossus" from whose lips came, "Mule-bray, pig-grunt and bawdy cackles."

cadence   the nonmetrical rhythm, flowing but irregular, used for poetic unity in **free verse** such as Whitman's *Leaves of Grass*.

caesura   a strong pause or break in a line of verse, usually falling about the middle of the line. See **scansion**.

canto   a division of a long poem, similar to the chapters of a book. Dante's *Divine Comedy* has one hundred cantos, thirty-four in the Inferno section, thirty-three in Purgatory and thirty-three in Paradise.

catalog   a list of objects, persons, cities, etc. Homer in Book 18 of *The Iliad* catalogs the goddesses of the sea, thirty-three in all from Glauke to Amathyia.

catastrophe   see **tragedy**.

catharsis   see **tragedy**.

character   a person in a work of literature. A character may be fully developed or *round* (*complex*) as Odysseus in *The Odyssey*; the poet presents him as warrior, athlete, penniless beggar, husband, father, king, adventurer, and lover. Or a character may be *flat* (*simple*), seen from one dimension only as is the servant-panderer Lisabetta in Hawthorne's "Rappaccini's Daughter." Flat characters may also be *stereotypes*. Stereotypical characters include such types as the warrior, the femme fatale, the clown, the innocent, the villain, and the gull. A *static* character does not change; a *dynamic* character does. In Lawrence's "The Horse Dealer's Daughter," Mabel and the doctor are dynamic; Mabel's brothers are static. The *protagonist* is the principal character, usually one for whom the audience feels sympathy; the *antagonist* is the person or force opposed to the protagonist. In Stephen Crane's "The Open Boat," the sea is the antagonist opposed to the four men in the boat, the protagonists. The main character, the leading character, may be a *hero* or *heroine*, a person of great strength and personality, as Aeneas or Medea are, or may be an *antihero* like Prufrock in Eliot's "The Love Song of J. Alfred Prufrock." The *foil* serves as a contrast to a more central character; Shakespeare's Gloucester is a foil to Lear as is Horatio to Hamlet; a *confidant* is a character like Polonius who is permitted to hear the confidences of a more central character.

characterization   the portrayal of a real person or the creation of a fictional one by showing the person in action and conversation or by describing the character's thoughts and motives to the reader. See **point of view.**

chorus   performers in Greek drama whose singing, dancing, and narration developed, explained, and elaborated the main action. T. S. Eliot uses such a chorus in *Murder in the Cathedral.* In Elizabethan drama the chorus dwindled to a single performer who spoke the prologue or epilogue or commented on the action. Thornton Wilder's Stage Manager in *Our Town* is such a character.

climax   see **plot.**

closed couplet   see **stanza.**

closet drama   a play meant to be read, rather than acted, such as Shelley's *Prometheus Unbound* or Milton's *Samson Agonistes.*

comedy   a work of literature (drama or narrative) in which the conflicts are usually resolved happily and which customarily reflects a hopeful view of human life and potential. Thus, the war of the sexes in *Lysistrata* ends in reconciliation. The plot structure of comedy has been described by Northrop Frye as U-shaped, beginning in a settled situation and, after sinking in the complication, rising again to a happy ending.

comic relief   a humorous element in a tragedy, usually performed by someone unaware of the impending or ongoing horror. The gatekeeper provides comic relief in *Macbeth.*

common meter   see **stanza.**

complication   see **plot.**

conceit   see **metaphor.**

confidant   see **character.**

conflict   see **plot.**

consonance　the repetition of final accented consonant sounds at close intervals, as in bea*r*s, boa*r*s and ha*r*es.

couplet　see **stanza**.

crisis　see **plot**.

denouement　see **plot**.

deus ex machina　literally, the "god from the machine," referring to the appearance of a god lowered by a crane in Greek and Roman tragedy, now used to refer to an implausible solution to a plot problem.

dialect　the form of spoken language peculiar to a certain time, region, society, or occupation. Eugene O'Neill uses New England dialect in *Desire Under the Elms*; Gwendolyn Brooks reproduces street lingo in "We Real Cool."

dibrach　see **meter**.

didactic　literature whose primary purpose is to teach. Pope's *Essay on Criticism* is didactic.

dirge　a funeral or mourning poem, also called a **lament**. Shelley's "A Dirge" mourns the evil in the world.

dissonance　inharmonious sound or combination of sounds, e.g., ". . . there's Vespers! *Plena gratia / Ave, Virgo*! Gr-r-r-you swine!" (Browning's "Soliloquy of the Spanish Cloister").

doppelganger　the supposed double (alter ego, ghost) of a living person. Henry James' "The Jolly Corner" and Conrad's "The Secret Sharer" explore the theme of the double.

dramatic irony　see **irony**.

dramatic monologue　see **monologue**.

elegy　a poem of mourning and praise for the dead, as Shelley's "Adonais"; sometimes used loosely to refer to any poem in a mournful and contemplative tone such as Thomas Gray's "Elegy in a Country Churchyard." The pastoral elegy such as Milton's "Lycidas," whose mourners are shepherds, follows the conventions of the **pastoral**.

end rhyme　see **rhyme**.

end-stopped line　a line of poetry which ends with a natural pause, usually marked by punctuation: "Then you shall go no further" (*King Lear* 4:2).

enjambment　a line of poetry that does not end with a pause because the thought continues to the next line: "He'll not feel wrongs / Which tie him to an answer. Our wishes on the way / May prove effects" (*King Lear* 4:2). (Also *run-on line*)

envoy see **stanza**.

epic a long narrative poem concerning the adventures of an historical or legendary national hero. Typical epic conventions include serious subject matter, a formal or elevated style, beginning in the middle of the action, elements of the supernatural, an invocation to a muse, catalogs, and warfare. *The Iliad, The Odyssey,* and *Paradise Lost* are epics. The *mock epic* treats a trivial subject with epic conventions for a satiric or derisive effect; Pope's *The Rape of the Lock* is a mock epic.

epigram a brief, witty, poetic statement of a seeming truth, e.g., "And she who scorns a man must die a maid" (Pope, *The Rape of the Lock*).

epigraph a quotation at the beginning of a poem, book, or chapter giving a clue to the theme or creating an atmosphere. Eliot's *The Waste Land* begins with a quotation from the *Satyricon* of Petronius in which the Sibyl, who has been granted a thousand years to live but who has forgotten to request youth, is asked what she wants and replies that she wants to die.

epilogue a closing section which adds further information. In a play it is often a monologue by an actor who returns to the stage after the concluding action to make a final comment. For example, in Marlowe's *Dr. Faustus* the chorus returns to the stage and exhorts the audience not to imitate Faust's ungodly ambition.

epiphany a moment of revelation for a character or the scene bringing forth such a moment. In Joyce's *Portrait of the Artist as a Young Man*, Stephen Dedalus experiences an epiphany when he looks at a girl standing in water with her skirts kilted up and realizes he is seeing her with an artist's eyes.

epitaph a short tribute to a dead person, either prose or poetry, suitable for engraving on a tombstone. Ben Jonson's "On My First Daughter" and "Epitaph on Elizabeth, L. H." are examples.

epithalamium a wedding song or poem whose conventions include an invocation to the muses, the homecoming of the bride, a celebration, and the preparation for the wedding night. The Song of Songs, a book of the Old Testament, contains an epithalamium.

epithet a descriptive term, sometimes with a negative connotation. Examples include Homer's "wine-dark sea," death as "The Destroyer," Jesus as "Prince of Peace."

essay a short, nonfiction prose composition on a single subject, usually written from a personal point of view. Essays may be formal or informal; persuasive, argumentative, descriptive, narrative, or reflective. Bacon's essays are justifiably well-known; modern essayists include E. B. White, Loren Eisley, Joan Didion, Nora Ephron, and Russell Baker.

eulogy   a speech or composition of praise, especially for a dead person; e.g., Christina Rossetti's "Cardinal Newman."

euphony   a combination of sounds with a pleasing, smooth, frequently musical, effect, often achieved through an emphasis on vowels and soft consonants — the opposite of **cacophony**. Milton's description of Eve at work in Eden in Book 9 of *Paradise Lost* is euphonious:

> . . . oft stooping to support
> Each flower of slender stalk, whose head though gay
> Carnation, purple, azure, or specked with gold,
> Hung drooping unsustained. . . . (427-430)

exact rhyme   see **rhyme**.

exemplum   a story told to illustrate a moral. Chaucer's *Pardoner's Tale* illustrates the moral that money is the root of all evil.

explication   a detailed, line-by-line explanation of a literary work or part of a work.

exposition   see **plot**.

eye rhyme   see **rhyme**.

fable   a short narrative, prose or verse, with animals or inanimate objects as actors and speakers, used to illustrate a moral; e.g., Chaucer's "Nun's Priest's Tale" and Orwell's *Animal Farm*.

fabliau   a racy, short, colloquial story told in verse with common people as actors, realistic detail, and blunt, often coarse, humor; e.g., Chaucer's "Miller's Tale" and "Reeve's Tale."

falling action   see **plot**.

farce   a broadly humorous comedy; *Run For Your Wife* is currently a popular London farce.

feminine rhyme   see **rhyme**.

figurative language   as opposed to literal language, language which represents one object in terms of another. Red used to represent courage or blood or war or hate and a rose used to signify love or romance or tribute would be figurative uses.

figure of speech   an expression using words in a nonliteral sense. In Coleridge's poem "This Lime-Tree Bower My Prison," the reader does not expect the bower to be a literal prison.

first-person narration   see **point of view**.

flashback   see **plot**.

fly-on-the-wall technique   see **point of view.**
foil   see **character.**
foot   see **meter.**
foreshadowing   see **plot.**
free verse   non-metrical verse characterized by unusual or irregular stanzaic form, irregular or no rhyme schemes, and rhythmic variation. Free verse achieves unity by repetition, image patterns, alliteration, assonance, and cadence.

> I celebrate myself, and sing myself,
> And what I assume you shall assume,
> For every atom belonging to me as good belongs to
>   you.

> I loaf and invite my soul,
> I lean and loaf at my ease observing a spear of
>   summer grass.

> (Walt Whitman, *Song of Myself*)

frontier tall tale   an anecdote characterized by exaggeration or understatement with realistic details. It often uses dialect and other characteristics of oral literature such as Mark Twain's "The Celebrated Jumping Frog of Calaveras County."

genre   a type or division. Literature can be divided into poetry, fiction, drama, and nonfiction prose; fiction is divided into the genres of novel, novella and short story; and the novel could be further divided into subgenres.

haiku   see **verse forms.**
hamartia   see **tragedy.**
hero (heroine)   see **character.**
heroic couplet   see **stanza.**
homily   a sermon or religious discourse such as Edwards' "Sinners in the Hands of an Angry God."
hubris   see **tragedy.**
hymn   a song of praise, devotion, and honor, often to God or a god, e.g., Donne's "Hymn to Christ, at the Author's Last Going into Germany."
hyperbole   exaggeration or overstatement used for ironic purposes. In Swift's *Gulliver's Travels*, the Lilliputian emperor (all six inches of him!) is described in hyperbolic terms as "Monarch of all Monarchs;

taller than the sons of men; whose feet press down to the center, and whose head strikes against the sun; at whose nod the princes of the earth shake their knees."

iamb   see **meter**.

idyll   a short poem or prose work with a pleasant, rustic setting. Examples include Tennyson's *Idylls of the King* and the Old Testament Book of Ruth.

image   descriptive language which appeals to any of the senses:

> That orbed maiden with white fire laden
> Whom mortals call the Moon,
> Glides glimmering o'er my fleece–like floor,
> By the midnight breezes strewn.
>
> (Shelley, "The Cloud")

imagery   literal and figurative descriptions which appeal to the senses. The imagery in the lines from Shelley quoted above is visual ("orbed maiden," "white fire," "fleece-like floor"), tactile ("fleece-like floor," "midnight breezes"), auditory ("midnight breezes"), thermal ("white fire," "midnight breezes"), kinesthetic and mobile ("glides glimmering"). Images can also appeal to the senses of taste (gustatory) and smell (olfactory) and, as seen above, to more than one sense at the same time (the latter is called *synaesthesia*). Imagery also refers to patterns of images; one can say, for example, that a specific poem contains religious or scientific imagery.

incident   see **plot**.

initial rhyme   see **rhyme**.

initiation story   a story in which a person, usually young, undergoes some kind of growth experience and thus gains a level of maturity. Hawthorne's "My Kinsman, Major Molineux" and Alice Munro's "Boys and Girls" are initiation stories about young people, while Paule Marshall's novel *Praisesong for the Widow* describes the ordeal and growth of a middle-aged widow.

in medias res   "in the middle of things," the typical epic beginning. Previous events are revealed through flashbacks and narration.

innuendo   an insinuation, an indirect reference, usually derogatory. In Browning's "My Last Duchess," the Duke comments ". . . she liked whate'er / She looked on, and her looks went everywhere," implying that her warmth and childish happiness were perhaps not so innocent.

interior monologue   see **monologue**.

internal rhyme   see **rhyme**.

invocation   a prayer addressed to a divine power, often for inspiration at the beginning of a work. At the beginning of *Paradise Lost*, Milton asks for help from the Holy Spirit: "Sing, Heavenly Muse, . . . I thence / Invoke thy aid to my adventurous song" (1:6, 12-13).

irony   language or situation in which the intended meaning or expected outcome is the direct opposite of the stated words or action. Devices of *verbal irony* are *hyperbole* (exaggeration), *understatement* (meiosis), and *litotes* (negative statement). In *situational irony* the action that occurs is the opposite of what one may have expected; in Crane's "The Open Boat" the oiler, who has been shown as the strongest of the shipwreck survivors, is the one who drowns. In *dramatic irony* the audience knows what the actor does not; Sophocles' Oedipus does not know he has killed his father at the crossroads, but the audience does. *Sarcasm*, similar to irony, is broader, with an element of personal humiliation, as in Lowell's *A Fable for Critics*.

Italian (Petrarchan) sonnet   see **sonnet**.

lament   a poem of complaint over loss or death. Chaucer's "Complaint to His Purse" is an amusing treatment of the genre.

literal meaning   language in which the stated words say exactly what is intended; opposed to figurative meaning.

litotes   see **irony**.

long meter   see **stanza**.

lyric   a short poem expressing emotion and personal response rather than detailing external events or actions. Examples include Shelley's "Ode to the West Wind," Keats' "Ode on a Grecian Urn," and Hopkins' "The Windhover."

malapropism   a ridiculous misuse of words, especially confusion caused by a resemblance in sound. Saying "progeny" for "prodigy" would be an example.

masculine rhyme   see **rhyme**.

metaphor   a figure of speech in which identity is stated or implied between two dissimilar objects; a comparison using "like" or "as" is a *simile*. In Maxine Hong Kingston's *The Woman Warrior*, the statement, "I had not noticed before that she had such a protruding melon of a stomach" contains the metaphor "protruding melon of a stomach," while a following sentence, "Like a great saw, teeth strung with lights, files of people walked zigzag across our land, tearing the rice" contains the simile "like a great saw, teeth strung with lights." A fanciful and extended metaphor is a *conceit*.

metaphysical poetry   poetry written largely in the early seventeenth century relying heavily on unusual metaphors (*conceits*) and paradox. As Samuel Johnson described it: "The most heterogeneous ideas are yoked by violence together; nature and art are ransacked for illustrations, comparisons, and allusions   " ("Cowley" in *Lives of the Poets*). John Donne's "A Valediction: Forbidding Mourning" is a metaphysical poem containing the famous comparison of two lovers to a compass:

> If they be two, they are two so
> As stiff twin compasses are two;
> Thy soul, the fixed foot, makes no show
> To move, but doth, if th' other do.

meter   the rhythmic pattern of a line or a whole poem, described by type of *foot* (combination of stressed and unstressed syllables) and number of feet per line. This rhythmical pattern provides much of the charm of poetry, but meter should always be subservient to sense. The most common foot in English is *iambic* (an *iamb*), an unstressed syllable followed by a stressed syllable, "thĕ bóy." A *trochiac* foot (*trochee*) is a stressed syllable followed by an unstressed one, "lyŕ ĭč." An *anapestic* foot (*anapest*) is two unstressed syllables followed by a stressed, "iň teř cépt." A *dactylic* foot (*dactyl*) is a stressed syllable followed by two unstressed, "mí cřo scŏpe." A *spondaic* foot (*spondee*) is two stressed syllables, "lifé stýle," and a *pyrrhic* foot (also called a *dibrach*) is two unstressed syllables, "tŏ thĕ." (These last two are unusual in English.)

The line of poetry is defined by the number of feet per line: *monometer* (one), *dimeter* (two), *trimeter* (three), *tetrameter* (four), *pentameter* (five), *hexameter* (six), *heptameter* (seven), *octameter* (eight). Reading and marking poetry for its rhythmic pattern is *scanning* or **scansion**.

metonomy   the use of a word associated with something to substitute for the thing itself. "The pen is mightier than the sword" states indirectly through metonomy that a writer can accomplish more than a warrior.

milieu   the environment of a work or of the artist.

miracle play   a form of medieval drama based on a Bible story or a saint's life. Well-known miracle plays include *Noah* and *The Harrowing of Hell*.

mock epic   see **epic**.

monologue   one person is represented as speaking alone yet has an implied audience. A verse monologue is a *dramatic monologue*; Browning's "Fra Lippo Lippi" is an example. A character speaking to himself in fiction uses *interior monologue* as seen in Joyce's *Ulysses*. A character speaking to herself aloud on stage is presenting a *soliloquy*, a device used most effectively by Shakespeare.

moral   a principle of conduct or behavior taught by a work of literature, not to be confused with **theme**.

motif   a thematic element with a recurring pattern such as the three wishes common in fairy tales.

myth   a narrative, often passed down from a long oral tradition, which attempts to explain the customs, culture, and history of a people, sometimes based on fact and sometimes not. Myths often have a hero or heroine and frequently deal with the supernatural. Myths also often propose an explanation for the origins and causes of natural phenomena. For example, most cultures have a creation myth; the Greeks believed that Chaos gave birth to Night and Erebus who in turn gave birth to Love which created Light and Day; the Hebrews believed that a Creator God fashioned the world in six days.

narration   see **point of view**.

nonfiction novel   a contradiction in terms according to the definition of **novel** below. Yet today the term is frequently used to describe a work of literature which, while based on fact, treats factual elements with fictional freedom. Norman Mailer's *Armies of the Night* and Truman Capote's *In Cold Blood* are nonfiction novels.

novel   a long work of fiction with a continuous story and many characters and incidents. It is difficult to be more precise than this because the genre includes so many diverse works: Daniel Defoe's *Moll Flanders*, Jane Austen's *Emma*, D. H. Lawrence's *The Rainbow*, James Joyce's *Finnegan's Wake*, John Dos Passos' *USA*, Ralph Ellison's *Invisible Man*, Lisa Alther's *Kinflicks*, Alice Walker's *The Color Purple*.

novella   a long short story such as Melville's "Bartleby the Scrivener." (Also *short novel, novelette*)

objective point of view   see **point of view**.

occasional verse   poetry produced to celebrate or commemorate a particular occasion, often the responsibility of a poet laureate. An example would be Tennyson's "Ode on the Death of the Duke of Wellington."

ode   a serious, dignified lyric poem of some length, usually with an irregular stanzaic structure, sometimes written to praise someone or something (Wordsworth's "Ode to Duty"); at other times, written more as a meditation on a human problem (Allen Tate's "Ode to the Confederate Dead"),

omniscient point of view   see **point of view.**

onomatopoeia   the sound of the word echoes its sense, e.g., "buzz," "hum," "growl." Note also the concluding lines of Tennyson's "Come Down, O Maid": "The moan of doves in immemorial elms, / And murmuring of innumerable bees."

overstatement   see **irony.**

oxymoron   a figure of speech composed of two opposite terms: "sweet sorrow," "cold fire," "darkness visible."

parable   a narrative which teaches a moral lesson as a fable does. However, the details of a parable are more realistic than those of a fable. The parable of the good Samaritan in the New Testament is well known.

paradox   a statement that seems contradictory or absurd but that may, in fact, be true. The speaker in Gwendolyn Brooks' "The Mother" states paradoxically that, "You remember the children you got that you did not get."

parody   a literary work imitating an established style, convention, or genre with the intention of ridiculing the form or the subject. Lowell's *A Fable for Critics* parodies both the style and subject matter of such writers as Cooper and Poe.

pastoral   a literary work which treats the rustic life in an ideal and artificial manner such as Spenser's *The Shepheardes' Calendar*. The pastoral can be a lyric, an elegy, a romance, or even a drama.

persona   the speaker or narrator of the work, the mask of the author. The narrator may be very similar to the author (the narrator of Whitman's *Song of Myself*) or quite dissimilar (the narrator of Dostoevsky's *Notes from the Underground*).

personification   a figure of speech treating a thing, object, or creature as though human; for example, the rational and idealized horses in *Gulliver's Travels* are personifications.

picaresque   a work of fiction dealing with the adventures of a rogue or vagabond, often presented autobiographically; Defoe's *Moll Flanders* is a picaresque novel.

plot   the arrangement of events causally related, involving conflict for the characters and suspense for the reader or spectator. The plot events usually consist of *exposition* (background information explaining the *conflict*); *rising action* (the complications generating the plot); the *crisis* (the point at which the action definitely turns); the *climax* (the peak of the audience's response to the protagonist's choice); *falling action* (leading to the conclusion); the *denouement* (final revelation); and *resolution* (which ties together any loose ends). Plots may also contain *flashbacks* (the interruption of chronological progression by a scene returning to an earlier time), *foreshadowing* (the anticipation of a future event), or *reversals* (sudden change of fortune for the protagonist). An *incident* or *episode* is an event, a unit of the action. A *subplot* is a secondary or minor plot.

point of view the angle or vision from which a literary work is presented; who tells the story and from what perspective. In the *omniscient author* or *third-person omniscience*, the author moves freely into the thoughts and minds of any of the characters, presenting internal action as well as external events, and commenting subjectively on them. This point of view is more typical of the novel than the short story, particularly of the eighteenth- and nineteenth-century novel. Sometimes the author may choose to limit his omniscience (*limited omniscient author* or *limited third-person omniscience*) to the thoughts of only one character while describing the actions of the others. James' "The Beast in the Jungle" is a good example of such a narrative perspective. In the *objective* point of view, the author permits himself omniscience in time and space, and in and out of the characters' minds, but avoids all subjective comment. Hemingway in "The Short, Happy Life of Francis Macomber" relates the thoughts of the three main characters and even the thoughts of the lion they hunt but does not comment on their behavior. The *dramatic* (or *fly-on-the-wall*) technique is severely limited to observation of the action with the author presenting events as though a spectator only. Despite four brief authorial comments, Hemingway's "The Killers" is primarily an example of this technique.

When the author chooses to become involved in the story, the narration can be *first person*, either *first-person protagonist* (main character) or *first-person witness* (minor character). Sometimes the first-person witness is plural; Faulkner's "A Rose for Emily" is narrated by a "we" who represents the community. The narrator can tell the story as it happens or after it happens, either as the same person or as one who has changed greatly. The narrator of Anderson's "I Want to Know Why" narrates his story only six months or so after the event, and yet he is not the same boy at all; the episode at the races has changed him. (Also *narration, narrative perspective*)

protagonist see **character**.

proverb   a short statement of a well-known truth such as "Hell hath no fury like a woman scorned." (Also *axiom, adage, maxim, aphorism*)

quatrain   see *stanza*.

refrain   see **stanza**.
resolution   see **plot**.
reversal   see **plot**.
rhyme   matching or corresponding sounds, usually at the end of lines of verse. *Masculine rhyme* is one syllable, end-stressed (away, obey); *feminine rhyme* is two syllables (mother, brother); *triple rhyme* is three syllables (listening, glistening). A close but not exact rhyme is called *slant* (or *approximate*) *rhyme* (obey, bee). *Eye rhyme* words look as if they should rhyme, but they are not pronounced as rhymes (proved, loved; anger, danger). Rhyme is also classified by placement. *End rhyme* falls at the end of the line of verse, *initial rhyme* occurs at the beginning of the line, and *internal rhyme* occurs within the line.
rhyme (rime) royal   see **stanza**.
rhyme scheme   the pattern of rhyme in a specific poem or stanza; in a stanza in which the first and third lines, and the second and fourth, rhyme, the rhyme scheme would be marked *abab*.
rhythm   the pattern of sound in a poem. See **meter**.
riddle   an ingenious verbal puzzle. Emily Dickinson's "A Narrow Fellow in the Grass" is a riddle; the reader must discover that a snake is described.
rising action   see **plot**.
romance   a narrative with a courtly background; an ideal of chivalry with stress on mercy to an opponent, good manners, bravery, loyalty, and preservation of honor; sometimes fantastic events. *Sir Gawain and the Green Knight* is a romance, and Cervantes intended *Don Quixote* to be a parody of romances.
run-on line   see **enjambment**.

satire   any literary work whose primary purpose is to ridicule or criticize wickedness or folly. The satirist usually claims to write to reform as Swift does in *A Modest Proposal*. The range of satire is enormous, from mild deprecation to burlesque to invective. Milder, witty satire is known as Horatian; Juvenalian satire is harsh, contemptuous, and bitter.

scansion   the art of scanning, of marking a line of poetry according to meter and feet. In the traditional form, ´ is used for an accented syllable, ˘ for an unaccented, ‖ for the caesura, and | for feet, as in the following example. (Note, however, that scansion is not an exact art; not everyone would scan this poem identically.)

> Thăt tíme| ŏf yéar‖ thŏu máyst| ĭn m̋e| bĕhóld|
> Whĕn yél|lŏw leáves,‖ ŏr nóne,| ŏr féw,| dŏ háng|
> Ŭpón| thŏse boúghs‖ whĭch sháke| ăgáinst| thĕ cóld,|
> Baŕe rúin|ĕd chóirs,‖ whĕre láte| thĕ swéet|biŕds śang.|
>
> (Shakespeare, Sonnet #73)

scene   an episode or smaller division of an act, or, in some modern drama, of the entire play. Tennessee Williams' play *The Glass Menagerie* is composed of seven scenes.

setting   the environment of a work; its time, culture, place, class, season, etc. The details the author uses to describe setting usually create an atmosphere and have a bearing on characterization and theme. In Kate Chopin's "Beyond the Bayou," the setting of cabin and plantation reflect and are symbolic of the different psychological states of the protagonist.

simile   see **metaphor**.

soliloquy   see **monologue**.

sonnet   a fourteen-line, iambic pentameter poem with varying rhyme schemes. In the *Italian* or *Petrarchan sonnet*, the rhyme scheme is *abba abba cdecde* or *cdcdcd*; a two-part division of thought is indicated with the octave setting up a situation or asking a question and the sestet providing the turn or answer. Milton's "When I Consider How My Light Is Spent" is a Petrarchan sonnet. In the *English* or *Shakespearean sonnet*, the rhyme scheme is *abab cdcd efef gg*. In the *Spenserian*, the rhyme scheme is *ababbcbc cdcd ee*. The Shakespearean and the Spenserian invite a division of thought with three examples and a close or summary in the couplet. Keats' "When I Have Fears That I May Cease to Be" is a Shakespearean sonnet.

sonnet sequence   a series of sonnets on a given theme or to a given individual. Each sonnet retains its integrity as an independent poem but gives the effect of stanzas in a longer work. Spenser's *Amoretti* and Donne's *Holy Sonnets* are sonnet sequences.

spondee   see **meter**.

stanza   a grouping of lines to form a unit within a poem. Stanzas may be based on patterns of sound or thoughts or both; they may consist of regular numbers of lines or the lengths may vary. Some of the most common stanza patterns in English are described below; for examples of the patterns, see the subheading "Stanzas — Patterns of Sound and Sense" in Chapter 7.

A *couplet* is two rhyming lines. An *heroic couplet* is written in iambic pentameter; a *closed couplet* ends with a strong mark of punctuation and completes a thought. A *tercet* is a unit of three lines, sometimes rhymed and sometimes not. A *quatrain* is a four-line stanza which includes the forms *common meter* (alternating lines of tetrameter and trimeter) and *long meter* (four lines of iambic tetrameter). A *quintain* (*quintet, cinquain*) is a stanza of five lines rhyming *ababa or ababb*. *Rhyme* (or *rime*) *royal* is a seven-line iambic pentameter stanza rhyming *ababbcc* which Chaucer used in *Troilus and Criseyde*. *Ottava rima* is an eight-line stanza rhyming *abababcc* used most successfully by Byron in Don Juan. Finally, the *Spenserian stanza* developed by Spenser for *The Faerie Queene* is a nine-line stanza rhyming *ababbcbcc*.

The *verse paragraph* is a stanzaic pattern based on sense rather than structure. A *refrain* is a set phrase or line repeated throughout a poem, usually at the end of each stanza. An *envelope* is two or more repeated or similar lines which enclose several other lines. An *envoy* is a concluding stanza, usually shorter than the others.

stream of consciousness   a narrative technique recording the thoughts of one or more characters with no attempt at order, interruption, or analysis; often disjointed and irrational. Well-known examples of stream-of-consciousness novels are Joyce's *Ulysses* and Faulkner's *The Sound and the Fury*.

stress   see **accent**.

subplot   see **plot**.

symbol   a physical object, event, or person standing for both itself and something else, particularly something abstract, for example, a flag representing the quality of patriotism; a circle, perfection; and a lamb, innocence. Most readers respond similarly to *conventional symbols*; white usually symbolizes good and black, evil. Similarly, *natural symbols* are objects in nature whose meanings are generally recognized: dawn represents hope and beginnings while night symbolizes death and endings. However, a *literary* or *private symbol* such as the lottery box in Jackson's "The Lottery" achieves its symbolic significance only in its work.

synecdoche   a figure of speech using a part of a thing to represent the whole. When Clytemnestra invites Agamemnon to come down from his chariot and not to place the "foot that trampled Troy" upon the ground, she is using "foot" to refer to his own and his army's prowess.

synopsis a very brief review or summary of a work.

theme the assertions or doctrines embodied in a literary work; those conclusions which may be drawn from the work and applied to life outside the work. A work may contain more than one theme, and readers may not agree on the existence or importance of themes in a specific work. Do not confuse themes with subjects or topics; for example, the subject of "I Want to Know Why" is a boy's trip to the horse races, but one of the themes of the story is the recognition that good and evil can be intertwined in the same person.

third-person limited omniscience see **point of view**.

third-person omniscience see **point of view**.

tone the attitude of the author towards his audience and his subject; for example, the tone of Jonathan Edwards' sermon "Sinners in the Hands of an Angry God" is relentless wrath, intended to shock his congregation into repentance and conversion.

tragedy a serious literary work in which the action ends disastrously for the main character. Originally, a tragedy was a play in which the protagonist, a good person with a special vulnerability (*hamartia*) such as pride or *hubris*, is brought down through this flaw from good to bad fortune. The final disaster, usually a resolution of order, is called the *catastrophe*. Aristotle has said that a tragedy such as *Oedipus Rex* arouses pity and fear and thus provides a *catharsis* or purging of the emotions. However, the heroes of Shakespearean tragedies such as *Romeo and Juliet* do not always have an hamartia, and modern tragedies such as *Death of a Salesman* are more likely to feature an antihero than a hero. Thus, the audience may feel more compassion and empathy than catharsis. Drama in the eighteenth century began to feature ordinary middle- and lower-class people rather than the rulers and aristocrats of earlier tragedy, and is called *domestic tragedy*, a subgenre still popular today.

trochee see **meter**.

understatement see **irony**.

utopian any work projecting an ideal world of perfect political and social order, developed from the title of More's *Utopia* (literally "no place"). Utopian literature ranges from Plato's *Republic* to Bellamy's *Looking Backward*.

verisimilitude   the appearance of reality achieved by scrupulous attention to concrete details. Swift's account of Lilliput and Brobdingnag is remarkable for its seeming realism.

verse   a single line of poetry; a sequence of words arranged metrically according to an established pattern or the poet's design

verse forms   the shapes or structures of various poems. Some verse forms have been discussed under *stanza*; others include the *haiku*, a three-line poem of five syllables, then seven, then five; the *limerick*, a five-line humorous or nonsense poem in anapestic meter, rhyming *aabba*; and the *villanelle*, five tercets rhyming *aba* and a quatrain rhyming *abaa* (Roethke's "The Waking").

verse paragraph   see **stanza**.

vignette   a short, subtle, intimate verbal picture; Carlyle wrote perceptive vignettes of his contemporaries in his letters.

Index

A 9
B 0
C 1
D 2
E 3
F 4
G 5
H 6
I 7
J 8